Digitalization in companies

Thomas Barton • Christian Müller
Christian Seel

Editors

Digitalization in companies

From theoretical approaches
to practical

 Springer

Editors
Thomas Barton
Worms University of Applied Sciences
Worms, Germany

Christian Müller
Technical University of Applied
Sciences Wildau
Wildau, Germany

Christian Seel
Landshut University of Applied Sciences
Landshut, Germany

ISBN 978-3-658-39093-8   ISBN 978-3-658-39094-5   (eBook)
https://doi.org/10.1007/978-3-658-39094-5

This Springer imprint is published by the registered company Springer Fachmedien Wiesbaden GmbH, part of Springer Nature.
The registered company address is: Abraham-Lincoln-Str. 46, 65189 Wiesbaden, Germany

Paper in this product is recyclable.

Preface

It was in 2018 when the this book was published in German language. Three editors proudly presented it as the third part of the book series Angewandte Wirtschaftsinformatik. Years have passed since then. For the German e-book edition of the single volume, there are already more than 700.000 downloads. In 2024, the updated version of this book will be released in English language. On the one hand, we are really proud. On the other hand, we are thoughtful and sad, because only two of us are left. Christian Seel, one of the three original editors, is no more. Sadly, he died in 2019 at the age of 39. Our thoughts are with Christian Seel's parents.

Homburg, Germany   Thomas Barton
Berlin, Germany   Christian Müller

Contents

About the Contributors

Gunnar Auth *Professor of Information Systems and e-Government, Meissen University of Applied Sciences (HSF)*

Gunnar Auth is professor of Information Systems and e-Government at Meissen University of Applied Sciences (HSF), Germany. He completed his diploma degree in Business Information Systems at the University of Bamberg, Germany, and received a PhD degree in Information Management from the University of St Gallen (HSG), Switzerland. He started his professional career as an internal consultant at DaimlerChrysler where he later worked in several management positions in logistics, operations and quality management. Before assuming his current position, he was IT director and representative of the CIO board at Leipzig University. His research focuses on IT project management, IT service management and information management.

Email: gunnar.auth@hsf.sachsen.de

Thomas Barton *Professor of Computer Science with a focus on Business Informatics, Spokesperson of the advisory board for Universities of Applied Sciences within the German Informatics Society (GIBH)*

Prof. Barton studied and received his doctorate at the TU Kaiserslautern. He then worked for SAP SE for about 10 years with a focus on application development, also consulting, training and project management. Since 2006, he has been working at the University of Applied Sciences, Worms, as Professor of Computer Science with a focus on business informatics.

His main areas of activity are the development of operational applications, e-business and data science.

Email: barton@hs-worms.de

Web: https://prof-barton.de

Walter Brenner *Professor at the Institute for Information Systems at the University of St. Gallen, Switzerland*

Walter Brenner has been Professor of Information Systems at the University of St. Gallen and Managing Director of the Institute of Information Systems since April 1, 2001. He was Dean of the Business Administration Department at the University of St. Gallen for 2 years from February 1, 2011; before that, from 1999, Professor of Information Systems and Business Administration at the University of

xii   About the Contributors

Essen and, before that, from April 1, 1993, to March 31, 1999, Professor of General Business Administration and Information Management at the University of Essen. From 1989 to 1993 head of the research program Information Management 2000 at the Institute for Information Systems at the University of St. Gallen; from 1985 to 1989 employee of Alusuisse-Lonza AG in Basel, lastly as head of application development; from 1978 to 1985 studies and doctorate at the University of St. Gallen; research interests: Industrialization of information management, management of IT service providers, customer relationship management and use of new technologies. Prof. Brenner has published more than 30 books and more than 200 articles.

Email: walter.brenner@unisg.ch

Web: https://www.iwi.unisg.ch/ueber-uns/lehrstuehle/prof-dr-walter-brenner/

Christian Czarnecki *Professor at the Institute for Digitalization Aachen, FH Aachen University of Applied Sciences*

Prof. Czarnecki has been Professor of Business Informatics with a focus on Business Applications at the FH Aachen University of Applied Sciences since 2021. His academic career started with studying business informatics at the University of Münster. He then worked in different consultancies for over 10 years and managed a large number of national and international projects in Europe, Asia and Africa. In addition to his work as a management consultant, he received his doctorate from the Otto von Guericke University in Magdeburg. From 2015 he taught as a professor at universities of applied sciences in Leipzig and Lippstadt. He is the author of various scientific publications. His main research areas include the digital transformation, innovative business models, process management and enterprise architectures.

Email: Czarnecki@fh-aachen.de

Marco Graf *Marco Graf has a bachelor and a master degree in business informatics from Worms University of Applied Sciences. He is working as a free software developer*

Michael Gröschel *Professor of Business Informatics, Mannheim University of Applied Sciences, Mannheim*

Prof. Dr. Michael Gröschel is a professor at the Faculty of Computer Science at Mannheim University of Applied Sciences. For many years, the business informatics graduate has been involved in research and teaching on topics of business process management and the sensible use of IT in companies in the context of new business models and the effects on the IT landscape in companies. In addition, he works as a trainer with a focus on business process modeling in BPMN.

Email: m.groeschel@hs-mannheim.de

Web: https://www.taxxas.com

Lucas Hubinger *Innovation Manager for Digital Strategy, Versicherungskammer Bayern*

Lucas Hubinger completed a training-integrated course of study based on the Munich Model. This includes a Master of Science degree in economics and organization at the University of the Federal Armed Forces in Munich as well as training as an insurance and finance clerk. At the same time, he gained initial experience in the insurance industry. Since 2017, he has been innovation manager for digital strategy at Versicherungskammer Bayern and coordinates various digital projects. His work focuses on artificial intelligence, voice control and agile project management.

Email: lucas.hubinger@vkb.de

Norbert Ketterer *Professor for Business Informatics, University of Applied Sciences Fulda*

Prof. Dr. Norbert Ketterer has been working as Professor of Business Informatics at Fulda University of Applied Sciences since 2008. His main areas of activity within the scope of his professorship are in the fields of "business process modeling/ business process management" as well as the investigation and expansion of standard business software, in particular ERP, CRM and SCM software. His current special interest is in production control software and the question of how in-memory DBs can support current production control issues. Before his appointment, Prof. Dr. Norbert Ketterer worked as a management consultant from 1995 to 2008 on the implementation of standard software for a number of industrial companies. His focus was mostly on implementing complex logistics processes in ERP and SCM software or supporting the implementation as an architect. Prior to that, he worked as a research assistant at the Heinz-Nixdorf Institute in Paderborn from 1991 to 1995, where he received his doctorate on the topic of "Distributed Production Control" at the Chair of Information Systems, in particular CIM; before that, he studied computer science with a minor in business administration at the University of Frankfurt/Main.

Email: norbert.ketterer@cs.hs-fulda.de

Kathrin Kirchner *Associate Professor at Denmark's Technical University (DTU), Kgs. Lyngby*

Kathrin Kirchner is Associate Professor at Denmark's Technical University (DTU). Her research currently focuses on the role of social media for knowledge management, collaboration and communication in organizations and (virtual) learning environments. Furthermore, she has done research in data analytics (data and process mining) and on modeling and supporting knowledge-driven business processes – with applications in healthcare, agriculture and marketing. She has published more than 70 refereed journal articles, book and conference papers on enterprise social media, business process management and data mining.

Email: kakir@dtu.dk

Web: https://www.dtu.dk/english/service/phonebook/person?id=136111

Ute Klotz *Professor of Business Informatics, Lucerne University of Applied Sciences and Arts – Computer Science*

Prof. Klotz studied economics and information science at the University of Konstanz. She worked for various German and Swiss companies in the field of consulting. Since 2010, she has been Professor of Business Informatics at the Lucerne University of Applied Sciences and Arts.

Her work focuses on information management, technology assessment, design fiction, and social informatics.

Email: ute.klotz@hslu.ch

Web: https://www.hslu.ch/de-ch/hochschule-luzern/ueber-uns/personensuche/profile/?pid=228

Martina Königbauer *Professor of Systematic Product Development, Technical University of Applied Sciences Augsburg*

Prof. Königbauer studied industrial engineering at the Stuttgart University of Cooperative Education and completed her Master of Systems Engineering at the University of Applied Sciences Landshut. She received her doctorate in computer science from the University of Würzburg for adaptive reference modeling in hybrid project management. Since 2003, she has been working on or leading projects in hardware and software development as well as in the area of organizational development. Her work focuses on project management and project design as well as creative engineering. She has been a professor at Technical University of Applied Sciences Augsburg since 2022.

Email: martina.koenigbauer@hs-augsburg.de

Web: https://www.hs-augsburg.de/Elektrotechnik/Martina-Koenigbauer.html

Claudia Lemke *Professor for Business Informatics at the Berlin School of Economics and Law, Berlin*

Claudia Lemke has been Professor of Business Informatics at various universities of applied sciences for over 10 years, currently at the Berlin School of Economics and Law. Her research interests lie in the area of digital transformation and shaping of companies through IT. Through her authorship of the two-volume textbook on business informatics, she has also been involved for some time with the topics of design and implementation of digital teaching and learning environments. She has published several book and conference contributions as well as journal articles on these topics, has appeared as a speaker, has been involved in various children's universities and currently advises companies on the path of digital transformation.

Email: claudia.lemke@hwr-berlin.de

Web: http://www.hwr-berlin.de/fachbereich-duales-studium/personen/kontakt/claudia-lemke/

Sebastian Meissner *Professor of Production Management and Logistics, Landshut University of Applied Sciences*

Prof. Dr. Meißner received his doctorate from the Chair of Materials Handling, Material Flow and Logistics at the Technical University of Munich and subsequently held various management positions in logistics at the MAN Group, including head of logistics planning at MAN Truck & Bus. Since 2015, he has been Professor of Production Management and Logistics at HAW Landshut. He teaches at the Faculty of Electrical and Industrial Engineering and conducts research in the field of intelligent production and logistics systems and the efficient design of logistics interfaces at the Technology Center for Production and Logistics Systems (TZ PULS).

Email: Sebastian.Meissner@haw-landshut.de

Christian Müller *Professor of Business Informatics, Wildau University of Applied Sciences*

Christian Müller studied mathematics at Free University of Berlin and received his PhD on network flows with constraints. Later, he worked at Schering AG and at the Berliner Verkehrsbetriebe (BVG) in the area of timetable and duty schedule optimization. He is now a professor in the Business Informatics program at Wildau University of Applied Sciences.

Email: christian.mueller@th-wildau.de

Nikolai Nölle *Product Manager at Deutsche Telekom*

Nikolai Nölle is the Product Manager of "Frag Magenta", Deutsche Telekom's award-winning digital service assistant in Germany. Best in class service experience and simplify customers' lives is his prime focus. He designs and drives the product vision, innovative use cases, customer journeys, interactions or dialogs for superior customer experience. He achieves this by consistent application of Customer Experience Management methods.

Sachar Paulus *Professor for IT Security, Head of Bachelor Cybersecurity, Head of MBA IT Management, Mannheim University of Applied Sciences*

Prof. Paulus studied computer science at Saarland University and earned his doctorate in number theory at the University of Essen. After several years in SMEs, he worked at SAP AG from 2000 to 2008 in various management positions related to security, including Chief Security Officer. From 2009 to 2014, he was professor for business informatics and security management at the University of Applied Sciences Brandenburg. Since 2014 he has been at the Mannheim University of Applied Sciences. His work focuses on corporate IT security, especially information security management systems and secure software development, as well as digitalization in teaching. In addition to his university activities, he also runs a small consultancy for security.

Email: paulus@hs-mannheim.de

Web: https://www.paulus-consult.de

Thomas Rodewis *Head of Digitalization and Head of Department Digital Innovation, Versicherungskammer Bayern*

Dr. Thomas Rodewis is Head of Digitalisation and Head of Digital Innovation at Versicherungskammer. In addition to the Group's digitalisation strategy, he is responsible for the implementation of all initiatives and projects in the field of digitalisation. A particular focus is on the topic of innovation. Previously, he held various other management positions at VKB, including responsibility for the composite private customer business and, most recently, head of central operational organization and technology. Thomas Rodewis is a mathematician and started his career as a consultant at IBM.

Email: thomas.rodewis@vkb.de

Martina Romer *Research associate at the Technology Center for Production and Logistics Systems (TZ PULS), Landshut University of Applied Sciences*

Martina Romer studied Systems Engineering at the University of Applied Sciences in Landshut. She then took up employment as a research assistant at the Technology Center for Production and Logistics Systems (TZ PULS). In addition, she is doing her doctorate at the Chair of Conveying Technology Material Flow Logistics at the Technical University of Munich. The focus of her work in the research project iSLT.NET is the conception of target processes and services for the integration of an intelligent special load carrier into the supply chain of the automotive industry.

Email: Martina.Romer@haw-landshut.de

Gabriele Roth-Dietrich *Professor of Business Informatics, Mannheim University of Applied Sciences, Mannheim*

Prof. Dr. Gabriele Roth-Dietrich holds a degree in physics and a doctorate in business administration from the University of Mannheim on process optimization and automation in healthcare. She worked for almost 10 years as a project manager and system analyst in development and product management at SAP SE. After a professorship at Heilbronn University, she has been teaching business informatics at Mannheim University of Applied Sciences since 2011 and focuses on enterprise software, workflow management, business intelligence, project management and digital transformation.

Email: g.roth-dietrich@hs-mannheim.de

Web: https://www.informatik.hs-mannheim.de/fakultaet/professoren/prof-dr-gabriele-roth-dietrich.html

Dominik Schneider *Sales Consultant at Deutsche Telekom*

Dominik Schneider creates customer-centric experiences. He helps enterprise customers to add value powered by digitalization solutions in the context of Mobile Communications and Device as a Service. He holds a Master's degree in Business Information Systems from the Leipzig University of Applied Sciences for Telecommunications (HfTL) and has over 10 years of professional experience in Consulting and Salesy. His main topics are Device as a Service, Artificial Intelligence/Big Data Economics, Machine-to-Machine/Internet of Things and Smart Cities. He has gained experience on these topics in various projects in Germany and Europe and has written several publications.

Email: Dominik.Schneider02@telekom.de

Holger Timinger *Professor for Project Management, Co-Founder of the Institute for Project Management and Information Modelling (IPIM), University of Applied Sciences Landshut*

Prof. Timinger studied electrical engineering at the University of Ulm and the University of Massachusetts. He received his doctorate at the Institute for Measurement, Control and Microtechnology at the University of Ulm in cooperation with the research laboratories of Philips Technologie GmbH. After several years in the management of research and development projects at Philips, he followed the call of Landshut University of Applied Sciences in 2011 and took up the professorship for project management in the Faculty of Electrical and Industrial Engineering. In 2012, he won the "Professor of the Year" competition of UNICUM magazine and KPMG. In 2014, he founded the Institute for Project Management and Information Modeling together with Christian Seel. His main areas of activity are hybrid project management and information modeling. He is the author of numerous publications on these topics.

Email: holger.timinger@haw-landshut.de

Web: http://timinger.ipim.institute

Stefan   Unterbuchberger *Innovation   Manager   Digital   Strategy, Versicherungskammer Bayern*

Stefan Unterbuchberger has worked in the insurance industry for 25 years. He has worked there in various divisions, including as a project manager and in various management functions. From 2008, he was responsible for the operational area "Output Management" in the Group. In 2016, he then took over as head of the "IT Products Life Output" department. Since 2017, he has been responsible for coordinating digital initiatives with various technical and specialist focuses as Innovation Manager in the "Digital Strategy" area. The topics are in the areas of digital communication, app and cloud solutions, artificial intelligence, voice control, agile coaching and in the coordination of strategic cooperations. Stefan Unterbuchberger completed his studies to become an insurance specialist and a degree in business administration while working.

Email: stefan.unterbuchberger@vkb.de

Web: http://www.unterbuchberger.bayern

Frank Wisselink *Executive Product Manager*

Dr Frank Wisselink sets the strategy for a portfolio of services and products ranging from advisory to tools and partners. His expertise covers the complete spectrum for the digitization starting with communication technologies like Narrowband IoT to sustainable value creation with AI. He is an active member in several national and international working groups and delegations at DIN, CEN-CENELEC & ISO for the standardization of AI within the framework of the EU AI ACT.

Email: Frank.Wisselink@t-systems.com

Karsten Würth *App developer and UX designer at VICAMPO.de GmbH, master's degree (business informatics) from Worms University, freelance travel photographer*

Karsten Würth earned his master's degree in business informatics at the University of Worms. Since the end of 2017, he has been employed in the app development and UX design department at the online wine retailer VICAMPO. There, he is currently mainly responsible for the further development of the iOS app. In addition, he works as a freelance travel photographer.

Email: karsten@karstenwuerth.com

Web: http://www.karstenwuerth.com

Part I
Introduction

Digitalization: An Introduction

1

Thomas Barton and Christian Müller

Abstract

After a short introduction to the topic, a definition of digitalization is presented. The importance of digitalization for applied business informatics is pointed out on the basis of six topic areas. Starting with the topic area of influence on work and value creation, the focus is moved to business models and their changes. This is followed by a reference to new approaches for the management of processes and projects on the one hand and for the innovation management of product creation and production on the other hand. Interaction with customers is placed in the context of digitalization. A reference to opportunities and risks in implementation rounds off this introduction.

Digitalization is in full swing. It affects us all and is causing profound change in every area of life [1].

According to the Gabler business encyclopedia, the term digitalization can be understood as "digital revolution" or "digital turn" [2]. The replacement of SMS by messenger services such as WhatsApp is seen as an example of this turn or revolution [3]. This is because in a highly connected, global and fast-paced world, direct

---

Christian Seel was deceased at time of publication.

T. Barton (✉)
Worms University of Applied Sciences, Worms, Germany
e-mail: barton@hs-worms.de

C. Müller
Technical University of Applied Sciences Wildau, Wildau, Germany
e-mail: christian.mueller@th-wildau.de

© The Author(s), under exclusive license to Springer Fachmedien Wiesbaden GmbH, part of Springer Nature 2024
T. Barton et al. (eds.), *Digitalization in companies*,
https://doi.org/10.1007/978-3-658-39094-5_1

3

and fast interaction is becoming increasingly important. The optimization of interaction requires ideas and concepts. Its implementation by means of technology needs data. According to Mark Getty, intellectual property is the oil of the twenty-first century, and money is made out of intellectual property [4]. Digitalization is in full swing and is changing our lives.

The following definition of digitalization reflects the concepts, applications and application scenarios presented in the context of this volume:

Digitalization enables the exchange of services between market participants to create value and to organize a society by implementing business models, processes, products, projects and services based on software solutions. The software solutions interpret the semantics of the exchanged data. In this way, software takes over tasks that were previously handled by humans. Data from and interaction with market participants play a prominent role in digitalization. The shaping of society and work as well as the protection of privacy and the security of applications are the challenges of digitalization.

The significance of this definition can be well illustrated by the evolutionary development of the term e-business, whereby the term e-business has the following meaning: e-business (electronic business) refers to the exchange of services between market participants for the purpose of achieving value creation or organizing a company with the help of information and communication systems that use Internet technologies [5]. While enterprises required an electronic exchange of business documents in the past, voice-controlled user interfaces are applied now, and in the future, enterprises will prefer fully automated but human controlled business processing and inventory management.

The significance of digitalization is elaborated in this book. Concepts, applications and deployment scenarios of digitalization are examined by 24 authors in 14 contributions from different perspectives. The selected contributions are intended to ensure that the phenomenon of digitalization can be illustrated as comprehensively as possible. The book is divided into sections on the influence on the world of work and value creation, business models in transition, new approaches in process and project management, innovation in product creation and production, analysis of behavior and optimization of interaction with customers, and opportunities and risks in implementation.

Our society and our working world are affected by digitalization. In **Part II** on the **impact on work and value creation**, Ute Klotz deals with the topic in Chap. 2. Based on two scenarios that illuminate the strategies of digitalisation, she looks at the changes to which professions and job profiles are subject on the one hand and companies on the other. The author presents new forms of employment and points out the challenges for trade unions that can be derived from this. She concludes her presentation with studies that draw on books from the field of science fiction to derive statements about the work of the future.

In their contribution in Chap. 3, Kathrin Kirchner, Claudia Lemke and Walter Brenner highlight the outstanding importance of data and algorithms. They explain the potential opportunities and significant changes for corporate value creation that result from the targeted use of data and algorithms. Their contribution exemplifies disruptions in the entrepreneurial value chain.

The topic of **business models** in **transition in Part III** is explored through three contributions from three different teams of authors.

In the contribution in Chap. 4, Sebastian Meißner and Martina Romer explain their investigations into how services in a cloud-based implementation can enable new business models for the load carrier industry. They show that with the help of intelligent sensors the digitalization of products does not only create transparency, but also optimizes processes, especially through a cross-company operator model.

The contribution in Chap. 5 by Dominik Schneider, Frank Wisselink and Christian Czarnecki and Nikolai Nölle highlights how the Internet of Things acts as a technological driver for information-driven business models. To this end, a scenario is presented of how parking spaces are networked with the help of sensors and drivers are informed about available parking spaces in real time. The concept of information-driven business models is illustrated using this concrete use case.

Gabriele Roth-Dietrich and Michael Gröschel conduct an assessment of IT as an enabler for innovative business models in their contribution in Chap. 6. They present a methodology for the redesign of a business model based on business model patterns that has proven itself in practice. Depending on the combination of business model patterns, different requirements arise for information technologies and the selection and development of a suitable IT foundation.

Part IV on **New Approaches in Process and Project** Management highlights the topics of process management and project management under the influence of digitalization.

In their article in Chap. 7, Christian Czarnecki and Gunnar Auth present Robotic Process Automation (RPA), a new approach to process automation. So-called software robots take over tasks that were previously performed by clerks. They learn manual tasks and perform them automatically. The article discusses Robotic Process Automation as an innovative approach to process digitalization and presents its use based on three concrete application examples.

In their article in Chap. 8, the authors Stefan Unterbuchberger, Lucas Hubinger, and Thomas Rodewis explore the question of how the transformation of output management in the insurance industry can succeed. They present a successful project from the analysis of the existing architecture and the formulation of requirements to the development and commissioning of the applications.

The article in Chap. 9 by Holger Timinger and Christian Seel shows how digitalization can automate activities in projects and support decisions. The path to digitized project management is presented using a maturity model. The maturity model is used to determine the current situation and to derive a development path.

Part V looks at the subject area of **innovation in product creation and production**.

In her contribution in Chap. 10, Martina Königbauer describes the hurdles on the way to a product development process in the world of digitalization and Industry 4.0. Problems are presented in the contribution and dealt with in a pragmatic way using systems thinking. Experiences from consulting practice in product development departments of German SMEs are included here.

In Chap. 11, Norbert Ketterer focuses on manufacturing. The functionality of ME systems is presented and differentiated from the functionalities of surrounding systems. As a concrete example, processes within the "SAP Industry 4.0" landscape are considered in particular.

A contribution in **Part VI** on **analyzing behavior and optimizing interaction with customers** explains on the one hand how a variety of unstructured data can be used to study consumer behavior. On the other hand, Part VI uses a scenario from the online wine trade to show which possibilities mobile applications in the form of apps offer to intensify the interaction with customers.

Marco Graf and Thomas Barton examine in Chap. 12 how it is possible to obtain informative and location-based information about New Zealand from a larger number of travel blogs. The authors show that the analysis and visualization of travel blogs can be used to make travelers' experiences visible.

In their Chap. 13, Karsten Würth and Thomas Barton describe how the use of an online shop can not only be simplified but also optimized by a mobile app. The app is developed as a Minimum Viable Product (MVP) for the iOS operating system. An increase in the frequency of interaction is achieved through the use of so-called push notifications.

Part VII on **opportunities and risks in implementation** highlights the topics of security and risks in the environment of digitalization.

Claudia Lemke, Kathrin Kirchner and Walter Brenner present management tools for successful entrepreneurial change in Chap. 14. The focus of the article is on changing principles of digital leadership and the associated effects on the management of organizations.

The contribution in Chap. 15 by Sachar Paulus explains why digitalization cannot be seriously deployed without security. The author uses the legal requirements and the current state of the art to explain why the use of an information security management system becomes necessary. He explains that software architectures for digitalization must also take certain design patterns and procedures into account.

References

1. Bundesministerium für Wirtschaft und Klimaschutz (n.d.) Dossier Digitalisierung. http://www.bmwi.de/Redaktion/DE/Dossier/digitalisierung.html. Accessed on 6 March 2024
2. Gabler Wirtschaftslexikon (n.d.) Digitalisierung. http://wirtschaftslexikon.gabler.de/Definition/digitalisierung.html. Accessed on 6 March 2024
3. Berkemeyer K (2019) Der Absturz in einer Grafik: So krass zerlegt WhatsApp die SMS. http://www.chip.de/news/WhatsApp-Der-Vorgaenger-ist-chancenlos_114356381.html. Accessed on 6 March 2024
4. Getty M (2000) Blood and Oil. The Economist (March 4), 68
5. Barton T (2014) E-Business mit Cloud Computing. IT-Professional. Springer Vieweg, Wiesbaden

Part II

Influence on Work and Value Creation

The Future of Work

2

Ute Klotz

Abstract

Most people still live in a working society. Several experts have forecast that digitalization will result in machines or algorithms replacing parts of human work, however these projections vary in the extent of their impact. And yet, when it comes to digitalization, new technologies are not the only factor of digitalization determining the future of work. Other influencing factors include positive or negative guidelines for the use of technology, differentiated in each case for industrial and craft enterprises and politics, new forms of organisation and employment; and various possibilities for the participation of trade unions and employees. The future of work can also be explored through the lens of science fiction literature, which can inspire enthusiasm for the topic of the future of work on a personal level, perhaps despite all the fears and contradictions.

2.1 Introduction

The topic 'Future of Work' concerns us all. From employees to companies to trade unions, everyone would like to know more, in terms of how they are personally affected. But therein precisely lies the difficulty.

There are studies that estimate the extent of possible substitutability due to technological development in occupations and activities, and there are studies that relativize precisely this estimation, in the sense of "the number of employees will remain the same". However, it is not only the impact of technologies on employees and companies that needs to be considered, but also new forms of employment,

U. Klotz (✉)
Lucerne University of Applied Sciences and Arts, School of Computer Science and Information Technology, Rotkreuz, Switzerland
e-mail: ute.klotz@hslu.ch

© The Author(s), under exclusive license to Springer Fachmedien Wiesbaden GmbH, part of Springer Nature 2024
T. Barton et al. (eds.), *Digitalization in companies*,
https://doi.org/10.1007/978-3-658-39094-5_2

9

partly inadequate legal regulations, weakening social security systems, and the further education and training market. The diminishing sense of solidarity amongst employees is also particularly worrying, as it seems that everyone is increasingly fighting to secure their own position and their livelihood.

The earlier work utopias, which were intended to promote technological development and thereby free people from material hardship and enable reductions in working hours, have largely disappeared. It is thus now important and necessary to revisit work, and focus anew on its determinants and impact [1].

2.2   Digitalization

Technical developments and their impact on work have always existed. Networking as a new development, which affects private and professional life in equal measure, can be considered as one possible explanation for the term digitalization. Spatial distances and organizational boundaries are disappearing, while acceleration and anonymization are on the rise. Although technology plays a central role in work and employment, this does not imply a cause-and-effect relationship. Other crucial considerations are socio-economic trends (changing lifestyles) and strategies of technology use. And yet, it is not even the trends that appear to be entirely new, but more so their magnitude and speed of change and the confluence of different developments. However, the trends that could have an impact on the number of jobs are automation (see Sects. 2.2.1 and 2.2.2), the relocation of work and consumer work [2].

In terms of the strategies of technology use, two distinct scenarios or guidelines exist [2, 3]:

- Automation scenario – Technical processes are to be automated as far as possible and thus become independent of human intervention
- Tool scenario – The focus is on supporting the employed with systems in the sense of a tool.

In the automation scenario, job losses must be expected [2]. The involvement or mental contribution of skilled labor will no longer be required. Employees will receive instructions, but no information, and will have no decision-making authority. This in turn will change employees' task scope, moving away from routine activities and towards special or exceptional cases. If this scenario is expanded, then adjustments will need to be made in vocational education and training and in continuing education [3].

The situation is somewhat different in the tool scenario. Here, employees would retain their freedom of design and plan their work and tasks and the technology would be designed to support and assist them in his or her job or activities [3]. Job losses are to be expected in this scenario as well, however, not to the scale expected in the automation scenario since company managers still rely on the experience of the employed [2].

However, applying digitalization only to the vocational and professional education sector sector would be too short-sighted. Digitalization can also change fundamental cultural techniques such as reading and writing. This is evident in our growing tendency to handwrite primarily in the private, informal sphere. And as for reading, it is clearly on the decline. Reading takes place in small portions, often on the side and always interrupted. Digital texts are constantly available, which makes reading less essential. The rise in quality in automatic translation programs has rendered reading foreign-language texts unnecessary. And long texts are automatically summarized. Multimedia texts, i.e., texts enriched with videos, graphics and podcasts, could possibly lead to less reading of texts containing complex argumentation. Basically, reading without a computer has become harder to do [4].

Evgeny Morozov therefore thinks that the political task would be to promote the positive aspects of technology and to limit the negative ones [5]. And this is a complex task.

2.2.1   Occupations in Transition

There are two well-known studies that investigate the impact of digitalization on occupations, activities, and employment figures.

The first study, by Frey and Osborne [6] from 2013, investigated the extent to which technology will affect future employment. Together with experts they defined 70 activities, assessed them according to their automatability and then transferred them to occupations according to their activities. The period of automation remained undefined. A total of 702 occupations in the USA were assessed using this method. The authors concluded that around 47% of employees in the USA work in occupations with a high risk of automation. The industries affected here are transportation, logistics and production, but also employees in the office and administration sectors across all industries. Frey and Osborne believe that employees will only win the race against automation if they acquire creative and social skills. The study results were also applied to Germany in [7]. Bonin, Gregory and Zierahn concluded that the results of the Frey and Osborne study require a cautious interpretation, arguing that the study overestimates the automation potential and does not consider the legal, social and ethical factors on shaping the development. They point out that further research is needed to better understand the relationship between automation, vocational training, and job creation.

The study [8] presented for Germany by Dengler and Matthes examines the substitutability potential of activities by technologies available today and applies this substitutability potential to entire occupations. This study explicitly points out that this assessment is not conducted by technology experts, who often overestimate the deployment capabilities of technologies, but by experts from the Federal Employment Agency. Furthermore, the classification of occupations is based on the expert database BERUFENET and is therefore not subject to transfer errors between the various occupational classifications. One result of the study shows that 15 percnt of employees subject to social insurance contributions in Germany can expect a very high substitutability potential, affecting approximately 4.672 million people [9]. However, the use of such technologies would have to be economically worthwhile for the corporate organizations and the legal and ethical issues would also have to be clarified [2, 8]. Another result of the study is that the substitutability potentials differ in the individual occupations and within them depending on the level of demand (helper, skilled worker, specialist, expert).

Information that uses concrete examples to show the as yet inadequate applicability of technologies is rare. But it is precisely this information that would help assess the connections between technological development and the future of work in a more differentiated way. Thus, as mentionded in [9, 10]:

- In May 2017, the University of Texas at Houston MD Anderson Oncology Center's contract with IBM for cancer research was not renewed. After 6 years and $62 million in spending, it has failed to integrate IBM Watson into everyday clinical practice. Despite the length of time, the high investment, and the support of a renowned international company, the expected treatment recommendations for real patients had not been delivered.
- In Berlin, a pilot project compares the faces of volunteers with those of terror threats in a database. While the facial recognition algorithm managed to recognize 70% of the faces, about 1% of the people were incorrectly classified as 'wanted', posing a serious problem. With 160,000 people scanned every day, that would result in 1600 false alarms. This made it clear that the use of facial recognition under real conditions was far more difficult than originally anticipated.

Dengler and Matthes see people's ability to keep their skills relevant and up to date [8] as one of the major challenges. There may be several reasons for this. Firstly, education policy is primarily focused on first degree education [11]. Secondly, vocational and career counselling services are also reaching the limits of their counselling options, as they too are unsure about how and when occupations will change. And thirdly [12, 13], despite the first points mentioned, responsibility for education is increasingly being transferred to the workforce.

Against the backdrop of these challenges, the concept of employability takes on greater significance and involves both employers and employees.- employers who need to attract and retain employees by promoting and supporting them, and employees, who assume responsibility for their own qualifications, not necessarily to enable career advancement but simply to avoid career decline. In addition, employees have shifted the focus on the skills they feel they need. While the emphasis used to be on technical competencies, it has now shifted more to interdisciplinary competencies and maintaining health. Particularly with regard to the latter, it has been recognised that physical and psychological overload in the workplace can have a negative impact on health in the long term [12].

2.2.2 Corporate Organizations in Transition

On the corporate side, too, the opinion is that digitalization will develop gradually, i.e. evolutionarily. Overall, however, there is no uniform picture of what the digitized corporate environment should look like or what it currently looks like.

In order to get a picture of the current state of corporate organizations, [14] a survey was conducted with 1.183 Swiss companies all with more than 20 employees, with regard to digitalization. Among other things, they were asked specifically about 24 technologies or technology elements, ranging from ERP and CRM to social media and RFID to 3D printing, autonomous driving vehicles and IoT. Rather surprisingly, the proportion of investment in digitalization has fallen over time, which can be attributed primarily to the services sector. And overall employment has not changed for around 76% of companies. Rather as expected, differences emerge between large and smaller firms in terms of technology diffusion, with the former having an edge over the latter. To the question of what factors were preventing digititalization, reasons most often mentioned included lack of skills or financial resources, workflow inadequacies, and the complexity of building network infrastructures.

A somewhat more differentiated but still heterogeneous picture emerges for German small and medium-sized enterprises (SMEs) from the survey conducted by the Center for European Economic Research [15]. Thus, one third of the companies surveyed are in a fundamental phase of digitalization. This means that the familiar buzzwords such as Industry 4.0 and their implementation are not currently part of operational reality. As with the Swiss companies, the number of digitalization projects is lower for small companies than for large ones, but low expenditure is the same for all, regardless of company size. The most frequently cited obstacles hampering the advancement of digitalization are the shortage of IT skills among employees, data protection and data security, inadequate Internet connection speed and the slow adaptation of corporate and work organization.

SMEs also include the skilled crafts, which are closely associated with individual product creation. In 2020, this important economic sector in Germany included around 5.6 million employees and around 1 million companies [38]. Digital processes are already present in the skilled crafts: for example, roofers use drones to examine roofs, electricians network devices in the spirit of the smart home, and model makers and dental technicians use 3-D printers to manufacture their products. By highlighting important aspects of its "Digitale Agenda des Handwerks" (Digital Agenda for the Skilled Crafts), the ZDH German Confederation of Skilled Crafts has adjusted the framework conditions for the digitalization of the skilled crafts to match those for the large industrial companies. This also includes, among other things, research funding tailored to the skilled crafts sector, nationwide Internet access and net neutrality, support for digitalization, the possibility of constantly updated training and continuing education, and the creation of the legal framework to prevent undercutting competition between crowd workers, solo self-employed workers and skilled crafts businesses [16]. In 2020, the term crowd worker or crowd employment was replaced by the term platform worker or platform work because this form of employment has changed and now covers more types of tasks [63, 64].

The corporate and work organization was listed in [15], as one of the key obstacles to advancing digitalization. This is linked to expectations that the challenges of the future can be mastered through greater flexibility and more personal responsibility on the part of employees [17]. There are currently two organizational forms, Holacracy and Reinventing Organizations, which are being discussed in this context and have been adopted by a few companies [19]. Holacracy [20] does not describe an ideal organizational structure but defines the rules of how to reach decisions within an organization and this can be company specific. Here, one works in circles (group of employees) and with roles (functions). Each circle usually has two roles: Lead Link and Rep Link. The former manages the circle and the latter manages communication to the other circles. Holacracy, in its positive implementation, is designed to speed up the decision-making process by avoiding hierarchical leadership through information advantage. In its negative form, it can lead to competitive situations between the circles or the desire of the lead link to exclude employees for performance reasons. Such a situation may then require the help of organizational consulting or a supervisor to be clarified. In [19], reference is also made to the somewhat contradictory situation in companies. On the one hand, comapnies aspire to new forms of organization that give employees more personal responsibility. On the other hand, however, these same companies are promoting a precarization of labor, and the expansion of the Human Cloud, and thereby reinforcing an already present desolidarization among the employces.

Laloux [21], in his concept Reinventing Organizations, uses the metaphor of a living system that, like nature, is constantly changing and has no central authority. He defines three factors that are characteristic of this type of organization:

1. Self-Management: No hierarchy and no consensus.
2. Wholeness: Complete employee involvement.
3. Evolutionary purpose: The organization has its own sense of meaning and purpose.

Critical questions are raised about both forms of organization in [19], including: Who finally owns the company? How are the questions of profit and profitability dealt with? Is there not something totalitarian about the devotion demanded? Is self-exploitation the calculation basis of these new forms of organizations?

2.3   New Forms of Employment

The future of work will not only be influenced by technological innovations, but also by new forms of employment. In Germany, possible reasons cited for this are social contribution savings of up to 40% of gross income and the decreasing attractiveness of statutory pension insurance [22]. Today, this is compounded by the greater flexibility expected by both employees and employers. Eurofound [23], the European Foundation for the Improvement of Living and Working Conditions [24], published the results of a Europe-wide survey in 2016 and found that the majority of discussions on new forms of employment take place between the social partners. Governments, which might be expected to play an active role as part of their responsibility for labour and social policy, do not do so in this way. The flexicurity concept [25], i.e. seeking a balance between flexibility and security in working and living conditions, once important in the EU, has lost significance. However, Eurofound defined a total of nine groups of new forms of employment that have developed since 2000. Two of them, Employee Sharing and Crowd Employment, seem to be of particular interest [26]. Strategic employee sharing means that an employee is jointly hired by several companies in the same region to cover the proportionate volume of work in each company. This offers several advantages. The employee is thereby employed in a regular employment relationship, thus reducing possible precariousness. And employers share the employment risk, while ensuring access to qualified labor [27]. Eurofound believes that this new form of employment is underestimated in its potential. They also raise the question of why more precarious forms of employment are more widespread than strategic employee sharing, which offers advantages for both employees and employers [26].

Platform work, is a form of employment whereby employers advertise larger or smaller jobs on an online platform, which are then contracted out to workers [26]. Because there are no comprehensive and cross-national data on the number of platform workers and their exact working and living conditions, opinions differ on the prevalence of this form of employment and its precarious working and living conditions. Some authors think that platform work is increasingly spreading [28, 29, 30], while others, for example the Swiss Federal Council, are critical of their general growth forecasts and consider the extent of the platform economy in Switzerland to be low [31]. Without precise data, in terms of numbers, on the affected employees and the benefiting employers in the platform economy, it seems difficult to call for political action. The desired self-regulation of platform operators has also largely failed to materialize [1, 32]. What is known about the working and living conditions of platform workers, however, includes the following:

- Workers are expected to perform unpaid work and offer high availability in order to receive positive feedback, which they rely on for further contracting [28].
- Contracting can also be competitive, i.e. platform workers submit finished products, concepts, or proposals and are only paid if their input is accepted [28].
- In this case, the contractor could simply use the other unaccepted submissions/ proposals, unless the intellectual property issue is explicitly regulated [33].
- Intra-company platform work may intensify competition between employees [34].
- Platform workers do not have the legal rights of protection against dismissal, sick pay, and minimum wage [35].

In this context, Thomas Klebe says: "Poor working conditions are not a private matter" [35]. Eurofound makes the following policy recommendations concerning the new forms of employment [23]:

- Develop specific concepts for individual new forms of employment, based on a cross-national exchange of information and experience.
- Raise awareness among employers and employees of new forms of employment and their positive impact on the labor market.
- Establish safety nets in the form of legislation or collective agreements for workers of the new forms of employment.
- Extend the political discussion to the areas of regional and sectoral development.

2.4 Trade Unions and Participation

Digitalization is changing the world of work, and this world of work also includes the trade unions. They are involved in the daily, practical debate in companies, but also in the empirical debate within the framework of research projects. One such case is the current research assocation "Digitalisierung, Mitbestimmung und gute Arbeit" (Digitalization, co-determination and good work) of the Hans Böckler Foundation, which seeks, answers to the question "how the process of digitalization can be shaped in terms of co-determination and good work" [36]. Here, 15 research projects were selected from a competition of ideas that address this question and also take into account different perspectives or interest groups. The publications that have resulted from this research association can be seen here [18].

In addition to the issues of co-determination and good work, however, there are other challenges that trade unions face in the future of work due to digitalization. These include [36, 37]:

- The flexibilization of work locations and, as a result, a changed information and communication situation with existing or potential members.
- A further differentiated world of work, which seems to move between extreme simple work and extreme highly qualified knowledge work [39].
- The development of appropriate vocational training and continuing education in the direction of changed professions or activities.
- The development of possible corporate profit and capital sharing schemes for employees.

Irrespective of digitalization, trade unions are also facing the challenge of stopping or reversing the trend of stagnating or declining membership, in order to retain their position as a negotiating partner with bargaining power recognized by social partners [37].

It seems important to recognize digitalization as a megatrend, and to take advantage of the scope for shaping it, which undoubtedly exists [40]. Thus, it is worth remembering that future work cannot be derived from the use of new technologies alone, in the sense of a cause-and-effect relationship, but that the use of new technologies is also influenced by the legal, social and operational framework conditions [2, 40]. In the context of digitalization, there could be further scope for shaping the use of very specific technical systems. This goes beyond the usual opportunities for participation, such as in the design of user-friendliness [40], and may also require new or adapted opportunities for participation in order to meet the operational requirements resulting from digitalization [41]. While the studies listed in Sect. 2.2.1 do not agree on the automation potential of occupations and activities, they do agree on the direction of the shift, namely towards non-routine activities, flexible and interactive activities and more demanding tasks. The employment growth is expected to come from new business models in the service sector [37, 40]. Although very little is known so far about which new occupations, activities and business models will emerge, it is expected that new, higher qualifications will be necessary, but that knowledge gained from professional experience will still remain important. Here, too, there is scope for trade unions to turn this into an opportunity for employees [40]. Two trends affect this need for qualification. On the one hand, there is the emergence of multi-employer relationships, which may also require different qualifications [42]. On the other hand, a flattening of hierarchies combined with new, also virtual, forms of organization shifts the responsibility for further training even more to the employed, without them knowing the precise development of the company.

The same applies to trade unions as to companies and employees: a global perspective must be adopted [37]. Here an example to illustrate: the platform worker from Germany works on a Swiss platform for an American entrepreneur. In this case, physical borders no longer exists, and the value chains have become more global, creating. a situation that makes international cooperations increasingly important for trade unions.

2.5 Science Fiction and the Future of Work

The future of work, in this case very specifically the occupations and activities, can be forecast as in the studies mentioned in Sect. 2.2, by interviewing either technology experts [6] or experts from the Federal Employment Agency [8]. Another possibility would be to apply methods of futurology.

The purpose of futurology is to discover, invent and analyze possible futures, and this includes describing possible policy steps that would allow the desired future to be achieved. It is important here to distinguish the desired future from the plausible one, i.e. future scenarios that describe Western European countries without an increasingly ageing population and without migration flows do not appear plausible. If political measures then support this future scenario, the problems are exacerbated [43].

The methods of futurology are diverse and range from the scenario technique [44] (a method with the help of which positive and negative factors are developed mentally in such a way that images of the future are created [45]) to the Delphi method (a special form of expert survey [46]) [47, 48]. However, there is a general shift towards participative methods, as the assumption that only a few people deal with their future and that of society in a very concrete and detailed way, but this is precisely what participatory methods expect [47].

Science fiction plays a significant role in this regard because society's images of the future are often based precisely on it [49].

In the project "Die Zukunft der Arbeit in der Vergangenheit des Science Fiction" (The Future of Work in the Past of Science Fiction) at the Lucerne University of Applied Sciences and Arts, approximately 50 electronically available science fiction books written between 2011 and 2013 were therefore analysed. Using analysis software, these books were then searched for terms related to work and the passages found were analyzed. The idea was to infer the future of work with the help of science fiction books of the present [50, 51].

The analyzed books contained different descriptions of work [50]. For example, there are societies in which work is done by robots so that people can live according to their own ideas [52]. In [53] the work could actually be done by robots, but they are not trusted, and so some work is done by humans. In the meantime, the robots do not want to take over dangerous jobs because they do not want to die. In [54], robots can be made cheaply, get by without sleep, and feed on a protein mush until they break. In another society [55], work is mandatory but highly regulated. For example, people generally work only 3 days and from the age of 55 this is gradually reduced. In [56] work can be so strenuous that after seven to 8 years people are exhausted and cannot continue working. More than half of people work shifts in home offices, in part because the earth is overpopulated and transportation capacity is exhausted [57]. Technological developments have not been held back to allow people to adapt. But, from the state's point of view, this led to a faulty or no professional adaptation, i.e. people were not prepared to let go of their old professions. That is why the employment office is also called "Office for Human Adaptation" [58].

In [59] public administration is provided by artificial intelligence. When humans are accused, the charges are dropped if they take over 5 years of construction and administration tasks [60]. The highest positions in the public administration had the so-called "Machinavellians", who are people who want to be machines [61].

Interestingly, some of the science fiction books analyzed do not describe a utopia, but rather a dystopia. And this often does not reveal the scope of development. In a sub-field of futurology, namely critical futurology, the focus is on averting precisely these negative future scenarios. It is also assumed that technologies are not value-neutral, but often linked to targeted interests, [48] and that everyone, not only futurologists, writers or fortune tellers, can think about the future and develop their own ideas about it [62].

2.6 Outlook

In most countries, work is still the structuring element in society [1]. This makes it both important and difficult to systematically find out which new occupations will emerge despite and because of automation. It is also crucial to create the necessary legal framework so that the workers of today and tomorrow can make appropriate use of the social security systems. The following questions also must be clarified: To what extent can the tool scenario be the guiding model for companies, society, and politics [2]? How can the existing opportunities for shaping the development be used by trade unions within the framework of automation? How can training and further education be adapted to the requirements of the world of work in a timely manner? And what measures must workers take for their health care in order to be able to cope with the current and future requirements of the world of work?

References

1. Negt O (2011) Arbeit und menschliche Würde. Essay. Aus Politik Zeitgeschichte (APuZ) (15):3–5
2. Flecker J, Schönauer A, Riesenecker-Caba T (2016) Digitalisierung der Arbeit: Welche Revolution? Auszug aus WISO 4/2016. WISO 39(4):18–34
3. Windelband L, Spöttl G (2012) Diffusion von Technologien in die Facharbeit und deren Konsequenzen für die Qualifizierung am Beispiel des "Internet der Dinge". In: Fasshauer U, Fürstenau B, Wuttke E (eds) Berufs- und wirtschaftspädagogische Analysen – aktuelle Forschungen zur beruflichen Bildung (Schriftenreihe der Sektion Berufs- und Wirtschaftspädagogik der Deutschen Gesellschaft für Erziehungswissenschaft (DGfE)). Budrich, Opladen, pp 205–219
4. Lobin H (2014) Engelbarts Traum. Wie der Computer uns Lesen und Schreiben abnimmt. Campus, Frankfurt
5. Morozov E (2015) Digitale Technologie und menschliche Freiheit. Neue Ges Frankf Hefte 3:30–34
6. Frey CB, Osborne MA (2016) The future of employment. How susceptible are jobs to computerisation? Technol Forecast Soc Chang 114:254–280
7. Bonin H, Gregory T, Zierahn U (2015) Übertragung der Studie von Frey/Osborne (2013) auf Deutschland. Research Report. ZEW Kurzexpertise Nr. 57. Zentrum für Europäische Wirtschaftsforschung (ZEW), Mannheim
8. Dengler K, Matthes B (2015) Folgen der Digitalisierung für die Arbeitswelt: Substituierbarkeitspotenziale von Berufen in Deutschland. IAB-Forschungsbericht Nr. 11, Nürnberg. http://doku.iab.de/forschungsbericht/2015/fb1115.pdf. Accessed on 15 Apr 2017
9. Bundesagentur für Arbeit (2015) Sozialversicherungspflichtige Beschäftigte nach ausgewählten Merkmalen nach Arbeits- und Wohnort – Deutschland, Länder und Kreise (Quartalszahlen)
10. Fuest B, Michler I (2017) Künstlich? Ja. Intelligenz. NEIN! Welt Sonntag 52:31–32
11. Weber E (2017) Digitalisierung als Herausforderung für eine Weiterbildungspolitik. Wirtschaftsdienst 97(5):372–374
12. Rump J, Eilers S (2017) Das Konzept des employability management. In: Rump J, Eilers S (eds) Auf dem Weg zur Arbeit 4.0. Innovationen in HR. IBE Reihe. Springer Gabler, Berlin/Heidelberg, pp 87–126
13. Gaylor C, Schöpf N, Severing E (2015) Wenn aus Kompetenzen berufliche Chancen werden. Wie europäische Nachbarn informelles und non-formales Lernen anerkennen und nutzen, 1st edn. Verlag Bertelsmann Stiftung, Gütersloh

14. Arvanitis S, Spescha A, Wäfler T, Grote G, Wörter M (2017) Digitalisierung in der Schweizer Wirtschaft. Ergebnisse der Umfrage 2016: Eine Teilauswertung im Auftrag des SBFI
15. Zimmermann V (2016) SMEs and digitalisation: the current position, recent developments and challenges, No. 138. KfW Research, Frankfurt am Main, pp 1–7. https://www.kfw.de/PDF/ Download-Center/Konzernthemen/Research/PDF-Dokumente-Fokus-Volkswirtschaft/Fokus-englische-Dateien/Fokus-2016-EN/Fokus-Nr.-138-August-2016-Digitalisierung_EN.pdf. Accessed on 14 July 2021
16. Schulte K-S, Barthel A, Dohle A (2018) Anforderungen des Handwerks an Prävention 4.0. In: Cernavin O, Schröter W, Stowasser S (eds) Prävention 4.0. Analysen und Handlungsempfehlungen für eine produktive und gesunde Arbeit 4.0. Springer Fachmedien, Wiesbaden, pp 95–107
17. Häusling A, Rutz B (2017) Agile Führungsstrukturen und Führungskulturen zur Förderung der Selbstorganisation – Ausgestaltung und Herausforderungen. In: von Au C (ed) Struktur und Kultur einer Leadership-Organisation. Holistik, Wertschätzung, Vertrauen, Agilität und Lernen. Leadership und Angewandte Psychologie. Springer, Wiesbaden, pp 105–122
18. Hans-Böckler-Stiftung (n.d.) Forschungsverbünde: Digitalisierung, Mitbestimmung, Gute Arbeit. https://www.boeckler.de/de/digitalisierung-mitbestimmung-gute-arbeit-18485.htm. Accessed on 14 July 2021
19. Döller M (2017) Die "Human Cloud" und die Organisationsberatung einer seltsamen Zukunft. Zeitschrift für Psychodrama und Soziometrie 16(S1):185–199
20. Mitterer G (2014) HolacracyTM – ein Fleischwolf für organisationale Entscheidungsprozesse. http://www.opmschmiede.net/wp-content/uploads/2015/03/2015_gm_Einf%C3%BChrung_ in_Holacracy.pdf. Accessed on 17 Feb 2018
21. Laloux F (2015) Reinventing organizations. Ein Leitfaden zur Gestaltung sinnstiftender Formen der Zusammenarbeit. Verlag Franz Vahlen, München
22. Dilger A (2002) Neue Beschäftigungsformen als Antwort auf alte Sozialsysteme. Zeitschrift für Personalforschung 16(4):563
23. Eurofound (2016) Neue Beschäftigungsformen. Zusammenfassung, Eurofound. Reference Nr.: EF14611. https://www.eurofound.europa.eu/de/publications/executive-summary/2015/ working-conditions-labour-market/new-forms-of-employment-executive-summary. Accessed on 11 Feb 2018
24. Eurofound (n.d.) Über Eurofound. https://www.eurofound.europa.eu/de/about-eurofound. Accessed on 11 Feb 2018
25. Klammer U, Tillmann K, Schwarze J, Hanesch W, Rabe B, Bäcker G et al (2001) Flexicurity: Soziale Sicherung und Flexibilisierung der Arbeits- und Lebensverhältnisse. Forschungsprojekt im Auftrag des Ministeriums für Arbeit und Soziales, Qualifikation und Technologie des Landes Nordrhein-Westfalen, Düsseldorf. http://www.sozialpolitik-aktuell.de/tl_files/sozialpolitik-aktuell/_Politikfelder/Sozialstaat/Dokumente/flexicurity.pdf. Accessed on 11 Feb 2018
26. Eurofound (2016) New forms of employment. Publications Office of the European Union, Luxembourg
27. Eurofound (2016) New forms of employment: developing the potential of strategic employee sharing. Research Report. Publications Office of the European Union, Luxembourg
28. Schörpf P, Flecker J, Schönauer A, Eichmann H (2017) Triangular love-hate. Management and control in creative crowdworking. New Technol Work Employ 32(1):43–58
29. Hammon L, Hippner H (2012) Crowdsourcing. Wirtschaftsinformatik 54(3):165–168
30. Leimeister JM, Zogaj S, Durward D, Blohm I (2016) Systematisierung und Analyse von Crowd-Sourcing-Anbietern und Crowd-Work-Projekten. Reihe Praxiswissen Betriebsvereinbarungen, Nr. 324. Hans-Böckler-Stiftung, Düsseldorf
31. Der Bundesrat (2017) Auswirkungen der Digitalisierung auf Beschäftigung und Arbeitsbedingungen – Chancen und Risiken. Bericht des Bundesrates in Erfüllung der Postulate 15.3854 Reynard vom 16.09.2015 und 17.3222 Derder vom 17.03.2017 (242.3–00001\COO.2101.104.4.2577057). https://www.newsd.admin.ch/newsd/message/ attachments/50248.pdf. Accessed on 12 Feb 2018

32. Dänische Gewerkschaft der Vertriebs- und Büroangestellten (HK), IG Metall, International Brotherhood of Teamsters, Local 117, Kammer für Angestellte und Arbeiter (Österreich), Österreichischer Gewerkschaftsbund (ÖGB), Service Employees International Union et al (2016) Frankfurter Erklärung zu plattformbasierter Arbeit. Vorschläge für Plattformbetreiber, Kunden, politische Entscheidungsträger, Beschäftigte und Arbeitnehmerorganisationen. https://www.igmetall.de/docs_20161214_Frankfurt_Paper_on_Platform_Based_Work_DE_1c33819e1e90d2d09e531a61a572a0a423a93455.pdf. Accessed on 11 Feb 2018

33. Durward D, Blohm I, Leimeister JM (2016) Is there PAPA in crowd work?: a literature review on ethical dimensions in crowdsourcing. http://pubs.wi-kassel.de/wp-content/uploads/2016/07/JML_563.pdf Accessed on 30 July 2016

34. Kawalec S, Menz W (2013) Die Verflüssigung von Arbeit. Crowdsourcing als unternehmerische Reorganisationsstrategie – das Beispiel IBM. Arbeits- und Industriesoziologische Studien 6(2):5–23

35. Redaktion IG Metall (2016). Schlechte Arbeitsbedingungen sind keine Privatsache. Interview mit Arbeitsrechtler Thomas Klebe. https://www.igmetall.de/interview-mit-arbeitsrechtler-thomas-klebe-zum-thema-14335.htm. Accessed on 12 Feb 2018

36. Hans-Böckler-Stiftung (2018) Digitalisierung: Aktivitäten der Abteilung Forschungsförderung. https://www.boeckler.de/67477.htm. Accessed on 13 Feb 2018

37. Eichhorst W, Hinte H, Spermann A, Zimmermann KF (2015) Die neue Beweglichkeit: Die Gewerkschaften in der digitalen Arbeitswelt. IZA Standpunkte Nr. 82, Bonn. http://hdl.handle.net/10419/121270. Accessed on 13 Feb 2018

38. Zentralverband des Deutschen Handwerks (ZDH) (ed) (2021) Daten und Fakten zum Handwerk für das Jahr 2020 – Betriebszahlen – Berufliche Bildung – Beschäftigte und Umsätze. https://www.zdh.de/daten-und-fakten/kennzahlen-des-handwerks/wirtschaftlicher-stellenwert-des-handwerks-2020/#c2077 Accessed on 14 July 2021

39. Hirsch-Kreinsen H, Minssen H (2016) Arbeitswelten und industrielle Beziehungen – zwischen Einfacharbeit und hochqualifizierter Arbeit. Editorial Ind Bezieh 23(4):411–414

40. Kuhlmann M (2017) Digitalisierung und Arbeit – Thesen für die gewerkschaftliche Diskussion. In: Tagung (ed) "Digitalisierung der Arbeitswelt", Unveröffentlichtes Manuskript. Unia Schweiz, Olten

41. Oerder K (2016) MITBESTIMMUNG 4.0. Der Wandel der Arbeitswelt als Chance für mehr Beteiligung. WISO Direkt 24:1–4

42. Helfen M, Nicklich M, Sydow J (2014) Hybride Wertschöpfung als Herausforderung für die Tarifpolitik. Mehr-Arbeitgeber-Beziehungen als arbeitspolitische Herausforderung. Gegenblende – das DGB Debattenportal. http://gegenblende.dgb.de/++co++9999dda2-083b-11e4-816c-52540066f352. Accessed on 13 Feb 2018

43. Graf HG (2017) (n.d.) Über den Zweck der Zukunftsforschung, St. Galler Zentrum für Zukunftsforschung. http://www.institutfutur.de/_service/download/Graf_SuB2003_4.pdf. Accessed on 5 Aug 2017

44. Schäfer R (2014) Design Fiction. (iF Schriftenreihe 01/14). Institut Futur, Berlin. http://www.ewi-psy.fu-berlin.de/einrichtungen/weitere/institut-futur/_media_design/IF-Schriftenreihe/IF-Schriftenreihe_0114_Schaefer_Design-Fiction_Online.pdf. Accessed on 5 Aug 2017

45. Weinbrenner P (2016) Szenariotechnik. sowi-online. https://www.sowi-online.de/praxis/methode/szenariotechnik.html. Accessed on 20 Feb 2018

46. Steinmüller K (1997) Grundlagen und Methoden der Zukunftsforschung. Szenarien, Delphi, Techikvorausschau (Steinmüller K, Ed.) (Werkstattbericht No. 21). Sekretariat für Zukunftsforschung, Gelsenkirchen. https://www.steinmuller.de/de/zukunftsforschung/downloads/WB%2013%20Science%20Fiction.pdf. Accessed on 20 Feb2018

47. Helbig B (2013) Wünsche und Zukunftsforschung (Freie Universität Berlin, Ed.) (iF Schriftenreihe 01/13). Institut Futur. http://edocs.fu-berlin.de/docs/servlets/MCRFileNodeServlet/FUDOCS_derivate_000000004145/IF-Schriftenreihe_0113_Helbig_Wunschforschung_online.pdf. Accessed on 5 Aug 2017

48. Tiberius V (ed) (2011) Zukunftsorientierung in der Betriebswirtschaftslehre. Gabler Verlag/Springer Fachmedien, Wiesbaden

49. Steinmüller K (1995) Gestaltbare Zukünfte. Zukunftsforschung und Science Fiction. Abschlussbericht. Sekretariat für Zukunftsforschung, Gelsenkirchen. https://steinmuller.de/de/zukunftsforschung/downloads/WB%2021%20Grundlagen.pdf Accessed on 14 Feb 2018
50. Klotz U, Boos D (2016) Science Fiction zu zukünftigen Arbeitswelten. Blogpost. Accessed on 14 Feb 2018
51. CreaLab (ed) (2015) Science-Fiction und die Zukunft der Arbeit. Blogpost. https://sites.hslu.ch/crealab/wp-content/uploads/sites/5/2020/02/KG_DieZukunftDerArbeit_04.pdf. Accessed on 14 Feb 2018
52. Schmidt P (2013) Das Prinzip von Hell und Dunkel. Science-Fiction-Thriller. neobooks Self-Publishing, München
53. Anderson F (2009) Science Fiction Kurzgeschichten. Books on Demand, Norderstedt
54. Anton U (2008) Venus ist tot. Science-Fiction-Geschichten. Fabylon, Markt Rettenbach
55. Elsner R (2011) Rudolf Wundersam und das Arche-Noah-Prinzip. Eine Science-Fiction-Fantasy-Geschichte. Books on Demand, Norderstedt
56. Müller J (2014) Das Bbk-P. Science Fiction Kurzgeschichten. BookRix, München
57. Tholey P, Förster O (2013) Der Erneuerer. Zweite Geschichte des Space-Legion-Zyklus. BookRix, München
58. Simak CD (2010) Als es noch Menschen gab. Wilhelm Heyne, München
59. Müller J (2013) Das erste Mal. Science Fiction Kurzgeschichten. BookRix, München
60. Benninghaus E (2011) Futuristische Mord-Fiktionen. Frösche für den Mars, und andere Science-Fiction Erzählungen. Books on Demand, Norderstedt
61. Häusler M (2012) Die Zeitfälscher. Ein ausserirdisch cooler (Anti) Science Fiction Roman. Books on Demand, Norderstedt
62. Hideg É (2007) Theory and practice in the field of foresight. Foresight 9(6):36–46
63. Eurofound (2020) Crowd Employment. Dublin. Accessed on 14 July 2021
64. Lane M (2020) Regulating platform work in the digital age: Policy Note (OECD Going Digital Toolkit Policy No. 1). https://goingdigital.oecd.org/toolkitnotes/regulating-platform-work-in-the-digital-age.pdf

New Forms of Value Creation in the Digital Age

3

Kathrin Kirchner, Claudia Lemke, and Walter Brenner

Abstract

Data and information are the oil of the digital age; industrial and service robots and intelligent algorithms are becoming a decisive production factor and will have a lasting impact on classic value creation. At the same time, however, they also create new opportunities for entrepreneurial value creation, thus influencing industry and market structures. This article explains the changes in entrepreneurial value creation through the targeted use of digital technologies. In particular, the influences of hardware and software robotics, intelligent algorithms and advanced analytics are discussed and classified. Based on this, examples are used to demonstrate disruptions in the entrepreneurial value chain. The resulting changes and their consequences are discussed by using examples. The changing demands on the market, industry structures, and business models with their business processes in these value creation structures are highlighted. To conclude the article, changes in value creation are outlined by using the example of the healthcare sector.

K. Kirchner (✉)
Technical University of Denmark, Kgs. Lyngby, Denmark
e-mail: kakir@dtu.dk

C. Lemke
Berlin School of Economics and Law (HWR), Berlin, Germany
e-mail: claudia.lemke@hwr-berlin.de

W. Brenner
University of St. Gallen, St. Gallen, Switzerland
e-mail: walter.brenner@unisg.ch

23

T. Barton et al. (eds.), *Digitalization in companies*,
https://doi.org/10.1007/978-3-658-39094-5_3

3.1   Introduction and Case Studies

The economy and society worldwide are in a state of change. Digitisation has already and will have an even greater impact on our private lives, business processes and business models. Three central features characterise digitalisation: people and things are connected, processes and products are virtualised, and data and knowledge, as well as their exchange and networking, are becoming increasingly important.

The power of consumers is a key variable in the relevance and success of digital business models with their products and services and their influence on the principles of software development and use. The increasing presence of the intelligence of machines and objects and the accompanying progressive automation of the economy and society are forcing changes in value creation in companies and in society in the direction of software development or algorithms in general. In addition, scenarios in which data-driven software solutions can be applied have been increasing.

Leading companies from various industries have already fallen victim to far-reaching disruptions. For example, in 2006, the Finnish Nokia Group dominated the still small smartphone market, having over 50% of the market share. However, a year later, Apple's iPhone hit the market. Intuitive touchscreens and apps became the trend, but Nokia continued to rely on keyboard phones and on the power of its own brand [1]. However, Nokia's supremacy melted away, the Finns were acquired by Microsoft and the company lost its importance. The touchscreen smartphone can be described as a disruptive technology – that is, technology capable of replacing the success of existing technology or completely displacing it from the market. Such technologies are initially found at the lower end of the market or in new markets. A new market is initially uninteresting for established companies because it can serve only a few customers with low volumes. However, new markets can grow very quickly, displacing established products and their suppliers [2].

Automobile manufacturers are also facing the biggest revolution since the invention of the combustion engine; they are evolving from hardware manufacturers to infrastructure providers and integrated mobility service providers [3]. Vehicles generate vast amounts of data, process these data, and use the data to then make decisions (keyword Big Data, [4]). Audi AG in Ingolstadt started a new era of data processing in passenger cars when the new Audi A8 launched in autumn 2017. Part of the intelligence previously distributed among decentralised embedded systems to support the actual driving process was concentrated on a central processing unit, the driving assistance system (zFAS). In this central processing unit, all data from the sensors (ultrasonic, radar, camera and lidar sensors) of the vehicle converge, generating a data model (real world model) of the environment in real time. The interpretation of this data model is not only used to control automated driving, but also to increase safety. In the event of an accident predicted with a high degree of certainty by the data processing of the central control unit, the floor panel of the A8 is raised by a few centimetres at lightning speed to improve the crash behaviour of the vehicle. It is expected that in the next few years, by using the data from sensor technology, numerous other digital services will be offered in vehicles and will go far beyond automated or highly automated driving [5]. The knowledge derived from the collected data can be copied and disseminated virtually free of charge through digitisation. Unlike real products, there are hardly any costs for storage or warehousing.

According to Rutherford, the classic definition of value added is calculated as the difference between the market value of the goods produced by the company and the cost of these goods and materials procured from other producers [6]. Value is created from existing resources, such as materials, machines, employees and knowledge, which is then actually realised through the sale of products and services. In the age of digitalisation, however, value creation also occurs in other ways. New value creation patterns have emerged that, contrary to traditional concepts, are based on openness and are collaborative and decentralised in nature [7]. Via the internet, people can freely connect and work together (crowdworkers, e.g., at Amazon Mechanical Turk, https://www.mturk.com). In the maker movement, people organise themselves to together develop new products in open workshops (fablabs).

New opportunities are also emerging in companies through which additional value can be generated, for example, through the collection and analysis of data, greater proximity to customers or greater flexibility. This chapter examines new forms of value creation in the digital age. It first looks at technology-driven value creation in general before explaining some selected forms of digital value creation in more detail through the use of examples. Finally, new forms of digital value creation are specifically discussed using the example of eHealth.

3.2   Technology-Driven Value Creation

3.2.1   Importance of Technology

Digitisation and networking affect the entire company, including its business models with value creation, processes and structures, products and services, and culture. Focusing on the support provided by information and communication technology alone, for example, through the use of operational information systems such as an Enterprise Resource Planning (ERP) system, does not realise technology-driven value creation. Data and information as the raw material of digital value creation, the increasing quest for complete automation and robotics all offer the potential to completely redesign previous corporate structures and services. For example, innovative, smart, social and technologically open interaction and communication systems, which can be used to develop customer-centric solutions, stand for this in particular. For example, the data-driven algorithms of Big Data combined with the possibilities of machine learning [8] form the basis for the applications of Industry 4.0 or for the capabilities of increasing the robotisation of industrial and service-oriented fields of work [9]. The resulting disruption of existing business models, products and services creates new forms of technology-driven value creation for companies.

An early recognition of the trends and tendencies in these technology areas, an observation of new solutions and their assessment regarding development and maturation are indispensable to react appropriately to the associated changes and, above all, act in a future-oriented manner [10, p. 468].

3.2.2 Data and Information as Drivers of Digital Value Creation for Business Models

'If it can be digitalized, it will be.' [10, p. 5]. This mantra from Silicon Valley illustrates the fundamentally changed role of data and information in a company's entire value creation process. Moving away from its former supporting role, data are becoming the sole factor of production, primarily as completely digital business models with digital products and services are pursued. Digital value creation, however, is no longer subject to the logic of Porter's value chain [11, p. 35] but requires a new value creation process. Real value creation uses, among other things, the skilful allocation of resources of real quantities, such as raw materials, capital and labour, to generate a service.

In the digital world, the skilful combination of data, its processing and presentation, and its consumption provides added value. Since 2007, less than 2% of the world's information has been in paper form, that is, analogue [12]. Thus, data form the basis for implementing new digital business models, such as the Big Tech companies Amazon, Google (Alphabet Cooperation), Meta (former Facebook) and Apple have realised in an extreme manner [13]. Digital ecosystems can be developed from this, through which millions of users are bound in the long term and produce further data through their own use, which is then used by the operators for the further development of the business models through analysis. This results in self-reinforcing effects that generally bind users even more strongly to the digital ecosystem. Quasi-monopoly positions then consume competitive positions or make it more difficult for others to enter the market. In 2020, in Germany, one in eight euros was spent online [14], and this spending has grown exponentially during the corona pandemic, just as in most European countries [15]. Here, the market-dominating position becomes obvious. Comparing the market value of internet giants to traditional business models, data-driven value creation becomes particularly clear. The internet giants are among the most valuable listed companies in the world.

However, not only can completely new business models be created through the use of data, but products and services can also provide new – in some cases completely new – forms and functionalities through a combination with the actual properties of these goods. Products that have been material up to now will experience new areas of application through an expansion with sensor technology, optics and actuator technology of the Internet of Things. Autonomous driving or smart home applications would be inconceivable without hardware expansion with so-called embedded systems [20, p. 161], a reliable and secure network infrastructure and an appropriate data processing. New services such as those made possible by social networks, applications for fitness tracking and health monitoring biotechnology sector's current development around the topic of DNA [16] would not be possible without modern data processing.

3.2.3 Interaction of Digital and Real Value Creation

Various studies and surveys propagate different scenarios regarding how and to what extent automation can replace manual activities [9, 17, 18]. For example, more than 50% of all work activities worldwide have the technical potential to be automated through the use of current digital technologies [9, p. 2]. At the same time, it is assumed that there will be an increase in highly qualified jobs in some completely new occupational fields [9, 18]. The digitalisation of the structures and processes that go hand in hand with automation requires a changed, new interplay between real and digital value creation. This is because despite the increasing merging of the real and digital worlds [1, p. 22], companies will still have to think intensively about and implement the management of their physical value creation in the future. This interplay of digital and real value creation is shown in Fig. 3.1.

The ubiquitous and comprehensive informatisation of our world requires the simultaneous management of real and digital value creation. Digital goods are both digitally generated and digitally consumed. The combination of real and digital value creation leads to new forms of business models, products and services. Digital value creation generally begins with the collection of data that have emerged from the digital traces of users, from the data of embedded systems or through machine-to-machine communication. Structuring and production comprise the actual value creation, in which insights are drawn through analysis, evaluation and assessment, which, in the next step, are assembled into meaningful, new data or information structures to distribute them in a user-specific manner. The bundling of such data with real value creation enables new combinations at every level. The usage of digital twins shows the potential of hybrid value creation in different industry sectors likes manufacturing. Digital twins foster the creation of new approaches, for

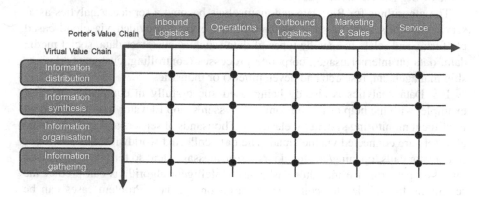

Fig. 3.1 Interplay of digital and real value creation according to Rayport and Sviokla [19]. ([20], p. 223)

example, the traceability and backtracking of a real product to the original equipment manufacturer (OEM) or to different offers. In sales, data are essential for creating customer-centric offers and solutions. Despite these simple connections, it is often difficult for companies to apply a hybrid view because doing so requires the targeted data management of structured data from their transactional systems, such as ERP systems, and unstructured data created daily by the internet. In the following section, three selected forms of digital value creation will be examined in more detail using examples.

3.3   Selected Forms of Digital Value Creation

3.3.1   Data-Driven Algorithms as the Basis for Business Decisions

An increasing amount of data are being generated in companies. Not only are structured data interesting, but also the amount of unstructured information, for example, from documents, emails or social media entries. Not only are the volumes of data getting larger (now in the zettabyte range), but they are also being created at an ever-increasing rate (e.g., through the collection of sensor data in autonomous driving). If data can be described as the fuel of digitisation, then algorithms are the engine. It is only through intelligent algorithms that computers can extract meaning from data and make it usable in the company. A Barc study of more than 500 companies in German-speaking countries identified better strategic decisions (69%), a better understanding of customers (52%) and cost reductions as added value for companies that can arise through Big Data analytics [21].

A study by NewVantage Partners, which included 85 blue-chip companies, came to similar conclusions. More than 48% of the companies were found to be driving innovation with data, and 39% managed data as business assets. Healthcare and life sciences are areas of growth in data usage. Nevertheless, 92% of companies struggle with organisational alignment and show a resistance or lack of understanding of the value of Big Data analytics [22].

The algorithms for Big Data can themselves become a service. Analytics-as-a-service comprises diagnostic and forecasting services provided via cloud-based platforms and relate to specific types of data (such as customer data, social media data, data on internet usage), corporate processes (controlling, customer relationship management, research and development) or industries.

Big Data analytics is already being used successfully in companies [4]. For example, with the help of IT companies, ThyssenKrupp Elevator has developed an intelligent monitoring system for elevators. Thousands of sensors and systems in the elevators are connected via the cloud. The data collected worldwide, such as times of elevator calls, opening/closing doors, error messages and so forth, are visualised on a key performance indicator dashboard. Intelligent algorithms can predict the remaining life of elevator components based on the data. Problem cases can be forwarded to technicians in real time. Through predictive and preventive services, maintenance can be significantly improved, which significantly increases elevator uptime. There are already around 12 million elevators worldwide that make 7 billion trips a day. With the help of the technologies used, elevator failures can be reduced by half. This is also interesting in view of the fact that in 2050, more than 70% of the world's population will live in cities, and buildings are becoming increasingly taller, so elevators are also becoming an increasingly important means of transportation, which requires regular maintenance [23].

A solution for Big Data analysis in industrial production was developed as part of the iProdict research project (http://www.iprodict-projekt.de) and used at the steel production company Saarstahl AG. In steel production, various internal and external factors (e.g., material properties, temperature fluctuations during melting) can lead to deviations in the quality of the steel. Therefore, almost one-third of the steel produced worldwide is scrap, but most of this passes through the entire production process and is only identified as scrap at the end. Early prediction of scrap steel in the production process using Big Data analysis means that scrap identified at an early stage no longer has to go through all the production steps, resulting in cost savings. By using sensors in production, materials can be measured using lasers, inclusions and defects in the steel can be detected in quickly using ultrasound, surfaces can be inspected, and temperatures and vibrations can be measured. This creates a continuous stream of data, reaching up to several hundred terabytes per year. The collected data are aggregated and visualised in a dashboard to provide process managers with a basis for quick decisions. Furthermore, algorithms can recognise patterns in the data based on which deviations in the production process can be predicted in the future. In the long term, changes in the production process then become possible [4].

The use of data analysis algorithms is also helpful when dealing with customers. Every day, letters or emails arrive, or customers comment directly on the products or on the company on Twitter or Facebook. Here, it is important to recognise the different opinions (especially the negative ones) to react to them quickly and appropriately. Sentiment analysis (analysis of opinions and moods in unstructured texts) can be used for this purpose. An example is the assignment of customer letters to a large insurance company [10, p. 163]. The large volume of letters arriving daily (by letter or mail) makes it impossible to presort the mail quickly by hand. The sentence 'Please send me an offer in this regard' can be assigned without doubt by an employee of the insurance company to the category 'request for offer'. An ideal set of hand-presorted training data for such an assignment contains a variety of phrases along with markings (annotations) as to which parts of the training data allow assignment to which category. A suitable algorithm can learn classification models from the training data, which can then be assigned to categories on new data (customer letters not yet presorted). This can save a lot of time in an insurance company: urgent letters with complaints can be filtered out and processed quickly – the number of angry customers and cancellations can then be reduced.

3.3.2 Artificial Intelligence and Robotics as the Drivers of Full Automation

Self-learning algorithms can be seen as a special form of machine learning algorithms within the field of artificial intelligence (AI). Algorithms can recognise images and language, translate or win in strategic games against human opponents, diagnose disease patterns and assist in therapy [10].

Industry 4.0 combines current information and communication technologies with production and automation technology, aiming to reach a new level of organisation and control of the entire value chain over the complete life cycle of products and services. This will achieve greater transparency, flexibility and improvement of value creation, as well as individualisation of the products and services through intensive customer-company interaction and networking [24, p. 5]. According to a McKinsey survey, 22% of the respondents say that more than 5% of their organisations' enterprise-wide earnings before interest and taxes in 2019 was attributable to their use of AI. Thirty percent of the companies use deep-learning as a form of machine learning algorithms. Forty-three percent of the AI high performers have a clearly defined AI vision and strategy, and show a better year-over-year-growth overall than other companies [25].

An important prerequisite for machine learning in industry is the equipment of plants and systems with smart sensors. Cognitive machines are industry-specific solutions based on machine learning, natural language processing, image recognition and infrastructure such as cloud computing, the Internet of Things and Big Data, with novel capabilities that can be usefully described as higher-level cognitive processes [26]. AI-equipped products that continuously optimise themselves and benefit from the experiences of all product users are now determined not only by the build series, but also by software updates. As a result, it is precisely this software – no longer the hardware – that becomes the decisive value driver. The integration of AI is an important asset for companies: Accenture found that 84% of executives believe that they have to leverage AI to achieve their growth objectives [27].

By using AI, employees spend less time on routine activities. According to Accenture, these 20% of nonroutine activities account for 80% of value creation. AI algorithms also contribute to intelligent automation and, thus, to changes in processes. Further added value is generated through the intelligent combination and evaluation of the collected data [28].

Machine learning can also be used in robotics. Usually, a robot in production performs a precise, strictly prescribed sequence of movements. Programming the robot is required only once, and this time-consuming work pays off because the robot performs the same movements over a very long time. Adjustments to motion sequences are time-consuming and costly. The robot cannot adapt to a change in production flow on its own. With the help of cognitive robotics, robots can respond more autonomously. Robots should perceive, recognise and act by using specific smart technologies. The robot collects data through its sensors, processes these data and adjusts its reactions accordingly. This enables the production company to react flexibly and economically to short product life cycles and increasing variants [29].

According to a study by Frost/Sullivan, the global market for intelligent robots in the industry is expected to double by 2023 and reach more than 70 billion US dollars [30].

Another field of application for flexible robots is the care of the elderly. Against the backdrop of an ageing population, more geriatric caregivers are needed, and the existing staff members are overworked. In Japan, where there are already 5.7 million people in need of care, work on care robots has been underway for some time. The focus is on lifting aids, mobility aids, toilets and monitoring systems for patients with dementia. In Germany, Fraunhofer IPA is working on intelligent care robots (also called service robots). Elevon is specifically designed to provide support when lifting people. Caregivers can request it electronically so that it can travel autonomously to where it is needed. People can be picked up from bed and transported in both lying and sitting positions. Using sensors, Elevon automatically detects the person and can position its pick-up system accordingly, making it easier to operate [31]. The use of nursing robots can minimise costs and increase the quality of care. Simply by saving the travel time to fetch a lift, costs can be saved and time for care better used [32].

3.3.3 Digitisation of Processes as a Consequence of Digital Value Creation

Reliability and trust are of great importance for the digitalisation of processes, for example, between business partners, but also between customers, suppliers and via digital platforms.

The support of knowledge-intensive processes in companies today often already takes place via digital platforms. Companies use Slack for corporate communication, Asana for project management, Teams or Zoom for videoconferencing and collaboration and LinkedIn for a business social network. These tools increase transparency in the company, improve collaboration across departmental boundaries and promote a self-organised, network-like work culture (cf. Chap. 14), thus enabling a more effective and efficient way of working.

A study among Danish companies in various industries investigated the perceived value created by the use of social media for corporate communication, collaboration and project management. The analysis of the quantitative data (number of respondents: 114, Fig. 3.2) showed that among other things, faster communication and more effective knowledge sharing with other employees make important contributions to value creation. Additional interviews in the companies showed a similar picture. Here, managers explicitly mentioned increased productivity and greater transparency. The induction process for new employees was also found to be easier because relevant company and project knowledge was openly available and the relevant experts became more easily accessible for questions [33].

The value created by supporting knowledge-intensive processes through time savings (faster communication, fewer emails, faster finding of experts) and cost savings (lower travel costs) has not yet been measured in companies. However, today's

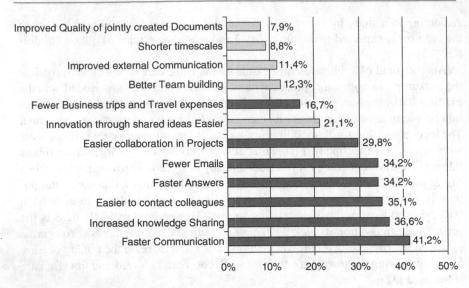

Fig. 3.2 Value creation through internal social media use in the company [33]

tools offer simple options for evaluation. For example, it is easy to determine how many employees have participated and how many posts have been generated [33].

Further added value will result if the data and knowledge modules collected in the tools are intelligently evaluated with the help of algorithms in the future. This will allow contributions to be summarised and categorised and, thus, also found more easily. Digitisation creates easier, cheaper and faster access to knowledge in the company. Measuring the influence and the added value of social media in companies can lead to these tools being used even more effectively and intensively [34].

In agriculture, too, processes are being optimised through digitalisation. Many tractors can drive autonomously. Because of track-precise driving, the machines are more precise and less distance is driven. This consumes less fuel and saves on costs. Sensor technology, electronics and software in agricultural machinery also significantly contribute to value creation. For example, the sensors can examine soil samples or determine plant density at a certain point in the field. In addition, precipitation and soil maps can be used to determine the optimum amount of fertiliser for this location. Thus, fertiliser (and hence cost) is saved, and plants grow more uniformly [35]. The greatest benefit of digitalisation in agriculture is seen in the increase in productivity through savings in working hours and operating resources [36].

In the financial sector, the direct processing of transactions between customers through blockchains is being tested. This could leave banks with little chance of survival with their traditional business models. In addition, new intermediaries are emerging that, for example, develop platforms for customer transactions (FinTechs). A blockchain offers the possibility of storing transactions in a tamper-proof and irreversible way. Blockchain technology is based on encryption and consensus building [37].

With FinTech companies, a new financial industry has emerged that relies on technology to improve financial activities. According to a study commissioned by the German Federal Ministry of Finance, the total market volume of FinTech companies operating in Germany in 2015 was 2.2 billion euros in financing and wealth management. Financing worth 270 million euros was brokered via crowdfunding platforms [38], whereby not a bank but a large number of supporters raise the funds for a goal to be achieved. The funds can be provided either as a donation or in exchange for something (e.g., a product is then produced using the funds). The funds are raised with the help of a corresponding portal, for example, StartNext (https://www.startnext.com/). StartNext is financed through voluntary commissions.

Another FinTech is Wikifolio (https://www.wikifolio.com), a platform that offers social trading. On this platform, anyone can share their trading ideas for everyone to see, and the performance of the corresponding Wikifolio (stock portfolio) is constantly available. The traders do not need any formal training or qualification; the platform is not subject to banking supervision. If a Wikifolio finds enough supporters, an exchange-traded certificate can be issued on its basis, in which anyone can invest via their bank or online broker. This allows financial products that can be traded directly on the stock exchange to be launched. Before the introduction of platforms created by FinTechs, this involved a lot of financial effort, high fees and long waiting times. The platform shortens this process and costs nothing. Wikifolio.com expects only 10 backers in the span of 3 weeks. Interested investors can follow the Wikifolios and copy well-performing portfolios. Any risks are partially covered by the platform. Investors who invest through the platform pay a fee to fund the platform.

InsurTechs can be considered a special form of FinTechs. These technology companies develop new services or business models in the insurance industry. In doing so, they are responding to criticism from customers who complain that insurance contracts are difficult to understand and nontransparent and who are dissatisfied with accessibility. According to InsurTech Radar, InsurTech companies are active in the fields of supply, sales and operations, with 33% of InsurTechs being active in sales (e.g., comparison portals) [39]. An example of a successful InsurTech in the field of 'offer' is the company Haftpflichthelden (https://haftpflichthelden.de), which cooperates with NV-Versicherung. A liability insurance policy can be taken out quickly and easily with an app. The insurance documents are sent by email. Daily insurance can be easily cancelled. Claim notifications are also possible via the app. In addition, the focus is on the community idea – customers receive a discount on their insurance premium if they refer their friends as customers.

LegalTech comprises software and online services to support legal processes that are developed by start-ups. The use of algorithms to clarify legal cases is changing the legal work previously done in analogue form, shifting the contact between lawyer and client to online platforms. One example is the company flightright (https://www.flightright.com). Passengers whose plane has been delayed can register on the platform. Algorithms can be used to check whether there is a claim for compensation at all and, if so, how much. Flight data, weather information on the day of the flight, strikes and current court decisions are collected and automatically checked by means of algorithms, and a possible compensation amount is calculated. The customer can decide whether a lawyer should take on the matter. Normally, this is not lucrative for the lawyer, but if several similar cases can be combined, the effort is significantly reduced.

3.4   Digital Value Creation Using the Example of eHealth

The healthcare industry has been in a state of flux worldwide for a long time. Online pharmacies are competing with stationary pharmacies, and Hospital 4.0 patient records are becoming digital. HealthTech start-ups are developing apps and solutions for a fast, transparent and innovative healthcare system. This digital transformation is continuing. The term eHealth covers electronically supported activities and systems that collect, make available and evaluate patient and other medical data across distances and use new technologies to do so [40].

The health tech start-up Klara (www.klara.com), for example, was launched in Berlin in 2014 with an app that simplifies communication between doctors and patients. Patients can take a photo of a suspicious skin spot and have it evaluated by doctors via the app. Based on the photo alone, it is often possible to decide whether the spot is just a harmless mole or whether a visit to the doctor is necessary. This can save unnecessary waiting time for an appointment, doctor's visits and costs. The platform has been further developed and can centralise the communication between a patient and respective doctors. Additional doctors and labs can gain access to communicate with the patient, speeding up patient diagnosis and treatment. Klara now only operates in the USA – the laws there are – unlike in Germany – open to remote treatment [41].

Although the healthcare industry is one of the largest sectors of the German economy, it is still one of the least digitised sectors [42]. Digitisation in the healthcare sector ranges from electronic health cards to telemedicine. The potential of digital health in the EU is estimated at more than 100 billion euros, covering, for example, savings through paperless data, workflow automation and patient selfservice [43].

Data in medicine today are largely captured digitally. These are used for documentation and patient management, but also for clinical decision support, for example, in making a diagnosis and selecting suitable treatments. However, these data are stored in different systems, and the lack of interfaces between them and the nonstandardised storage of data make it difficult to use.

To be able to act more efficiently, multiple examinations should be avoided, and the overall treatment of the patient should become more transparent. One possibility is digitisation along the clinical treatment pathway [44]. Here, data on individual treatment steps are collected in various clinical information systems. These data can be linked to the electronically mapped treatment process and evaluated. Figure 3.3 shows the digitally mapped clinical treatment process for liver transplantation, which is linked to corresponding patient-related treatment data [45].

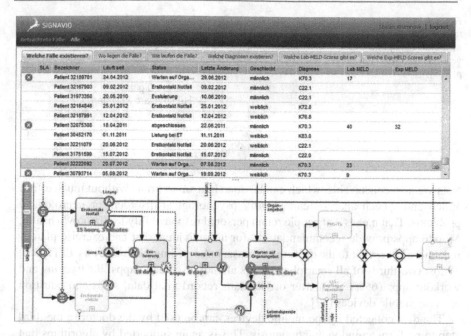

Fig. 3.3 Liver transformation process with process monitoring, screenshot Signavio (2014) (www.pige-projekt.de)

This makes the treatment process more transparent for both the doctor and patient; it is possible to track where the patient is currently in the treatment process and which steps follow next. The patient currently shown was admitted to the hospital as an emergency, has undergone the evaluation tests, has been listed for a transplant at Eurotransplant (ET) and is currently waiting for a liver donation. The next open treatment step is surgery. By monitoring the typical course of treatment, duplicate examinations are avoided and the treatment process can be better planned and carried out more efficiently. This can also shorten the hospital stay, resulting in lower costs. In the specific case of liver transplantation, for example, a reorganisation of examinations succeeded in halving the inpatient stay of a potential living liver donors for evaluation for donation [46].

Another example of digitalisation in medicine is individualised medicine (precision medicine), which enables an individual approach to a patient by means of intelligent software solutions (Fig. 3.4). The information cycle comprises four steps. In the first step, an individual risk factor for a person is determined based on that person's family history and genetic disposition, as well as socioeconomic and ecological environmental factors. For example, the spread of diseases, new knowledge about genes or even the current state of fine dust pollution can lead to an adjustment of the individual risk factor. Here, intelligent algorithms are indispensable in linking and evaluating large amounts of data. The second step in the cycle of individualised medicine is health monitoring. Today, smartphones already measure the number of steps per day, and smartwatches can determine one's pulse. In the future, laboratory

Fig. 3.4 Information cycle for individualised medicine. (Simplified version taken from [48, p. 325])

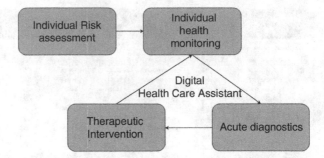

tests are also conceivable, which can be done in a smart home without much effort. Video and speech analysis can identify psychological disorders or neurological problems. That means that people retain personal responsibility for their own health. Mobile apps provide recommendations for an individual diet and exercise plan or indicate when a visit to the doctor is necessary. According to a survey by BITKOM, almost two-thirds of all smartphone users already use health apps like tracking and workout apps (65%). A quarter of Germans record vital data, steps and nutrition apps on mobile devices [47].

The data collected by the mobile devices can be used by the doctor in the third step to perform an individual diagnosis. This is again supported by algorithms that link the data collected by the mobile devices to other examination results performed on site at the doctor's office, hence being able to better identify patterns. Based on these analyses, a digital health assistant can then suggest therapy options (step 4). This can include medication, surgical interventions and coaching. However, the final decision on treatment remains with the doctor. The digital health assistant takes over intelligent data analysis. Data can be evaluated based on the latest medical and scientific findings. Predictive analysis is also possible for predicting possible future diseases or abnormalities resulting from the collected data.

In the future, a great amount of potential is attributed to eHealth applications, for example, improved medical care and its more efficient design [49]. The greater integration of the patient into the treatment process makes the acceptance of the technologies used particularly important. Only if solutions are accepted by all the parties involved can they reach their full potential. In addition to the costs and usability of the technical components, however, concerns about data protection and security also represent important acceptance factors for eHealth solutions [50].

3.5   Summary and Outlook

Digitalisation is primarily characterised by the networking of people and things, the virtualisation of products and processes and the exchange of data and knowledge. Numerous new opportunities follow from digitalisation, such as the use of data from machines and sensors, more targeted use of resources, individualised products and greater customer proximity. The implementation of these opportunities in all areas of the economy can lead to additional new forms of value creation. This means that further added value can also be created beyond the narrow economic concept of value creation, for example, through increased productivity, lower costs and greater flexibility [51].

The integration of human and machine intelligence will become increasingly important in the future, where machines will not only learn from humans, but where humans will also learn from machines. Although machines are getting better at recognising patterns, it takes humans to evaluate and make sense of those patterns. Machines are getting better at relieving humans from routine tasks, leaving them more time for creative activities. The joint generation of innovative ideas in teams – as supported by digital platforms – can create the potential for new value creation.

In the future, intelligent machine assistants will have numerous sensors to better recognise the user's situation and will have improved methods to evaluate large amounts of sensor data. In addition, moods can be detected based on facial expressions and voice pitch so that customers can be addressed even better in the future [26]. Products can be adapted even more precisely to the customer based on the analysis of large amounts of data, thus generating additional added value. Of course, ethical and social issues, as well as data protection aspects, must be discussed more in this context.

References

1. Lamberg J-A, Lubinaite S, Ojala J, Tikkanen H (2021) The curse of agility: the Nokia Corporation and the loss of market dominance in mobile phones, 2003-2013. Busi Hist 63(4):574–695
2. Christensen CM, Raynor ME, McDonald R (2015) What is disruptive innovation. Harv Bus Rev 93(12):44–53
3. Deloitte (2017) The Future of the Automotive Value Chain. 2025 and beyond. https://www2.deloitte.com/content/dam/Deloitte/us/Documents/consumer-business/us-auto-the-future-of-the-automotive-value-chain.pdf Accessed on 24 Nov 2021
4. Marr B (2016) Big data in practice: how 45 successful companies used big data analytics to deliver extraordinary results. Wiley, Hoboken
5. Dremel C, Wulf J, Herterich MM, Waizmann JC, Brenner W (2017) How AUDI AG established big data analytics in its digital transformation. MIS Q Exec 16(2):81
6. Rutherford BA (1977) Value added as a focus of attention for financial reporting: some conceptual problems. Account Bus Res 7(27):215–220
7. Redlich T, Moritz M (2016) Bottom-up economics. Foundations of a theory of distributed and open value creation. In: The decentralized and networked future of value creation. Springer, Cham, pp 27–57
8. Dean J (2014) Big data, data mining, and machine learning: value creation for business leaders and practitioners. Wiley, Hoboken
9. Manyika J (2018) Technology, jobs, and the future of work. McKinsey Global Institute. https://www.mckinsey.com/global-themes/employment-and-growth/technology-jobs-and-the-future-of-work Accessed on 24 Nov 2021
10. Lemke C, Brenner W, Kirchner K (2017) Einführung in die Wirtschaftsinformatik. Band 2: Gestalten des digitalen Zeitalters. Springer Gabler, Berlin/Heidelberg
11. Porter ME (1998) Competitive advantage. Creating and sustaining superior performance. Free Press, New York

12. Mayer-Schönberger V, Cukier K (2013) Big data: a revolution that will transform how we live, work, and think. John Murray, London
13. Brenner W, Lamberti H-J, Wieske L (2014) Walk like internet giants: Konsequenzen für die Forschung und Lehre in der Wirtschaftsinformatik. In: Brenner W, Hess T (Hrsg) Wirtschaftsinformatik in Wissenschaft und Praxis. Springer Gabler, Berlin, pp 15–39
14. Ecommerce News (2021) Ecommerce in Germany was worth €83.3 billion in 2020. https://ecommercenews.eu/ecommerce-in-germany-was-worth-e83-3-billion-in-2020/ Accessed on 24 Nov 2021
15. Ecommerce News (2021) Amazon still leader in German ecommerce. https://ecommercenews.eu/amazon-still-leader-in-german-ecommerce/ Accessed on 05 Jan 2022
16. Hale C (2020) Illumina launches whole-genome analysis software to help identify rare diseases. FierceBiotech. https://www.fiercebiotech.com/medtech/illumina-launches-whole-genome-analysis-software-to-help-identify-rare-diseases Accessed on 24 Nov 2021
17. Frey CB, Osborne MA (2013) The future of employment. How susceptible are jobs to computerisation? Technol Forecast Soc Chang 114:254–280
18. Arntz M, Gregory T, Zierahn U (2016) The risk of automation for jobs in OECD countries. A comparative analysis. OECD social, employment, and migration working papers (189). OECD Publishing, Paris
19. Rayport JF, Sviokla JL (1994) Managing in the marketplace. Harv Bus Rev 72(6):141–150
20. Lemke C, Brenner W (2015) Einführung in die Wirtschaftsinformatik. Band 1: Verstehen des digitalen Zeitalters. Springer Gabler, Berlin
21. BARC (2015) Big data use cases: getting real on data monetization. https://www.sas.com/content/dam/SAS/bp_de/doc/studie/ba-st-barc-bigdata-use-cases-de-2359583.pdf Accessed on 15 Feb 2018
22. NewVantage Partners (2021) Big data and AI executive Survey 2021. https://c6abb8db-514c-4f5b-b5a1-fc710f1e464e.filesusr.com/ugd/e5361a_76709448ddc6490981f0cbea42d51508.pdf Accessed on 26 Nov 2021
23. thyssenkrupp Elevator (2016) Elevator technology MAX. The game changing predictive maintenance service for elevators. https://max.thyssenkrupp-elevator.com/assets/pdf/TK-Elevator-MAX-Brochure_EN.pdf Accessed on 04 Mar 2018
24. Salkin C, Oner M, Ustundag A, Cevikcan E (2018) A conceptual framework for industry 4.0. In: Industry 4.0: managing the digital transformation. Springer series in advanced manufacturing. Springer, Switzerland, pp 3–23
25. Balakrishnan T, Chui M, Henke N (2020) The state of AI in 2020. McKinsey Global Survey https://www.mckinsey.com/business-functions/mckinsey-analytics/our-insights/global-survey-the-state-of-ai-in-2020 Accessed on 05 Jan 2022
26. Magility (2021) Cognitive technologies conquer the economy. https://www.magility.com/en/cognitive-technologies-conquer-the-economy/ Accessed on 24 Nov 2021
27. Awalegaonkar K, Berkey R, Douglass G, Reilly A (2019) AI: Built to scale. Accenture. https://www.accenture.com/_acnmedia/Thought-Leadership-Assets/PDF-2/Accenture-Built-to-Scale-PDF-Report.pdf. Accessed on 26 Nov 2021
28. Accenture (2017) Why is artificial intelligence important? https://www.accenture.com/t20170628T011725Z__w__/us-en/_acnmedia/PDF-54/Accenture-Artificial-Intelligence-AI-Overview.pdf. Accessed on 26 Nov 2021
29. Atkinson RD (2019) Robotics and the future of production and work. Information Technology & Innovation Foundation. https://itif.org/sites/default/files/2019-robotics-future-production.pdf Accessed on 26 Nov 2021
30. Frost & Sullivan (2017) The dawn of artificial intelligence – Foreseeing manufacturing in the cognitive era. Report. https://www.researchandmarkets.com/research/b9rfft/the_dawn_of Accessed on 28 Feb 2018
31. Graf B (2021) Service robots as residential care facilities. Fraunhofer IPArobo https://www.ipa.fraunhofer.de/content/dam/ipa/en/documents/Expertises/Roboter%2D%2Dund-Assistenzsysteme/Servicerobots_residential_care.pdf. Accessed on 26 Nov 2021

32. Locsin RC, Ito H (2018) Can humanoid nurse robots replace human nurses. J Nurs 5(1). https://doi.org/10.7243/2056-9157-5-1
33. Razmerita L, Kirchner K, Nielsen P (2017) The perceived business value of social media at work. Int J Multidiscip Bus Sci 3(4):52–59
34. McKinsey (2015) Transforming the business through social tools. https://www.mckinsey.com/industries/high-tech/our-insights/transforming-the-business-through-social-tools Accessed on 28 Feb 2018
35. Wolfert S, Ge L, Verdouw C, Bogaardt MJ (2017) Big data in smart farming – a review. Agric Syst 153:69–80
36. Trendov NM, Varas S, Zeng M (2019) Digital technologies in agriculture and rural areas. Briefing Paper. Food and Agriculture Organization of the United Nations. https://www.fao.org/3/ca4887en/ca4887en.pdf Accessed on 26 Nov 2021
37. Tapscott D, Tapscott A (2016) Blockchain revolution: how the technology behind bitcoin is changing money, business, and the world. Portfolio Penguin, London
38. Dorfleitner G, Hornuf L, Schmitt M, Weber M (2016) The FinTech market in Germany. https://papers.ssrn.com/sol3/papers.cfm?abstract_id=2885931 Accessed on 26 Nov 2021
39. Oliver Wyman, Policen Direkt (2019) The future of Insurtech in Germany. The Insurtech Radar 2019. https://www.oliverwyman.com/content/dam/oliver-wyman/v2-de/publications/2019/jul/insurtech-092019/MUN-MKT40506-001_InsurTech_E_20190913_Online.pdf Accessed on 26 Nov 2021
40. Hallberg D, Salimi N (2020) Qualitative and quantitative analysis of definitions of e-health and m-health. Healthc Inform Res 26(2):119–128
41. Landi H (2020) Klara scores $15M financing round backed by Google's AI venture fund. Fierce Healthcare. https://www.fiercehealthcare.com/tech/google-s-ai-focused-venture-fund-invests-digital-health-company-klara Accessed on 26 Nov 2021
42. Richer L, Silberzahn T (2020) Germany's e-health infrastructure strengthens, but digital uptake is lagging. McKinsey. https://www.mckinsey.com/industries/life-sciences/our-insights/germanys-e-health-infrastructure-strengthens-but-digital-uptake-is-lagging Accessed on 26 Nov 2021
43. McKinsey & Company (2020) Digital Health @ Worldwebforum. Digital health ecosystems, hybrid care pathways and data ethics in healthcare. https://www.mckinsey.com/~/media/mckinsey/locations/europe%20and%20middle%20east/switzerland/our%20insights/worldwebforum/digital-health-at-worldwebforum.pdf Accessed on 26 Nov 2021
44. Kirchner K, Scheuerlein H, Malessa C, Habrecht O, Settmacher U (2012) Klinikpfade in der Chirurgie: Überblick und praktischer Einsatz. Chir Allg Z 13(10):538–541
45. Kirchner K, Herzberg N, Rogge-Solti A, Weske M (2013) Embedding conformance checking in a process intelligence system in hospital environments. In: BPM 2012 Joint Workshop, ProHealth 2012/KR4HC 2012. Springer, Berlin/Heidelberg, pp 126–139
46. Kirchner K, Scheuerlein H, Malessa C, Krumnow S, Herzberg N, Krohn K, Specht M, Settmacher U (2014) Was ein klinischer Pfad im Krankenhaus bringt. Evaluation klinischer Pfade am Uniklinikum Jena am Beispiel des PIGE-Projekts. Chir Allg Z 15(7–8):475–478
47. Engberg A (2019) Bitkom study: Germans are in favor of eHealth. Healthcare IT News. https://www.healthcareitnews.com/news/emea/bitkom-study-germans-are-favour-ehealth Accessed on 26 Nov 2021
48. Hahn H, Schreiber A (2018) E-health. In: Neugebauer R (Hrsg) Digitalisierung. Springer Vieweg, Berlin/Heidelberg, pp 321–345
49. Task Force Health Care (2019) E-health in Germany. Market Study. https://www.tfhc.nl/wp-content/uploads/2019/08/eHealth-in-Germany-barriers-and-opportunities.pdf Accessed on 26 Nov 2021
50. Robles T, Bordel B, Acarria R (2020) Enabling trustworthy personal data protection in eHealth and wellbeing services through privacy-by-design. Int J Distrib Sens Netw 16(5):1–23
51. Sorbe S, Gal P, Nicoletti G, Timiliotis C (2019) Digital Dividend: Policies to Harness the Productivity Potential of Digital Technologies, OECD Economic Policy Papers, No. 26. OECD Publishing, Paris. https://doi.org/10.1787/273176bc-en. Accessed on 26 Nov 2021

Part III

Business Models in Transition

New Business Models Based on Smart Transport Container and Data-Based Services

4

Sebastian Meissner and Martina Romer

Abstract

The Internet of Things, Data, and Services is changing markets and competitive environments of most industries. The modularization and digitalization of products enable a fundamental change of business models. Based on the systematic analysis of product and process data, product-related services with significant usage improvement potential can be offered to the customers.

This chapter presents the creation of new service-system-based business models by the example of the transport container industry. The findings presented are based on the results of the research project "iSLT.NET", that was funded by the German Federal Ministry for Economic Affairs and Energy. The project has pre-competitively applied technologies of the "Internet of Things" in automotive supply chains, by constructing intelligent loading equipment and by designing and implementing a cloud-based service system for smart container management. Core target of this "cross-company network for smart load carrier" is to enable fundamentally new business models for the load carrier industry with hybrid – data-based and container-based – services and cloud-based implementations. In particular, data platforms and IT-services such as cross-company management of load carrier enable hardware-independent revenues and offer manufacturers the opportunity to escape from the downward spiral of cost competition by transforming their business model. The digitalization of transport

This article was written based on the research project "iSLT.NET", which is funded by the German Federal Ministry for Economic Affairs and Energy (BMWi) as part of the program "Digital Technologies for the Economy" (PAiCE) under the code 01MA17006F and supervised by the project management organization German Aerospace Center (DLR).

S. Meissner (✉) · M. Romer
University of Applied Sciences Landshut, Landshut, Germany
e-mail: Sebastian.Meissner@haw-landshut.de

43

container offers the customers, among other things, more transparency of the material flows and of the actual conditions of the loaded goods by smart sensors, cross-organisational optimization of the supply chain processes, and lower costs by network operator and pay-per-use payment models.

4.1 Introduction: Transformation of Logistics Driven by the Internet of Things, Data, and Services

The technological transformation of products by digitalization and communication technologies revolutionizes value chains and also enables manufacturers of industrial goods to rethink their current business models – from development and manufacturing to support and management of products in use by customers [1]. The target of the application of Internet of Things technology is not just to gain advantages through collecting data, but to offer new services to the customer and, thus, to change the accessible market so that new customers can be acquired and other forms of revenue generation can be realized. For the implementation of this hybrid value creation, cross-company IT platforms, data-based services, and operator models are gaining more and more importance.

Targeted product development based on modularization and digitization leads to smart, scalable products in an "Internet of Things" (IoT) [2]. Their basic capabilities, such as identification, localization, and decentralized networking are particularly promising for the logistics industry, whose very own task is the orchestration of the material flow and the necessary information flow within and between companies. The further development of material flow technologies by integration of information and communication technologies enables to gain actual information on the material flow across system and company boundaries and, thus, is key to the holistic optimization of logistics processes. By merging the real with the digital world, transparency of material movement and inventory data and decentralized process control is offered [3].

The cross-product and inter-manufacturer consolidation of data in data platforms (as cloud systems in the "Internet of Data") generated during the use of products enables the digital integration of value creation networks. Based on data integration and analysis, new services can be developed in the sense of the "Internet of Services" (IoS). The development of these "service systems" should start from the customer perspective and focus on process and product optimization. Cross-company process transparency in the logistical context enables advantages for efficiency and error detection and increases in-time-delivery. Especially the real-time detection of disruptions in the material flow offers improvements in risk management within supply chains. The permanent identification of process improvements and, thus, optimization potential of the customer's value chain through hybrid products and services significantly increases the revenue potential of the manufacturers. Moreover, by means of operator models, steps of the customers' value chain can be taken over in order to create higher turnover. And resulting long-term partnerships can sustainably strengthen the market position.

The potential of the Internet of Things, Data, and Services for the development of business models can be divided into three stages – starting with the optimization of the value chain and leading to market disruption:

- Short-term: Reduction of costs and risks through digitalization and optimization of the value chain
- medium-term: Increase in turnover through new services and products
- long-term: Growth in profitability through the acquisition of new customers up to the creation of new markets.

Figure 4.1 summarizes the fields of action and targets of the Internet of Things, Data and Services.

The development of new business models based on the digitalization of products is explained in the following, using the example of special load carrier manufacturer. Due to the increasing "commoditization" of their products and due to global competition, manufacturers of containers are under high pressure, so that their main value creation increasingly is shifted to countries with low labor costs. The opportunities that arise from a transformation of the business model through modular, reconfigurable load carrier design and the use of IoT technologies open up a path to future value creation. The research project "iSLT.NET" was funded by the German Federal Ministry for Economic Affairs and Energy. The project partners were GEBHARDT Logistic Solutions GmbH, BMW AG, DRÄXLMAIER GROUP, Chair of Materials Handling, Material Flow, Logistics of the Technical University of Munich, Fraunhofer Working Group for Supply Chain Services and TZ PULS of the University of Applied Sciences Landshut. The research project explored technological solutions for the design and cross-company use of modular and smart special load carriers (SLT) and furthermore investigated the general potentials of data-based services for all relevant stakeholders. By a prototypical implementation of an operator model a sustainable business model was finally proven.

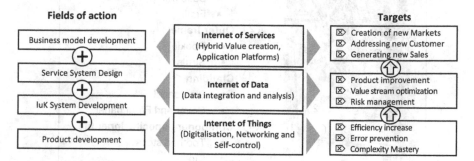

Fig. 4.1 Fields of action and targets of the internet of things, data, and services

4.2   Challenges of Today's Load Carrier Management Within the Automotive Supply Chain

According to DIN 30781, load carrier are a mean to bundle goods to a unit load. Load carrier are, thus, the central logistics objects for enabling the transport, handling, and storage of raw materials, components, and products in value-added networks. Barely any cargo is moved in logistics today without load carrier. With the increased demands on product and component quality, the importance of the constructive design of load carrier for consistent protection of the transported goods against damage and contamination is increasing. In addition, load carrier ensure that the material is positioned correctly and ergonomically at the point of use. These requirements lead to the increasing use of component-specific load carrier, so-called special load carrier, especially in the automotive industry. These are used in particular for components with a large number of variants or sensitive surfaces – such as center consoles or door panels. For this purpose, they are usually manufactured in small quantities and designed for the respective logistic process. Today, special load carrier consist primarily of a frame made of welded steel modules and inlays – sometimes made of individual plastic components – to carry the transport goods (Fig. 4.2).

Special load carrier cause high costs for the companies due to product-related, and thus, short usage cycles and complex cross-company processes in the container management [4]. This challenge particularly affects the automotive industry with its frequent product changes and susceptible just-in-time logistics. A model changeover in the automotive industry leads to a change in the geometry of components, to a reorganization of the supply chain, and to a change in requirements for the process of delivery and supply of materials to the assembly line. The consequence is that on average every 4–6 years the special load carrier of the current model are in most

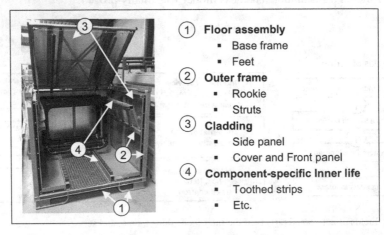

①	**Floor assembly**
	▪ Base frame
	▪ Feet
②	**Outer frame**
	▪ Rookie
	▪ Struts
③	**Cladding**
	▪ Side panel
	▪ Cover and Front panel
④	**Component-specific Inner life**
	▪ Toothed strips
	▪ Etc.

Fig. 4.2 Structure of an exemplary special load carrier. (Courtesy of © Martina Romer & Gebhardt Logistic Solutions GmbH 2018. All Rights Reserved)

cases no longer usable for the new car line and have to be scrapped. Due to its typical manufacturing method, modifications to the load carrier are usually only possible with high effort. For the model changeover, special load carrier have to developed simultaneously with the product development under time pressure, since components have to be transported and supplied in time for the start of production. This requires consistently a high level of coordination between all the partners involved, such as the manufacturer, the suppliers, and logistics service providers, as well as the OEM, and is associated with numerous time-intensive change loops that could jeopardize the start of series production.

There are also numerous challenges in today's industrial environment with regard to the control and monitoring of container flows in the supply chain. For example, in heterogeneous value chains often a suitable IT and communication infrastructure is missing to determine a cross-company transparency of material movements and stocks . It is not uncommon that load carrier are counted by employees for inventories and manually recorded in proprietary systems. Often the data synchronization with the other companies in the supply chain is conducted via e-mail. Losses and damages cause ongoing financial expenses and cannot be allocated according to their root cause. The lack of transparency of load carrier stocks and movements often leads either to overstocking or low availability at the point of need. This can lead from extra expanses for alternative packaging to late deliveries and up to disruptions in the supply chain, thus, in the worst case, to interruptions of the OEM manufacturing line.

4.3   From the Transformation of the Product to a New Business Model

In order to meet the challenges of container management, technologies of the Internet of Things can be integrated into load carrier and the data generated by intelligent handling units can be used for significant process improvements [5]. The future development of special load carrier by integration of information and communication technologies and the consistent modularization of hardware and product-related services within the scope of the Internet of Things, Data, and Services enables manufacturers also to implement new business models.

Today, load carrier manufacturers offer customers the design, construction, and manufacturing on project basis, though the potential of an operator model with a cross-company load carrier pool has already been demonstrated and partly implemented into practice [6]. Due to the modularization and the resulting possibility to re-assemble modular load carrier, the waste of resources by scrapping can be minimized. Cross-company reconfiguration and reusability of the special load carrier modules in the network's load carrier cycles enable a high scalability of use life and of quantity of special load carrier [7]. In particular, customers can profit from short-time load carrier use without high investments.

Furthermore, the digitalization of transport equipment through smart sensors and communication technologies enables manufacturers to develop new business models and specifically expand their portfolio of product-related services for customers. Thus, load carrier manufacturers transform to a platform operator and offer their load carrier coupled with enhanced functions and services as part of a "container-as-a-service" operator model [8]. Due to the permanent generation and analysis of load carrier data, disruptions can be detected at an early stage and customer's supply chain risk management can be significantly improved. In addition, based on the transparency gained, the customer's load carrier stocks and logistics processes can be dynamically optimized. For the realization of this service system, a comprehensive transformation of the business model of the load carrier manufacturers from the conventional sale of industrial goods to a provider of smart products and product-relevant services is necessary.

Figure 4.3 summarizes this interaction of modular load carrier, digitization, and service system. In the following chapters, the three key elements of the new business model are presented in detail.

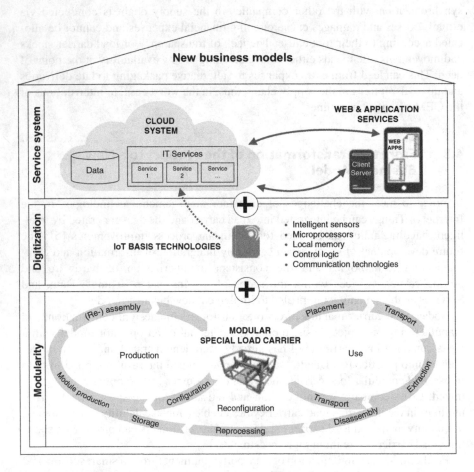

Fig. 4.3 Key elements of the network for intelligent special load carrier

4.4   Modularity: With Modular Load Carrier to Reuse and Scalability

Conventional special load carrier mainly consist of individual steel components that are welded together. After the end of use, a modification of the special load carrier is not possible in most cases. In order to avoid this disadvantage, in recent years industrial companies have developed more sustainable concepts, so-called modular special load carrier (MLT), which allow reconfigurability and reusability of the individual modules for the next use cycle (see for example [4]). Modules of the MLT can, for example, be joined together by bolted connections. This allows the modular load carrier to be disassembled at the end of use and the individual modules can be reassembled for further use cycles. The useful time of an individual module is then decoupled from the usage period of a specific load carrier [7].

The modular system of the smart special load carrier (iSLT) developed within this project is based on a modular system and is shown in the variant tree in Fig. 4.4. It consists of different standardized load carrier modules that can be configured into a specific special load carrier according to customer requirements. The modules are each available in different variants. The modular structure of the basic module is made up of sub-assemblies: e.g., platform, frame, base, and forklift pockets as well as folding or fixed stayers. Optionally, the bottom, panel and top as well as sensor and communication technologies can be configured. During configuration, a wide range of dependency relationships between the modules must be considered. In the last step of the configuration process, the component-specific inlay has to be selected or specially developed and, if required, it has to be integrated into the frame.

Load carrier manufacturers can achieve significant economies of scale in procurement and manufacturing by producing standardized modules for different user of the modular system. Due to the combinatorics of the modules, the load carrier manufacturer can offer to their customer flexibility in design despite the standardization of selected modules. Simultaneous, the load carrier manufacturer can guarantee high availability of its modules due to pre-production of modules that are frequently in demand. In addition, the reuse of the modules over several usage cycles leads to an improvement in sustainability and to cost benefits for the load carrier manufacturer and its customers [6].

4.5   Digitalization: From Smart Load Carrier to Transparent Processes

By equipping conventional load carrier with technologies of the Internet of Things, they are developing to cyber-physical systems. The integrated "IoT module" consists of hardware (e.g., sensors and microprocessors), software (e.g. control logic) and communication technology (e.g. radio technology, interfaces, and antennas). Smart sensor technology and the ability to communicate with other systems transform load carrier into identifiable, localizable, and self-active smart objects of the Internet of Things [5]. Smart load carrier can independently capture and filter

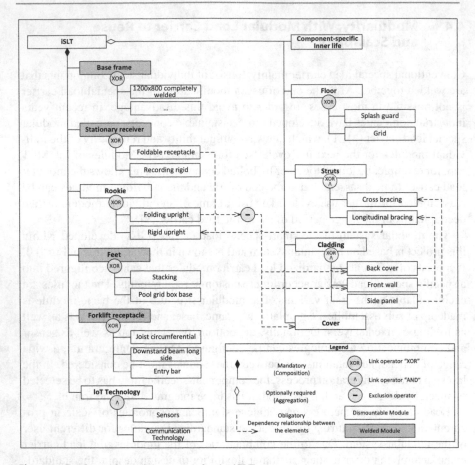

Fig. 4.4 Configurable modular system for the iSLT

relevant status and local environmental data within the supply chain and share this information with other logistics objects and IT systems via wireless technologies. Thus, for example, damages to the load carrier and the transport goods can be detected and rule-based quality processes can be initiated.

Depending on the use-case, multiple sensors can be attached to the smart load carrier. Figure 4.5 shows an overview of potential sensor modules and their functions for load carrier. As part of the "iSLT.NET" project, a modular sensor system has been developed. In a first prototypical implementation, location and temperature data are initially recorded.

The captured data from the smart load carrier can be filtered and temporarily stored locally before been forwarded to other IT systems via radio-based communication technologies such as LPWAN, Bluetooth LE, or narrow band IoT. The data is processed and stored in the cloud-system. The cloud system links this data with the data streams of other logistics objects, in addition, it can be analyzed by various IT services. Moreover, it is available for analysis via web and application servers or

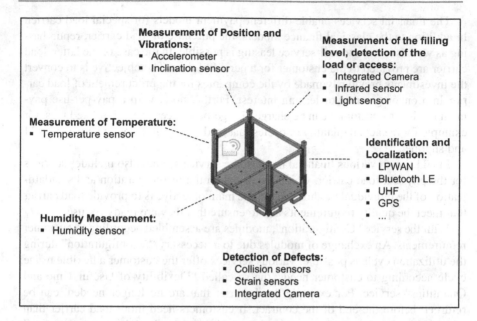

Measurement of Position and Vibrations:
- Accelerometer
- Inclination sensor

Measurement of the filling level, detection of the load or access:
- Integrated Camera
- Infrared sensor
- Light sensor

Measurement of Temperature:
- Temperature sensor

Identification and Localization:
- LPWAN
- Bluetooth LE
- UHF
- GPS
- ...

Humidity Measurement:
- Humidity sensor

Detection of Defects:
- Collision sensors
- Strain sensors
- Integrated Camera

Fig. 4.5 Exemplary functions and sensors for smart load carrier

forwarded to other IT systems (such as ERP or SCM systems). As a result, the physical and virtual worlds in the load carrier management merge and a so-called cyber-physical system is created. The load carrier has a digital twin. In particular, by means of the captured and digitized data from the material flow, a wide range of services and IT services can be derived to monitor, control and optimize the supply chain [8].

4.6   Service System: From Data Integration to a Service Platform

With the transparency on the load carrier movements and status data of the supply chain processes obtrained, a wide range of services can be offered to customers via a cloud-based service system [8]. By linking the functions of the physical load carrier with "software services", new benefits can be created.

The operator of the iSLT network plays a central role in setting up the service system. The operator offers via its integrated product platform, the physical iSLT and product-related services, and IT services. They can be chosen via a digital marketplace on a modular basis. The IT services of the smart, modular load carrier are accessible to the customer via web applications and IT interfaces.

Figure 4.6 shows the services for iSLT. These go far beyond the classic four services of the load carrier industry: repair, modification, maintenance, and cleaning. Based on IoT technologies, new types of finance and data-based services can be developed in particular for this industry.

The financial services enable different payment models for special load carrier. In addition to the classical finance models, the purchase of load carrier, repurchasing as well as rental and full-service leasing is possible. In the case of the latter, load carrier are provided to the customer for a period of time. The objective is to convert the investments previously made by the companies for the procurement of load carrier into ongoing rental or leasing interest. Furthermore, with a pay-per-use payment model, the customer can be charged usage-based fees instead of fixed fees, for example for the actual quantity of cycles that load carrier go through between OEM and supplier.

In addition to various financial models, the service system also includes services for the physical load carrier, which are based on the reconfiguration and standardization of the individual modules. Here, the main objective is to provide load carrier that meet the quality requirements and to ensure that they are ready for use.

With the service "Configuration", modules are assembled according to customer requirements. An exchange of modules due to a necessary "reconfiguration" during the utilization cycle is possible. Various services offer the customer a flexible usage cycle according to customer needs, the so called "Flexibility of Useful Time and Quantities" service. For example, load carrier that are no longer needed, can be returned before the end of the contract. If customers need more load carrier than agreed due to unexpected demands, these additional load carrier can be provided promptly with the "Ad hoc delivery" service. For this purpose, the operator has to keep a stock of component-specific modules to be able to deliver additional load carrier immediately.

A condition check of the load carrier in regular intervals is part of the service "Maintenance", and defines reconditioning measures, such as the replacement or oiling of hinges for folding load carrier. In the cloud system, the measures for each load carrier can be tracked and planned. Damaged modules of the load carrier during its use can be repaired by using the "Repair" service. Supported by the modular

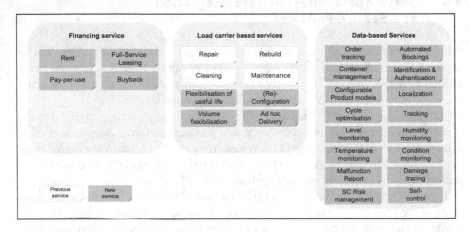

Fig. 4.6 Potential services within the iSLT network

structure of the load carrier, spare parts can be ordered specifically and damaged modules can be replaced more quickly and with less effort.

Further services are based on the analysis of captured data during the life cycle of the iSLT. A digital product configurator supports load carrier planners in the design of iSLT. With the web-based product configurator, different modules can be virtually assembled according to the modular system and as s so called "Configurable Product Model". This significantly simplifies and accelerates the load carrier development process. From the inquiry to the delivery of the load carrier, customers also get more transparency in their order process by "order tracking" and have, for example, information on the quantity of produced load carrier.

The "Load Carrier Management" controls the load carrier cycles of customers across company boundaries and manages the iSLT stocks. With the "Inventory Transactions" service, load carrier movements can be automatically triggered and the manual bookings in proprietary systems can be replaced simultaneously. With the "Circulation Optimization", the demand for load carrier within logistic processes can be automatically determined and planned in advance. Measures to avoid bottlenecks are, e.g., additional procurement or to avoid overstocks a return of load carrier to the pool.

In addition to the "Identification and Authentication" of each individual load carrier, "Tracking" can be used to locate the load carrier within the plants or on the transport route with an accuracy of a few meters, depending on the technology. The service "Tracking" processes and analyzes the localization data. The "Humidity or Temperature Monitoring" service provides information on the environmental conditions of load carrier. Based on that, user can define individual limits for humidity or temperature and will be informed in case of deviations via "disruption reporting". If limits for e.g. temperature are exceeded during the use of the load carrier, a message will be sent to the user as a "supply chain event". The individual limits depend on the physical processes. User can react directly and efficiently to avoid further problems.

The "Filling Level Monitoring" service continuously measures the fill level of the load carrier. The "Condition Monitoring" service reports all the captured condition data of load carrier and analyze this over specific periods of time. Sensors are able to continuously capture tilting, vibrations, or collisions. If a damage occurs, the user receives information about the condition of the load carrier. Quality assurance measures can be initiated in the process via the service "Disruption Report". This service is closely linked to the "Damage Tracking" service that focus on the identification of error pattern for load carrier. Following repairs or configuration changes of the load carrier can be planned and tracked.

Within the "SC Risk Management" service, user can define rules, that initiate a blocking or even a reordering of transport goods. These reduce the risk of disruptions in the supply chain up to a production stop. With the "Self-Control" service, customer-specific data can be stored on the IoT modules of the load carrier to enable decentralized communication between smart objects and to provide required information for process control.

4.7 Transformation of the Business Model by Setup of a Partner Network

The transformation from a provider of industrial goods to a container-as-a-service operator entail many new requirements on the competencies of a load carrier manufacturer. In addition to the product "load carrier", the IT infrastructure, the development and operation of software services are new key competencies of the operator. The setup of a company network and the development of long-term partnerships are mandatory requirements for success, as today's load carrier manufacturers basically do not have these competencies. Figure 4.7 shows an overview of the different network partners that are necessary for the realization of the iSLT.

The operator bundles the competencies of its partners from the areas IT infrastructure, load carrier, and services. Module suppliers deliver plastic and steel components and, if required, component-specific inlays. Assembly service providers are responsible for the disassembly and reassembly of the load carrier modules in accordance with customer requirements. Logistics service providers take care of the storage of the modules as well as the transport of the load carrier to and from the customers. Financial service providers enable the various financial models. IoT-hardware-providers develop and manufacture the sensor modules for the load carrier and are responsible for the information and communication infrastructure in the supply chains of the users. Based on the services of software providers, the cloud provider offers the database, IT services, and applications with defined access rights for the network and ensures data security.

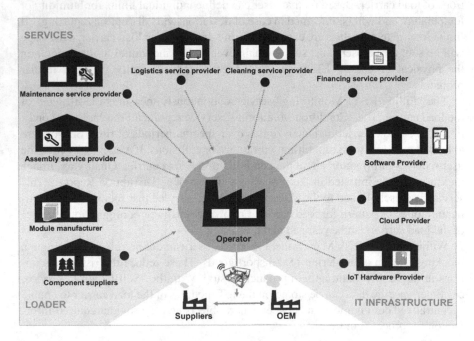

Fig. 4.7 Eco-system of the network for smart, modular special load carrier

Service providers for maintenance and cleaning are necessary during the use of the load carrier. A stationary implementation is recommended for large customers and a temporary mobile implementation for small customers. For non-reusable modules, defective IoT hardware or damaged load carrier for which a repair is uneconomical, the operator commissions disposal service providers.

4.8   Conclusion: Sustainable Market Change by the Internet of Load Carrier

The Internet of Things, Data, and Services changes the business model of companies. On the one hand, this is an immense challenge, especially for manufacturers of conventional industrial goods such as load carrier, but on the other hand, it also opens great opportunities. Customer orders do no longer relate only to the development and manufacture of physical products, but also include services that require a setup of a partner network with different key competencies. Figure 4.8 summarizes the possible transformation of the business model in the load carrier industry based on smart load carrier as an "Internet of load carrier".

Revenues of the new business model are no longer generated solely by the purchase price of the load carrier, but also by the alternative financing models such as pay-per-use and the revenue of the services. In particular, the data platform and IT services enable a long-term relationship with customers and offer hardware-independent and constant revenue. The enables to break free from the downward spiral of cost competition through the "commoditization" of industrial goods. In this context, the customer relationship is changing from contract manufacturing to process consulting and to customized IT services provision. The fundamental change of the value proposition for the customers is in the center of the new business model. Using the example of the smart special load carrier, this includes not only the promise of high-quality products, but above all an increase of the availability of load carrier and of the transparency of the goods' movements and conditions in the supply chain, thus, reducing the probability of Supply Chain disruptions.

The container-as-a-service operator model enables the renting of load carrier and the entry into smart container management without high initial investments and entry barriers. This is particularly attractive for small and medium-sized companies, which have not been willing to shoulder the investment in special load carriers. In addition, the usage-based payment of services makes it also easier to implement cross-company projects. In this way, investments that are difficult to break down to individual companies can be avoided. The supply chain partners – in the sense of cost-benefit sharing – can be individually charged according to usage and expenditure. This offers load carrier manufacturers a great opportunity to win new customers from other industries and to significantly expand the market for special load carrier to smart container services, thus, to ensure their future in global competition in the long term.

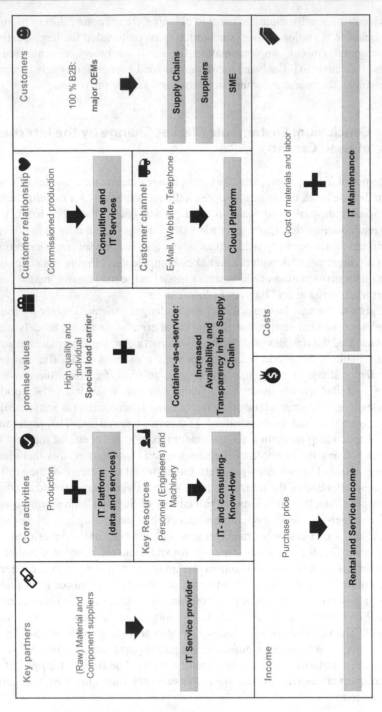

Fig. 4.8 Transformation of the business model by the iSLT. (Own representation, structure based on [9], see also strategyzer.com)

References

1. Porter M, Heppelmann J (2015) How smart, connected products are transforming companies. Harv Bus Rev 2015:96–112
2. Mattern F (2005) Die technische Basis für das Internet der Dinge. In: Fleisch E, Mattern F (Hrsg) Das Internet der Dinge. Ubiquitous computing und RFID in der Praxis: Visionen, Technologien, Anwendungen, Handlungsanleitungen. Springer, Berlin, pp 39–66
3. Günthner W, ten Hompel M (2010) Internet der Dinge in der Intralogistik. Springer, Berlin/ Heidelberg
4. Meißner S (2015) Adaptive Materialflusstechnik: modulare Transportwagen und Sonderladungsträger für die Materialbereitstellung. 24. Deutscher Materialfluss-Kongress, VDI-Berichte 2234, Düsseldorf
5. Zeiler J et al (2018) Entwicklung des Sonderladungsträgers der Zukunft. ZWF 113(1–2):37–40
6. Kampker A et al (2012) Geschäftsmodell für den Betrieb von Pools modularer Sonderladungsträger. ZWF 107(12):932–936
7. Attig P (2010) Komplexitätsreduktion in der Logistik durch modulare Sonderladungsträger. Apprimus-Verlag, Aachen
8. Romer M, Meißner S (2018) Das Internet der Behälter. Der intelligente Sonderladungsträger und dessen cloudbasiertes service-system. Industrie 4.0 Management 37(3). (submitted)
9. Osterwalder A et al (2015) Value proposition design. Campus, Frankfurt am Main

Benefits and Framework Conditions for Information-Driven Business Models Concerning the Internet of Things

5

Dominik Schneider, Frank Wisselink, Christian Czarnecki, and Nikolai Nölle

Abstract

In the context of the increasing digitalization, the Internet of Things (IoT) is seen as a technological driver through which completely new business models can emerge in the interaction of different players. Identified key players include traditional industrial companies, municipalities and telecommunications companies. The latter, by providing connectivity, ensure that small devices with tiny batteries can be connected almost anywhere and directly to the Internet. There are already many IoT use cases on the market that provide simplification for end users, such as *Philips Hue Tap*. In addition to business models based on connectivity, there is great potential for information-driven business models that can support or enhance existing business models. One example is the IoT use case *Park and Joy*, which uses sensors to connect parking spaces and inform drivers about available parking spaces in real time. Information-driven business models can be based on data generated in IoT use cases. For example, a telecommunications company can add value by deriving more decision-relevant information – called insights – from data that is used to increase decision agility. In addition, insights can be monetized. The monetization of insights can only be sustainable, if careful attention is taken and frameworks are considered. In this chapter, the

D. Schneider (✉)
Deutsche Telekom, Bonn, Germany
e-mail: Dominik.Schneider02@telekom.de

F. Wisselink · N. Nölle
Bonn, Germany
e-mail: Frank.Wisselink@t-systems.com; Nikolai.Noelle@telekom.de

C. Czarnecki
FH Aachen – University of Applied Sciences, Aachen, Germany
e-mail: Czarnecki@fh-aachen.de

concept of information-driven business models is explained and illustrated with the concrete use case Park and Joy. In addition, the benefits, risks and framework conditions are discussed.

5.1 The Internet of Things as a Technological Driver of the Digital Transformation

The term *digital transformation* is used in theory and practice to discuss fundamental changes in the business world, society and private life triggered by so-called disruptive technologies [1–3]. The challenge of digital transformation is a combination of strategic, organizational and cultural issues that go far beyond the mere use of technology [4, 5]. The goal must be to understand the connection between innovative technologies and digital business models as well as the resulting changes in organizations, value chains and markets [6–8].

In this context, the Internet of Things (IoT) is considered a promising disruptive technology [9], as it is developing two to three times faster than many innovations and technologies before [10]. The International Telecommunication Union (ITU) defines the IoT as a global infrastructure for the information society that enables advanced services by connecting physical and virtual things based on existing and evolving interoperable information and communication technologies [11].

In 2016, just a few years after its introduction, the IoT has led to the interconnection of about 6.4 billion devices [12]. In comparison, only about 3.9 billion active smartphone connections [13] and 3.4 billion Internet users [14] were predicted worldwide in 2016, as well as 1.6 billion TV households [15]. Thus, the IoT seems to be far from being a hype anymore, as which it was classified by Gartner in 2011 [16]. At that time, IoT for the first time appeared on the Gartner hype cycle along with machine-to-machine (M2M) communications [16]. A four-stage evolution of IoT began (Fig. 5.1) [17]. At this point, M2M included simple networking of mechanical or electronic devices, as well as automated exchanges between devices

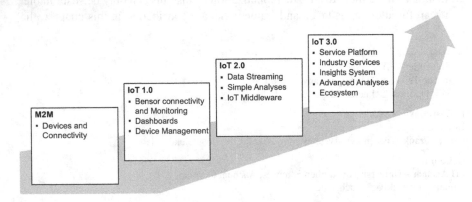

Fig. 5.1 The evolution from machine-to-machine to the internet of things. (Based on [17])

[18, 19]. The next evolutionary step was IoT 1.0, which additionally focused on the networking and monitoring of sensors and enabled device management with the help of dashboards. The subsequent IoT 2.0 created the possibility of exchanging data between IoT devices and performing initial analyses based on this data. Since then, IoT has been seen not just as an enabler for connecting devices, but rather as middleware on which applications can be built. Today, IoT is on the verge of becoming IoT 3.0, which will bring with it comprehensive ecosystems, new industry services and service platforms with advanced analytics capabilities.

Low Power Wide Area (LPWA) technologies are the catalyst for the breakthrough from IoT 2.0 to IoT 3.0. These are communication technologies that are characterized, among other things, by high energy efficiency and long ranges, but at the same time low costs. An example of an LPWA technology is NarrowBand Internet of Things (NB-IoT). NB-IoT was standardized in 2016 and enables devices to be networked and connected to the Internet over the cellular network in an energy-efficient and direct manner [20]. Devices thus become capable of communicating autonomously over long ranges. As of October 2017, 21 commercially available NB-IoT networks were already counted worldwide [21]. A total of 30 commercially available NB-IoT networks were forecast by the end of 2017 [21].

IoT is facing increased potential benefits with NB-IoT [22], as an increasing number of interconnected devices and the exchange of data between devices are feasible [20]. The sharp increase in the number of devices creates large amounts of data overall, even though each individual device sends only small packets of data over NB-IoT. The advanced analytics capabilities of IoT 3.0 help to generate more decision-relevant information – so-called insights – from IoT data, which can be used to increase decision agility. In the context of digital transformation, the IoT is therefore seen as a technological driver through which new business models can emerge in the interaction of different actors [2, 20]. Identified key actors include traditional industrial companies, municipalities and telecommunications companies (telcos) [23]. The latter, by providing connectivity, enable small devices with tiny batteries to be connected almost anywhere and directly to the Internet. Industrial companies provide, among other things, the development of hardware components with long-lasting batteries.

For example, NOWI in cooperation with T-Mobile in the Netherlands is developing sensors that use a technology to harvest energy from 4G networks [24]. The technology is called *energy harvesting* and makes it possible to extract small amounts of energy from e.g. communication signals. Energy harvesting can also harness energy from light, vibration and heat. Although the amount of energy extracted is limited, the low energy consumption of NB-IoT allows sensors to last a lifetime [25]. This provides the technological basis for use cases that would not have been possible before. For example, temperature sensors can be permanently installed in road asphalt, concrete slabs or tiles and assist in measuring surface temperatures [25]. The Dutch railway infrastructure company ProRail is testing such a use case in Delft, the Netherlands, by installing battery-free sensors from NOWI between tiles on the platform to measure temperature [26]. The sensors send a signal when the temperature approaches freezing. In this way, ProRail can target icy conditions on the platform by spreading salt at the right time. In the future, sensors with almost infinite operating times will also find application in the consumer market through the use of energy-efficient communication technologies. Philips already offers for sale *Philips Hue Tap*, a switch that uses the kinetic energy of the button press and therefore does not require batteries [27]. It can be used in houses or apartments as a remote control for preferred scenes, for example to turn off all lamps at once [27]. Other conceivable areas of application in the consumer market for wireless sensors that do not require battery replacement are smart watches or fitness wristbands [25, 28].

The examples illustrate the close connection between the technical development of IoT, the resulting new use cases, their innovation potential for business models and the resulting implementation in restructured value creation networks in which the collection and processing of information takes on a high priority. The added value from IoT use cases usually arises from a combination of connectivity and the provision of decision-relevant information. In this context, there are different approaches to dividing responsibilities between the individual players. For example, from the perspective of industrial companies, one possible proposal is to design ecosystems around industrial companies [29]. If connectivity is to be implemented over a public telecommunication network (e.g. mobile network), the involvement of a telco is essential. In the present chapter, we discuss the design of IoT use cases in the interaction of different actors from a telco's perspective. A distinction is made between the following two cases: By the telco (1) providing connectivity only or (2) providing services beyond that, enabled by marketing insights and referred to as information-driven business models in the following. As a basis, in Sect. 5.2 the use case of ProRail and NOWI is considered in more detail in terms of its value creation. Subsequently, in Sect. 5.3, the concept of new, information-driven business models is presented using the example of the *Park and Joy* [30] use case, which will be relevant for a large proportion of IoT use cases in the future. In particular, the benefits, risks and framework conditions of information-driven business models are discussed (Sect. 5.4). This chapter closes with a conclusion and outlook in Sect. 5.5.

5.2　　New IoT Use Cases Derive Value from Insights

In principle, many IoT use cases already exist on the market today that represent a simplification for end customers or that offer added value to society [22]. Since the standardization of NB-IoT in 2016, NB-IoT use cases in particular have become more important [31], as they realize the new evolutionary stage – the IoT 3.0. Why does NB-IoT have such high importance for new use cases?

Many applications require IoT devices to be very small. However, small IoT devices can only be equipped with appropriate batteries. IoT devices thus rely on energy-efficient communication technologies to benefit from long battery lifetimes [25]. Use cases such as *tracking*, which are geared towards mobile application, also rely on wireless communication among IoT devices. Use cases such as *smart metering*, where IoT devices are mostly placed in deep basements, also require high building penetration of communication technology [20]. Similarly, low device cost and low connectivity cost are paramount if, as predicted, over 20 billion IoT devices are to be networked by 2020 [12]. NB-IoT meets all these requirements and is therefore seen as a pathfinder for new use cases. In the following, the use case of NOWI and ProRail described in Sect. 5.1 is used as an example to explain how (NB-)IoT use cases can generally be technically or logically structured and which implementation options can be considered in the interaction of different partners. The main focus of this section is to highlight the role and business models of telcos in existing (NB-)IoT use cases. The focus of these use cases is thus on providing connectivity between different devices.

NB-IoT enables the use case of NOWI and ProRail, where battery-free temperature sensors on the platform in Delft are used to prevent slipperiness [26]. To realize the use case, the sensors are networked using NB-IoT, which sends a signal when the temperature falls below a certain level. It is assumed that the sensors transmit the measured temperatures to a cloud via NB-IoT. Figure 5.2 shows a simplified implementation option for the use case, which is based on assumptions and practical project experience. Historical and current data can be stored in the cloud, for example data such as the sensor ID, the sensor position, time and date of the temperature measurement, and the measured temperature. Using simple analysis methods, more decision-relevant information can be derived from the available data. More relevant information for ProRail is, above all, surface temperatures on the platform that are accurate to the position and the knowledge of when and at which point the platform is in danger of freezing. If more relevant information is available to ProRail as a result of the simple data analyses, ProRail can act faster and in a more targeted manner. Decision agility is created. By knowing exactly how cold it is on the platform at any given time, ProRail can spread salt in the appropriate places at the right time. When more relevant information leads to decision agility, value is added [20]. In this use case, added value is created for society, ProRail and Dutch Railways Ltd. On the one hand, slipperiness on the platform is avoided, which can be dangerous

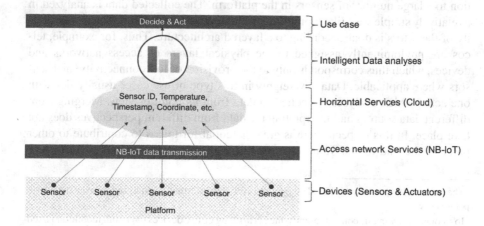

Fig. 5.2 Temperature sensors send data via NB-IoT to a cloud for analysis

for passengers and staff. Secondly, ProRail can save costs by spreading salt more efficiently. Avoiding icy conditions also means that passengers can board and disembark trains more quickly and unexpected incidents on the platform are avoided. This can ultimately increase the punctuality of train services in winter. These complex benefit relationships are typical of IoT use cases, often resulting in the implementation of an interplay of different actors.

In the following, the implementation options in the interaction of different actors are discussed using the ProRail use case as an example.[1] Fig. 5.2 not only shows how the use case can be implemented, but also the technical and logical layers into which it can be simplified. The use case is physically realized by installing the sensors on the platform. The sensors reflect the device layer, which includes sensors as well as other hardware components such as actuators. In the described use case, the sensors are developed and provided by NOWI in cooperation with T-Mobile Netherlands [25]. The layer above comprises the access network services. Since NB-IoT is a mobile standard, connectivity is typically provided by a telco, such as T-Mobile Netherlands. The middle layer describes horizontal services that function independently of the underlying devices and transmission technologies. This layer includes, among others, cloud services, which in practice are often provided by service providers such as IBM, Microsoft or SAP [32]. However, hardware vendors such as Dual Inventive [33] and telcos such as Deutsche Telekom AG also provide cloud services for controlling and monitoring IoT devices [34]. In the layer of intelligent data analytics, more relevant information is derived from existing data, which is used in the layer above for agile action and decision making. Smart data analytics are often an integrated component of the horizontal services below, but are also offered separately by different vendors. It can be assumed that the horizontal services and intelligent data analyses in the use case of NOWI and ProRail will be provided by corresponding service providers.

The NB-IoT use case described and its architecture (Fig. 5.2) can be seen as an example of a large number of existing use cases. The focus of these use cases is on the realization of connectivity; in the specific example, the focus is on the connection to a large number of sensors in the platform. The collected data is analyzed in a relatively simple way, like monitoring the temperature at ProRail. The responsibility of the actors is done according to a layered architecture. Thus, for example, telcos are predominantly assigned to the physical layers of access networks and devices, which thus corresponds only to the provision of IoT connectivity[2] and sensors where applicable. Data sovereignty in this type of use cases usually lies with one actor, which analyzes the collected data from its point of view. Merging from different data sources and interpreting the data from different perspectives does not take place. In this respect, there is great potential for telcos to contribute to other parts of the end-to-end value chain in the future, in addition to providing IoT

---

[1] The information presented is based on publicly available information analyzed from an outside-in perspective.

[2] IoT connectivity in this context refers to the networking of IoT devices over both mobile and fixed networks.

connectivity. Information-driven business models, which are located in the three upper technical or logical layers (Fig. 5.2), represent one possibility for this. Business models based solely on IoT connectivity are coming under increasing pressure because revenue from IoT connectivity is small in terms of a telco's total revenue, and the provision of IoT connectivity will become the core business in the long term. Therefore, telcos need to support and evolve traditional business models with information-driven business models to take a central role in the IoT market. How existing IoT use cases can be further developed through information-driven business models is explained in Sect. 5.3.

5.3 Decision Agility and Uniqueness Determine Value Creation

IoT use cases, in addition to providing IoT connectivity, offer telcos the opportunity to further contribute to value creation with information-driven business models. Therefore, telcos should push the development of information-driven business models to support and evolve traditional business models. Information-driven business models generally aim to first derive more relevant information (insights) from data and use it to increase decision agility to generate value. Algorithms or Big Data analytics are used to derive insights from large volumes of structured and unstructured data at a high speed [20]. Insights can also be monetized to generate additional value from the analytics business. Information-driven business models can be built on data generated in IoT use cases. In addition, insights from other information sources, such as social media, CRM or production systems, can be included and combined in Big Data analyses.

One example of information-driven business models is the IoT use case Park and Joy,[3] in which parking spaces are networked with the help of sensors and drivers are informed about available parking spaces in real time via an app. Park and Joy also enables users to book and pay for parking spaces directly via app [30]. This covers the entire parking process, from finding a parking space, to booking and parking, to payment [35]. Technically, Park and Joy is implemented by sensors on the parking spaces detecting whether a parking space is free or occupied [35]. The sensors send the data via NB-IoT to a secure cloud of Deutsche Telekom AG [35], which acts as a data source for data analyses. The analysis results are provided in real time in the app as an overall view of the available parking spaces in a municipality [35].

Use cases such as Park and Joy, like the ProRail use case, often also consist of the technical and logical layers shown in Fig. 5.2. However, the responsibility of the actors is distributed differently. In information-driven business models, telecommunication companies act as intermediaries. In addition to providing sensors and connectivity, they provide horizontal services (e.g. a dedicated cloud), smart data

---

[3] Note: This article is based on a German version from 2018. At that time the case study 'Park and Joy' was the digital parking service of the Deutsche Telekom AG. In the meantime, the assets of Park and Joy are operated by EasyPark.

analytics, and application delivery (e.g. an app). As a result, telecommunications companies have a significant share of the end-to-end value creation in these use cases. What is the end-to-end value creation of IoT use cases based on information-driven business models?

To analyze what the end-to-end value creation of an IoT use case looks like, several preliminary works have developed different models.

Schneider et al. [20] propose an analysis procedure whose central element is the investigation of the business relationships – especially the data and information flows – between the partners involved in an IoT use case. Value chain analyses using this model have shown that new partner models are required to realize IoT use cases [20]. Moreover, a use case can only achieve value if an explicit end-customer benefit is generated and the value to the customer is consistently the focus of the use case [36]. In most use cases, the end-customer value is generated by analyzing the IoT data using Big Data. According to a model by Wisselink et al. [37], Big Data analyses create added value when better information (insights) are derived from large volumes of structured and unstructured data and these are used for agile actions and decisions (decision agility) (Fig. 5.3) [37].

A Bitkom position paper [38] describes how automated decisions are derived from data, which is important for decision agility. Automated decisions are a central component of use cases such as Park and Joy, in which algorithms are used to determine, evaluate, and implement decision alternatives in real time based on data (e.g. the selection of free or occupied parking spaces) [38]. The better an algorithm evaluates these alternatives and derives appropriate decisions from them, the greater its added value [38].

The application of these models to smart parking use cases such as Park and Joy has shown that above all telecommunications companies, municipalities and end customers are key partners for the realization. By networking parking areas, deriving insights from the collected data and making agile decisions, added value can be

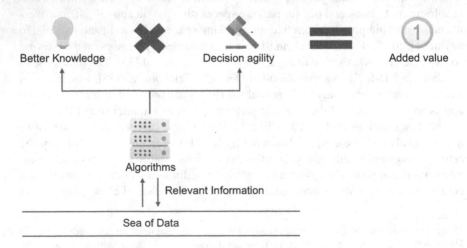

Fig. 5.3 Value creation through data and algorithms [38]

generated for all key partners. The focus must always be on the added value for the end customer that the players generate through the primary use case. In the specific use case of Park and Joy, more decision-relevant information can be offered to the end customer via the app through the cooperation between the municipality and the telecommunications company. Better knowledge of which parking spaces are available or occupied simplifies the end customer's search for a parking space. They are enabled to act agilely in that they can drive directly to an available parking space. This results in time savings and cost reductions as added values, as the search for a parking space is no longer necessary and fuel consumption and wear and tear on the vehicle are reduced. The minute-by-minute recording and display of the parking duration in the app also enables the end customer to extend the parking duration before the paid parking period expires. The added value of this is that the end customer does not have to buy an overly expensive parking ticket to safely cover the required parking duration, nor does he run the risk of receiving a ticket for exceeding the paid parking duration.

For the municipality or the public order office, control tasks become more efficient and effective through the availability of real-time parking information. Due to the availability of more relevant information, the public order office learns which parking space is occupied and whether the use of the parking space was paid for via the app. This better knowledge increases the decision-making agility of the public order office, as parking controls can be carried out selectively if a parking space is occupied but has not been paid for via the app. The added value for the municipality lies in the fact that the staff of the public order department can be deployed more efficiently and the unpaid use of parking spaces can be minimized through optimized control options. Furthermore, digital parking payment means that there is no longer a need for as many parking machines and paper for printing parking tickets, so that the municipality can save costs in this area. For the telecommunications company, the primary use case results in revenue from the provision of NB-IoT connectivity and parking sensors, as well as possible commissions from the municipality for parking ticket payments by the end customer via app.

Not directly from the primary use case, but from the analysis business based on the insights that can be generated from the data of the use case, further added values arise for the municipality and the telecommunications company. Parking statistics can be generated from the large amounts of parking data, such as parking locations, parking meter times, parking durations and vehicle types in parking lots. With the parking statistics, the municipality receives, for example, more precise information about the traffic volume at certain times, at different locations. This means, for example, that traffic routing can be agilely adjusted using traffic lights and digital road signs, and traffic jams can be minimized. Added values that result from this for the municipality include reduced carbon dioxide emission levels, increased attractiveness of the municipality, and possibly fewer traffic accidents. The telecommunications company can use the information from parking statistics, for example, to offer advice on traffic flows. Furthermore, the parking insights from the primary use case can be monetized to generate further added value.

Using a smart parking use case as an example, the application of the models has illustrated how insights can lead to greater decision agility and how this can create added value for various partners. Information-driven business models have the particularity that the end-to-end value creation is not only done by the primary use case, but also by the analytics business. The fact that telecommunications companies act as intermediaries makes it possible to use the generated insights in a variety of ways, which is different from the simple analyses of the connectivity-based use cases.

The model shown in Fig. 5.4 illustrates how end-to-end value creation of use cases based on information-driven business models works. In the model, it is assumed that an IoT use case is realized by two partners. In the Smart Parking use case, these two partners are the telecommunication company and the municipality, which realize the use case by installing and networking sensors in parking spaces, and providing a parking app. Through the IoT use case, the partners create value for a common business-to-consumer (B2C) customer. The value creation for both partners comes from the fact that the joint B2C customer is willing to pay for the added value or provide its data, which in return can be used to generate added value for both partners. In the Smart Parking use case, the B2C customer releases certain parking data to use the service and pays for the parking space via app, creating gratuitous and remunerated value. A characteristic of information-driven business models is that additional value is created from the analytics business. To do this, partners generate insights from the data in the primary use case and provide them to

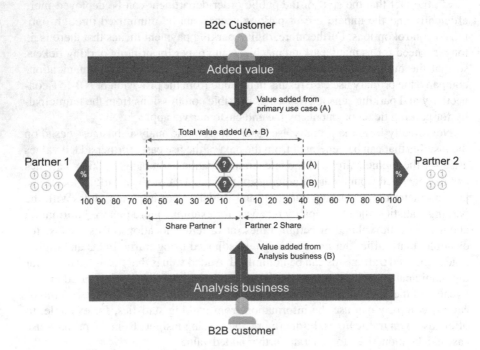

Fig. 5.4 Value added by the primary use case and analysis transactions

another end customer, a business-to-business (B2B) customer. If a B2B customer can use the insights to increase their decision agility and generate value, the insights can be monetized. In order to monetize Insights in general, they must not only bring decision-relevant information and decision agility, but also be unique in the market. This is because insights are only valuable if they cannot be offered by other providers or cannot be offered in a similar quality [39]. Therefore, the qualitative value creation model from Fig. 5.3 must be supplemented by the parameter uniqueness in order to take market effects into account (see Fig. 5.5).

From the provider perspective – i.e., the perspective of the partners – it is important to consider that the value creation balance can only be positive if the value created by the uniqueness of the insights is greater than the sum of the costs of generating the insights and the risk of application or monetization. In order to monetize insights sustainably, certain framework conditions must therefore be observed, which are discussed in Sect. 5.4. Value can also be created for both partners if they use the insights from the analysis business themselves to optimize their own business. The value added from the primary use case and the value added from the analytics business results in a total value added for both partners. The distribution of the total value added to the partners depends on the use case and is usually negotiated and contractually agreed. The distribution of the value added from the primary use case and the distribution of the value added from the analysis business between the partners do not necessarily have to be the same.

5.4   Framework Conditions for Information-Driven Business Models

The monetization of insights can only be sustainable [38] if careful action is taken and framework conditions are considered [39]. In this section, the essential framework conditions for the monetization of insights for telcos are explained.

Customer trust is a unique selling point for telcos compared to *over-the-top* (OTT) *providers* [40]. It is essential that customer trust is always maintained [41].

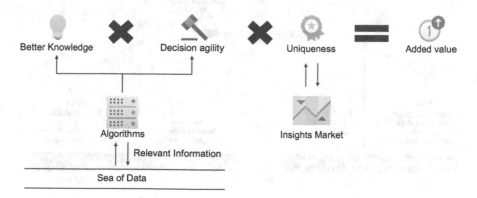

Fig. 5.5 Monetization of insights is shaped by their uniqueness [39]

To ensure customer trust is sustained, clear ethical principles and guidelines are required for information-driven business models. A recent example of this are the guidelines of Deutsche Telekom AG [42]. Among other things, such guidelines ensure that insights are handled in a sustainable manner. From the perspective of a telecommunications provider, the model shown in Fig. 5.6 represents the principles of sustainable insights monetization [39]. Before using a service, such as a smart parking app, customers must consent to the provider's use of data. In doing so, customers weigh the benefits of the offered service against the perceived costs of providing their data (see point 1 in Fig. 5.6). Therefore, providers must offer attractive services where the added value is higher than the perceived costs. If the customer has given his consent to the use of data, telcos may generate insights and monetize them sustainably (see point 2 in Fig. 5.6).

It must always be taken into account that the monetization of insights is a very sensitive topic that is associated with many risks. For telcos, customer trust is of high importance. Since the loss of customer trust affects the overall revenue, risks should be minimized and it should be ensured that the value creation is sustainable. If this is the case, insights monetization creates value for the telecommunications company and the customer – a *win-win situation* [39]. If the balance between value creation and risk tips, the customer's perceived costs increase and a *lose-lose situation* arises [39].

An exemplary application of the model to a smart parking use case is shown in Fig. 5.7 under the assumption that the use case is implemented solely by a telco and corresponding partners (e.g. a municipality). It can be assumed that the customer benefits of a smart parking use case such as Park and Joy are high and the perceived costs of consenting to data use are low. Therefore, based on an attractive service and the given trustworthiness of the telco, the conditions for consenting to data use and generating insights from parking data should be met. Since parking data is used and processed within the telco, the risk of customer and image loss is low. As parking

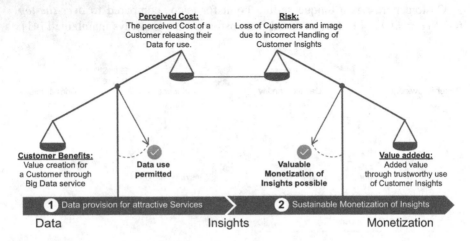

Fig. 5.6 Trade-off scenarios for customers of a Big Data service [39]

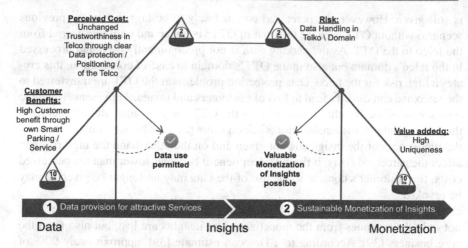

Fig. 5.7 Insights monetization in a smart parking use case of a telco [39]

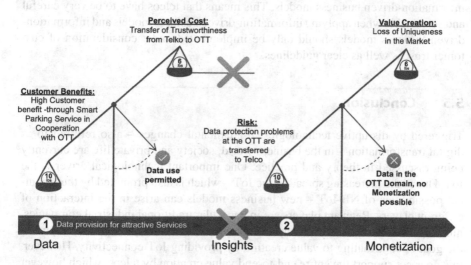

Fig. 5.8 Insights monetization in a smart parking collaboration between telco and OTT [39]

insights are likely to have a high uniqueness in the market, a high value creation can be assumed. As long as customer trust is maintained, the perceived costs are low, so that insights can be monetized sustainably.

The exemplary application of the model to a smart parking use case in Fig. 5.8 looks different if it is assumed that the use case is not implemented by a telecom-munications company and corresponding partners alone, but also by an OTT, for example. It would be conceivable to implement this in cooperation with an OTT in order to base the use case on existing map material of an OTT (e.g. Google Maps). If an attractive smart parking service is offered, the customer benefit is still likely to be higher than the perceived costs, which is why the customer's consent to data use is still given. However, the perceived cost is likely to be higher than the previous scenario without OTT because the trust in OTTs is lower and only transferred from the telco to the OTT. As the parking data is not predominantly used and processed in the telco's domain but also in the OTT's domain in case of cooperation, this creates a high risk for the telco. Data protection problems at the OTT are transferred to the telco and can directly lead to loss of customers and image. At the same time, the uniqueness of the insights is also lost, as the OTT can also generate insights from the parking data. A sustainable monetization is not possible because on the one hand the uniqueness of the insights is not given and on the other hand the high risk can affect the perceived costs. If the customer benefit becomes lower than the perceived costs, the customer's consent to the use of the data may no longer be given or may be revoked.

If a telecommunications provider loses its customer trust and customers migrate, not only the revenues from the monetization of insights are lost, but also from the core business [39]. According to a Detecon estimate [39], approximately 90% of revenues are generated from the core business and a maximum of one tenth from information-driven business models. This means that telcos have to be very careful and sustainable when applying information-driven business models and information-driven business models should only be implemented under consideration of customer trust as well as clear guidelines.

5.5 Conclusion

Triggered by disruptive technologies, fundamental changes – also referred to as digital transformation – in the business world, society and private life are currently being discussed in theory and practice. One important technological driver is the IoT. Due to the increasing spread of the IoT – which is also promoted by the technical possibilities of NB-IoT – new business models can arise in the interaction of different players. Relevant players are in particular traditional industrial companies, municipalities and telcos. In many IoT use cases, the latter predominantly pursue the goal of contributing to value creation by providing IoT connectivity. However, this does not support the entire end-to-end value creation by telcos, which however offers great potential. In addition to providing IoT connectivity, telecommunications companies should also participate in other parts of the end-to-end value creation in the future and support and further develop traditional business models with information-driven business models. In this chapter, the concept of information-driven business models is proposed and the benefits, risks and framework conditions are discussed.

Information-driven business models aim to first derive relevant information (insights) from data and use it to increase decision agility in order to generate added value. Simplified, an IoT use case is realized by two partners to create value for a common B2C customer. The realization of the primary use case creates paid or unpaid value for both partners, as the B2C customer is willing to pay for it or provide its data. Insights can be generated and monetized from the data of the primary use case. To do this, the insights are made available to a B2B customer. If the B2B customer can use the insights to increase their decision agility and thus generate value, monetization is possible. The benefits from the primary use case and the contribution of the insight monetization result in a total value proposition, the distribution of which must be negotiated among the partners. In order to monetize insights in general, they must be unique in the market. Insights are only valuable if they cannot be offered by other providers or cannot be offered in a similar quality. When monetizing insights, it is always important to keep in mind that this is a very sensitive topic that comes with many risks. For example, loss of customer trust due to insights monetization can effect the overall revenue of a company because if customers churn, not only the revenue from insights monetization is lost but also revenue from the core business. Therefore, risks should be minimized and it should be ensured that monetization is sustainable. This requires clear ethical principles and guidelines.

The present contents are based on the evaluation of initial application scenarios. The next step should be a further evaluation, for example, using practical projects or surveys. The concrete design of value networks for the implementation of NB-IoT business cases offers further questions for future research.

References

1. Fitzgerald M, Kruschwitz N, Bonnet D, Welch M (2013) Embracing digital technology. MIT Sloan Manag Rev (Research Report), 3–12
2. Urbach N, Ahlemann F (2017) Die IT-Organisation im Wandel: Implikationen der Digitalisierung für das IT-Management. HMD Praxis Wirtschaftsinform 54:300–312. https://doi.org/10.1365/s40702-017-0313-6
3. Cole T (2017) Digitale Transformation: warum die deutsche Wirtschaft gerade die digitale Zukunft verschläft und was jetzt getan werden muss!
4. Bensberg F, Buscher G (2016) Digitale Transformation und IT-Zukunftsthemen im Spiegel des Arbeitsmarkts für IT-Berater – Ergebnisse einer explorativen Stellenanzeigenanalyse. In: Tagungsband zur Multikonferenz Wirtschaftsinformatik (MKWI) 2016. Technische Universität Ilmenau, Ilmenau, pp 1007–1018
5. Jung R, Lehrer C (2017) Guidelines for education in business and information systems engineering at tertiary institutions. Bus Inf Syst Eng 59:189–203. https://doi.org/10.1007/s12599-017-0473-5
6. Kreutzer R, Neugebauer T, Pattloch A (2017) Digital business leadership: digitale transformation – Geschäftsmodell-innovation – agile organisation – change-management. Springer Gabler, Wiesbaden
7. Legner C, Eymann T, Hess T et al (2017) Digitalization: opportunity and challenge for the business and information systems engineering community. Bus Inf Sys Eng 59:301–308. https://doi.org/10.1007/s12599-017-0484-2
8. Morakanyane R, Grace A, O'Reilly P (2017) Conceptualizing digital transformation in business organizations: a systematic review of literature. In: BLED 2017 proceedings, Bled
9. Bensberg F, Buscher G (2017) Treiber der Digitalisierung – Transformationale Informationstechnologien im Spiegel des Arbeitsmarkts. Anwend Konzepte Wirtschaftsinform 6:76–85
10. International Business Machines Corporation (2004) Global innovation outlook. International Business Machines Corporation, New York, p 6

11. International Telecommunication Union (2012) Internet of things global standards initiative (ITU-T Y.2060). https://www.itu.int/en/ITU-T/gsi/iot/Pages/default.aspx. Accessed on 02 Jan 2018
12. Gartner, Inc. (2017) Gartner Says 8.4 Billion connected things will be in use in 2017, up 31 percent from 2016. https://www.gartner.com/newsroom/id/3598917. Accessed on 02 Jan 2018
13. GSMA Intelligence (2016) The mobile ecomony 2016: smartphones expanding beyond the developed world. GSMA Head Office, London, pp 14–15
14. Internet Live Stats (2016) Number of internet users. http://www.internetlivestats.com/internet-users/. Accessed on 02 Jan 2018
15. Digital TV Research Ltd (2017) Press release 12th June 2017: Global TV households by platform, p 2
16. Gartner, Inc (2011) Gartner's 2011 hype cycle special report evaluates the maturity of 1900 technologies. https://www.gartner.com/newsroom/id/1763814. Accessed on 04 Jan 2018
17. IBM (2014) Two worlds of technology are converging. https://sgforum.impress.co.jp/article/312?page=0%2C3. Accessed on 12 Feb 2018
18. Knoll T, Lautz A, Deuß N (2016) Machine-to-Machine communication: from data to intelligence. In: Vogel-Heuser B, Bauernhansl T, ten Hompel M (Hrsg) Handbuch Industrie 4.0: Produktion, Automatisierung und Logistik. Springer, Berlin/Heidelberg, pp 347–356
19. Czarnecki C, Dietze C (2017) Reference architecture for the telecommunications industry: transformation of strategy, organization, processes, data, and applications. Springer, Berlin
20. Schneider D, Wisselink F, Czarnecki C (2017) Qualitative Wertschöpfungsanalyse von Anwendungsfällen des Narrowband Internet of Things. In: Barton T, Herrmann F, Meister V, Müller C, Seel C (Hrsg) Angewandte Forschung in der Wirtschaftsinformatik: Prozesse, Technologie, Anwendungen, Systeme und Management. Aschaffenburg, pp 184–193
21. Huawei Technologies Co., Ltd (2017) NB-IoT commercial premier use case library. https://www.gsma.com/iot/nb-iot-commercial-premier-use-case-library/. Accessed on 04 Jan 2018
22. Nölle N, Wisselink F (2018) Pushing the right buttons: how the internet of things simplifies the customer journey. In: Krüssel P (Hrsg) Future Telco: successful positioning of network operators in the digital age. Springer International Publishing, Cham, pp 327–336
23. Schneider D, Wisselink F, Czarnecki C (2017) Transformation von Wertschöpfungsketten durch das Internet der Dinge – Bewertungsrahmen und Fallstudie. In: Eibl M, Gaedke M (Hrsg) Lecture Notes in Informatics (LNI) – proceedings, Bd P-275. Chemnitz, pp 2081–2094
24. BTG (2017) Nooit meer batterijen: IoT – sensoren van NOWI halen stroom uit 4G. https://www.btg.org/2017/08/09/nooit-meer-batterijen-iot-sensoren-nowi-halen-stroom-4g/. Accessed on 17 Jan 2018
25. Weber D, Schilling C, Wisselink F (2018) Low power wide area networks – the game changer for internet of things. In: Krüssel P (Hrsg) Future Telco: successful positioning of network operators in the digital age. Springer International Publishing, Cham, pp 183–193
26. ProRail (2017) Gericht strooien door slimme perrontegels. https://www.prorail.nl/nieuws/gericht-strooien-door-slimme-tegels. Accessed on 18 Jan 2018
27. Philips (2018) Hue Tippschalter. https://www.philips.de/c-p/8718696498026/hue-tippschalter/ubersicht. Accessed on 02 Feb 2018
28. Fellmann M, Lambusch F, Waller A, Pieper L, Hellweg T (2017) Auf dem Weg zum stresssensitiven Prozessmanagement. In: Eibl M, Gaedke M (Hrsg) INFORMATIK 2017. Gesellschaft für Informatik, Bonn, pp 863–869
29. Terrenghi N, Schwarz J, Legner C (2017) Representing business models in primarily physical industries: an ecosystem perspective. In: Maedche A, vom Brocke J, Hevner AR (Hrsg) Designing the digital transformation. DESRIST 2017 research in progress proceedings, Karlsruhe, pp 146–153
30. Deutsche Telekom AG (2017) Hamburg macht Parken einfach – Mit der Telekom freie Parkplätze finden, buchen und bezahlen. https://www.telekom.com/de/medien/medieninformationen/detail/hamburg-macht-parken-einfach-488342. Accessed on 27 Sept 2017

31. Statista (2017) Number of cellular Internet of Things (M2M and NB-ioT) connections world-wide from 2015 to 2021. https://www.statista.com/statistics/671216/global-m2m-and-nb-iot-connections-forecast/. Accessed on 22.01.2018

32. Evans B (2017) The top 5 cloud-computing vendors. https://www.forbes.com/sites/bobev-ans1/2017/11/07/the-top-5-cloud-computing-vendors-1-microsoft-2-amazon-3-ibm-4-salesforce-5-sap/#41e2b6666f2e. Accessed on 21 Feb 2018

33. Dual Inventive (2018) Services and products that serve to make working on railway infrastruc-ture safer. https://www.dualinventive.eu/en/services. Accessed on 24 Jan 2018

34. Deutsche Telekom AG (2018) Zentrale Plattform zur Steuerung und Überwachung. https://m2m.telekom.com/de/unser-angebot/cloud-der-dinge/cloud-der-dinge-details/. Accessed on 24 Jan 2018

35. Park and Joy (2018) Einfach parken. Einfach Zahlen. https://www.parkandjoy.de/. Accessed on 05 Feb 2018

36. Arnold HM (2015) Zum Geleit: Datability und Digitalisierung. In: Linnhoff-Popien C, Zaddach M, Grahl A (Hrsg) Marktplätze im Umbruch. Springer, Berlin/Heidelberg, pp 705–712

37. Wisselink F, Horn T, Meinberg R, Obeloer J, Ujhelyiová D (2016) The value of big data for a telco: treasure trove or pandora's box? In: Detecon international GmbH (Hrsg) future telco reloaded: strategies for successful positioning in competition. Detecon International GmbH, Köln, pp 151–161

38. Bitkom (2017) Entscheidungsunterstützung mit Künstlicher Intelligenz – Wirtschaftliche Bedeutung, gesellschaftliche Herausforderungen, menschliche Verantwortung. Bitkom, Berlin, pp 66–77

39. Wisselink F, Schneider D (2018) The Artificial Intelligence Challenge: How Telcos can obtain a Grand Prix for Insights Monetization. In: Krüssel P (Hrsg) Future Telco: successful posi-tioning of network operators in the digital age. Springer International Publishing, Cham, pp 337–345

40. Institut für Demoskopie Allensbach (2016) Sicherheitsreport Bevölkerung 2016. Deutsche Telekom/T-Systems, Bonn

41. Wisselink F, Meinberg R, Obeloer J (2016) Vertrauensvoll Mehrwert für Kunden schaffen. In: Hauk J, Padberg J (Hrsg) Der Kunde im Fokus der digitalen Transformation. Detecon International GmbH, Köln, pp 74–79

42. Deutsche Telekom AG (2018) Die neuen Leitlinien der Telekom zum Einsatz von künstlicher Intelligenz. https://www.telekom.com/de/konzern/digitale-verantwortung/details/ki-leitlinien-der-telekom-523904. Accessed on 07 June 2018

Matching Between Innovative Business Model Patterns and IT Impact Areas

6

Evaluation of IT as Enabler for Digital Business Model Innovations

Gabriele Roth-Dietrich and Michael Gröschel

Abstract

Under the pressure of digital transformation, companies are forced to constantly revise or even reinvent their business models. As many examples show, remaining in the so-called "red ocean" may have consequences that threaten the company's existence. However, **business model innovations** encounter various obstacles in corporate management. These obstacles can be overcome, for example, with the help of a structured approach of the **St. Gallen Business Model Navigator**, which provides a construction methodology for the redesign of a business model based on 55 business model patterns that have been proven in practice.

Empirical investigations of the patterns found in corporate reality led to the identification of a **business model DNA** consisting of 12 pattern combinations. The paper examines the relationship between this business model DNA and various **IT impact areas** such as different IT technologies (e.g. cloud or in-memory computing) and applications (such as process mining or blockchain), data sources tapped through digitalization (such as IoT or social media data), and types of digital customer access, for example via multi-sided platforms or smart services. Using concrete examples, the study relates these four areas of impact of IT for digital transformation to the clustered pattern combinations of the business model DNA.

In the process, it becomes apparent that these pattern combinations have different requirements for different IT areas. This paper is intended to provide an **overview of the interdependencies between business models and IT areas and technologies.** On the one hand, it provides answers to the question, which

G. Roth-Dietrich (✉) · M. Gröschel
Hochschule Mannheim, Mannheim, Germany
e-mail: g.roth-dietrich@hs-mannheim.de; m.groeschel@hs-mannheim.de

© The Author(s), under exclusive license to Springer Fachmedien Wiesbaden GmbH, part of Springer Nature 2024
T. Barton et al. (eds.), *Digitalization in companies*,
https://doi.org/10.1007/978-3-658-39094-5_6

business model DNA requires special efforts in which area of impact. It also gives indications for which pattern combination a company has to focus on which IT areas. On the other hand, it examines which possibilities technologies offer to make the implementation of patterns or pattern combinations more effective or more efficient. This provides assistance to companies in selecting suitable strategies for digital transformation, as well as in selecting and developing a suitable IT foundation.

6.1   Digital Transformation

The term **digital transformation** describes a fundamental, continuous change throughout society and especially in companies. A change that is driven by digitalization and networking and its design is the central challenge of our time [1, p. 3]. It calls for the fundamental reorientation of established companies in almost all industries in which traditional value chains are increasingly breaking down and new types of networking processes are taking hold. Start-ups are experimenting with innovative business models, penetrating market segments quickly and globally, and threatening to overtake and displace long-established market players [2, p. 3ff.].

The digital transformation has revolutionary features and joins the industrial revolutions of the past [3, p. 1ff.].

- The **first industrial revolution** from the middle of the eighteenth century on began with the invention and use of the steam engine to drive mechanical devices. While on the one hand this led to an improved basic supply of food and clothing for the population, on the other hand employment opportunities shifted away from handicrafts and agriculture towards factory work.
- From the middle of the nineteenth century on, mass production based on the division of labour with the aid of electrical energy and the assembly line work introduced by Henry Ford promoted above all the chemical, electrical and automobile industries as well as mechanical engineering (**second industrial revolution**).
- The economic miracle in Germany at the beginning of the 1960s is the **third industrial revolution**, which, driven by developments in electronics and information and communication technology, enabled companies to rationalise and automate production processes. Since then, fewer and fewer people have been working in production-related areas, and more and more in service sectors.

The **fourth industrial revolution** is the first one that is not only recognisable as such in retrospect. The Science and Industry Research Union and a project within the Hightech Strategy of the Federal Government coined the term **Industry 4.0** to emphasise the penetration of industrial production with modern IT technologies. Their goal is the largely self-organising production, the communication and cooperation of all human actors and machine components as well as the optimisation of the value chain in all phases of the product life cycle [4].

The **dynamics of the change processes** arise from the combination of several developments. First of all, the exponential increase in the performance of **IT technologies and systems** is driving. According to Moore's Law, which is consistently applicable, the available computing power doubles every 2 years. The possibilities for internet use are constantly improving due to the expansion and improvement of networks as well as the equipment of users with end devices of all kinds [5, p. 8ff.].

Digitalisation is finding its way into more and more **areas of life**. Sensors turn everyday objects into computers (Internet of Everything) which continuously deliver data and communicate with each other. Pattern recognition algorithms filter the data streams and convert them into a meaningful basis for decision-making. People communicate with each other and with machines via smart voice-, gesture- or facial expression-controlled user interfaces. The convergence of these developments is opening up new business areas, forcing companies to adapt their business models and helping innovative products, services and processes to achieve a breakthrough [5, p. 8ff.].

The new IT technologies have a **disruptive** effect because product, service and business model innovations based on them shake up entire industries. In most cases, new competitors with innovative offers, concepts and relationships appear unexpectedly because they are usually not attributed to one's own industry and are therefore noticed too late. Even services that are not very mature or tailored to niches can claim dominant market shares after a short time. According to the **zero marginal cost theory** for digitised or dematerialised products, the production costs for digital products and services are completely eliminated after the first copy is created (first copy cost effect), as they can be duplicated without effort. With standard flat rates for the use of internet services, there are also no delivery costs [6, p. 105ff.]. Rapid growth and global expansion of the range of services offered are also common in the case of services that start-ups ultimately provide with the help of physical resources, since the new market participants do not rely on their own facilities, but rather make the equipment of other value creation partners available to them through skilful networking. This central characteristic of **platform companies** is what makes them so dangerous to incumbent providers [7, p. 36].

6.2 Business Model Innovation and the Pattern-Based Construction of Business Models

In companies, the **digital transformation** is changing customer expectations, the competitive landscape, the data situation, value creation and the way innovation is handled, and thus key areas of corporate strategy and the business model [8, p. 1ff.].

A **business model** describes how a company creates, communicates and captures value, what benefits it provides to customers and partners, and how the benefits flow back to the company in the form of revenue. The central dimension of a business model are the target customers addressed by the business entity, with details of specific customer segments, channels and relationships. Further dimensions are the value proposition to the customers by providing products and services, the value chain explaining the service provision with the help of resources, capabilities, processes as well as partners, partner channels and relationships, and the profit mechanism showing the financial side with revenues and costs [9, p. 22f.]. A popular template for business model documentation is the **Business Model Canvas**, which summarises the business model dimensions in nine blocks and visualises them clearly [10, pp. 22f., 48].

The **digital transformation of a business model** can either be limited to the redesign of individual business model dimensions or fundamentally transform the business model with all its value chains and actors [11, p. 7]. If at least two of the four who-what-how-value business model dimensions are affected, it is referred to as a **business model innovation** [12, p. 4ff.].

The **St. Gallen Business Model Navigator™** provides a construction methodology for business model innovations. From a broad analysis of innovative business models in corporate practice, it draws the fundamental conclusion that 90% of all new business models can be traced back to a subset of 55 underlying patterns that companies "merely" put together with new combinatorics. What is needed is not a reinvention of the wheel, but creative imitation. A new business model is created through inspiration from successful role models, imaginative imitation and new recombination of the basic elements [12, p. 17ff.].

An example of a business model pattern is the razor-and-blade approach, which in its core idea offers a basic product at a low price or even free of charge, but generates high margins through the consumables required later for further basic product use. In addition to the namesake Gilette, Hewlett-Packard with inkjet printers and cartridges or Nestlé with espresso machines and coffee capsules also implement the razor-and-blade pattern [12, p. 19f.].

To generate new business ideas from the patterns, companies can proceed according to different **basic strategies** [12, p. 20ff.].

- **Transferring** a business model pattern that has already been successfully practiced in other industries to one's own industry sector helps to avoid the mistakes made by other companies. The company thus becomes an innovation leader in its own industry sector, but must ensure that it does not adopt a pattern 1:1, but rather pays attention to leeway in adapting the template.
- If a company accepts more complex planning and implementation processes, it can combine two or even three business model patterns in order to strengthen the effect of the individual elements. At the same time, the **novel combination** makes it more difficult for competitors to imitate.
- The **repetition** of a successful business model in another product area means, on the one hand, a balancing act between change and stability. On the other hand, the company can use experience and synergies and thus keep the risk manageable.

Barriers to business model innovations come, for example, from the **dominant industry logic**, in which managers orient themselves to the five-forces of industry analysis, tend to remain in the highly competitive "red ocean" and invest far too little innovation budget in the search for new market segments. Mental barriers manifest themselves in typical arguments about the specificity of the industry and its business processes, as well as customer expectations and acceptance. Managers also doubt the necessity of change as long as the company is profitable [12, p. 10f.]. Management tends to reject new ideas from the outside rather than their own impulses that originated within the company (**not-invented-here syndrome**).

Other obstacles include myths that companies adhere to, even though they do not correspond to the facts. For example, executives insist that only ideas that no one has had before lead to commercial success, although in practice business models transferred from one industry to another often prove successful (**first ascent myth**). The **think-big myth** only allows for radically new business model innovations, while reality also recognises incremental business model adjustments such as opening another distribution channel. The **technology myth** demands fascinating new technologies as a prerequisite for new products, when in fact many technologies have been known for a long time before a creative leap makes them usable through innovative applications. The **chance myth** doubts that companies systematically plan and work hard to create business model innovations, believing them to be a product of chance. The **Einstein myth** does not believe that interdisciplinary, cross-functional teams can achieve inspiration and looks, often unsuccessfully, for a single creative genius. Management also demands extensive resources, ignores the many business model innovations from outsiders (**size myth**) and sees only the R&D department as responsible for providing new impulses instead of placing the responsibility for this in the hands of all employees (**R&D myth**) [12, p. 11ff.].

6.3   IT Impact Areas for Digital Transformation with Disruptive Character

The digital transformation is driven by four areas of leverage, all of which can be assigned to the IT environment. These **IT leverage or impact areas** use IT technologies as enablers, resulting in new offers [13, p. 17ff.]. Depending on the industry considered, the impact areas take different priority (Fig. 6.1). The keywords in the outer ring are to be understood as examples that can be expanded as desired.

6.3.1   Networking and Data Processing Technologies

The basis for the use of digital data, innovative applications and multiple customer accesses is the mobile or wired networking of all participants as well as the scalable availability of storage space and computing power. Companies, for example, use **cloud computing technologies** such as software-, platform- and infrastructure-as-a-service to have flexible access to data and applications at a calculable cost and to react agilely to changes. Hybrid models that combine public and private cloud areas consider the demands for security, reliability and data protection [14, p. 31ff.]. For data preparation, companies are making supplementary use of so-called **NoSQL database technologies** in addition to classic relational databases, which accept the input of flexible data formats, can quickly search the dataset for fields outside the predefined indices in the event of spontaneous query requests, as well as handle datasets of different types and sizes [15, p. 59ff.]. The evaluation speed is increased by the **memory computing approach**, which initially manages and persistently stores data in main memory, and by the use of multicore processors [16, pp. 1, 14f.].

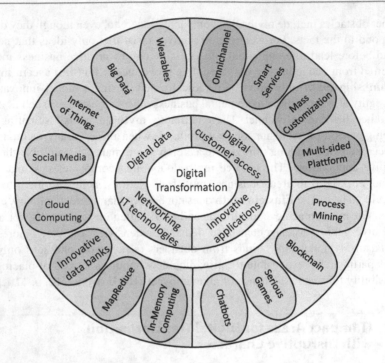

Fig. 6.1 IT impact areas for digital transformation

Some in-memory databases completely dispense with record updates, insert new data tuples for accelerated processing and mark these as the currently valid ones (insert-only) [17, p. 16f.]. Further performance improvements can be achieved by column-based data layouts, where a database maps column by column into the storage areas to make them quickly accessible for queries on individual fields across all rows. Compression procedures for fields that are frequently left empty or have low value cardinality further increase processing speed [16, p. 77ff., 17, p. 17, 59ff.]. The **MapReduce** model demonstrates a method for distributed search and analysis of large data sets on a cluster of commodity hardware. Via the stages splitting, mapping, shuffling and reducing, all cluster nodes contribute to the results analysis [18, p. 42ff.].

These and other IT technologies and networking possibilities have no direct counterparts in the business model patterns. Nevertheless, many business models presuppose the use of IT technologies or are promoted by technological developments.

6.3.2   Digital Data

With the four V's, volume, velocity, variety and veracity, **Big Data** formulates that the available volume of data is constantly growing and flowing at a quickening pace into companies, which have to deal with the high range of data types and formats and evaluate the trustworthiness of the data [19]. Analytics applications collect information from more and more areas of reality, which they make digitally analysable in the sense of datafication [15, p. 101]. The Internet of Things forces new business models by making any objects of reality addressable and controllable and thereby connecting physical and virtual objects [20, p. 14ff.]. With their applications for human interaction as well as information, identity and relationship management, social media generate a new kind of communication space and grant the world of Big Data access to competencies, interests, preferences, relationships, experiences, opinions, adventures and moods of users, as well as to multimedia content generated by them and to their expert knowledge [21, p. 11ff.]. **Wearables** augment the Big Data evaluation possibilities with insights into personal life worlds and open up self-measurement to improve one's own life according to social or individual demands of a systematic evaluation [22].

The comprehensive collection, processing, storage and evaluation of **digital data** is the prerequisite for customer focus, as propagated by many business model patterns. The data enable well-founded decisions and predictions to be made. The **Customer Loyalty** business model pattern, for example, provides incentives for long-term customer loyalty, usually using a card-based bonus program that records all purchases made and calculates the rewards. The bonus systems collect extensive customer data and document the purchasing behaviour of individual customers almost completely. Companies use the evaluation of customer profiles to optimise offers, to increase the effectiveness of advertising measures and to increase sales if customers redeem the rewards at the same company [12, p. 137f.].

The business model pattern **Leverage Customer Data** also makes use of the possibilities of comprehensive collection and processing of customer data as a profit-promising resource which, after suitable processing, leads to competitive advantages through the identification of savings potential, prompt market analyses and targeted advertising and improves the basis for strategic decisions [12, p. 207f.].

With its motto "**Sensor as a Service**", the **Digitalisation** pattern explicitly addresses products supplemented by sensors, which extend the real world with a digitally mirrored one. Companies connect with their customers in real time and learn from the most effective users and how they use products. They thus enhance the customer experience and also make the business model itself measurable along numerous recorded data points [12, p. 142ff.].

6.3.3   Innovative Applications

The abundance of available data leads to **novel applications** that use a wide variety of data sources and process them in many different ways. Thus, **process mining** draws a complete picture of the actual processes in the company by accessing data that the operational application systems hold and retrogradely generate actual process models including outliers and error cases. They show in detail which process instance went through which process path and how much time it took, where steps were omitted or executed more than once and what other deviations occurred. From historical paths, it is possible to predict the next steps for current instances and proactively detect missed deadlines or target deviations [23]. **Blockchain** combines well-known technologies such as encryption mechanisms and peer-to-peer networks for distributed and trusted data storage and makes intermediaries obsolete in transactions. Smart contracts use blockchain to digitally map and automatically settle contracts by allowing contract clauses to be partially self-executed or self-enforced, increasing security for parties and reducing transaction costs [24]. **Gamification** relies on playful elements for customer loyalty or on playful design of the work and learning processes of employees. Serious gaming in companies aims to improve business processes, contribute to knowledge sharing and absorption and even influence employee behaviour [25, p. 4ff.]. **Chatbots** aim at natural language communication between humans and computers. Text-based dialogue systems use a database as a knowledge base for recognition patterns and answers and are able to learn permanently due to artificial intelligence. They are increasingly developing into intelligent personal assistants, which conduct dialogues and provide services [26].

Many business model patterns also rely on – more or less – innovative applications. The **E-Commerce** pattern, for example, is based on exclusively or complementarily electronically processed sales and trade. The business partners exchange business information on the Internet, maintain their relationships and carry out transactions. In addition to the purchase or sale of goods and services, they also offer or make use of electronic services and support [12, p. 152ff.]. The shop systems in electronic sales take over the construction of product catalogues and the multimedia presentation of product and process data for the demanders. The online shopping cart and the applications for product ordering, payment and delivery represent the further steps in the purchasing process [27, p. 239ff.]. However, e-commerce applications are now so widespread that it is hardly possible to speak of novel applications.

The **Auction** business model pattern also requires applications that control participatory pricing. This is particularly evident in the auction format of real-time bidding, which auctions off online advertising spaces to the highest bidders in fractions of a second. Marketing companies thus optimally exploit the willingness of advertisers to pay and avoid empty advertising spaces [12, p. 110ff.].

The **User-Designed** pattern interprets the customers themselves as inventive entrepreneurs. The company sees itself in the role of a supporter of the entrepreneurial project and provides the customer with tools for product development, technical design and realisation of the submitted designs. It takes over the marketing of the products and sells them, for example, via the company's own online shop [12, p. 343ff.].

6.3.4 Digital Customer Access

The interplay of data, networking, IT technologies and applications increases market transparency for customers who can easily compare offers and take into account recommendations and experiences of other consumers into their purchase decision. At the same time, customers communicate via an increasing number of different channels and end devices and expect an uninterrupted shopping experience (**omnichannel**) from the initial expression of interest through to delivery, invoicing and service. **Smart services** around the product complement the purchase, collect usage data and analyse it for the user. Digital customer access reduces the importance of physically owning a product, which also develops its benefits when consumers use it as a service in sharing models. **Mass customisation** addresses the increasing demands of customers with individual and volatile preferences with personalised experiences and offers with extensive automation of product configuration and production and therefore controllable costs despite maximum individualisation. In the best case, companies thus anticipate changing customer expectations and fluctuations in demand [14, p. 29ff.].

In the course of digital transformation, those involved in value creation and use interact with each other directly and in real time. In many industries, **multi-sided platforms** are replacing the yet practiced pipeline model of a linear value chain from supplier to customer. Platforms are value creation networks in which the people, machines and resources involved largely organise themselves and respond flexibly to one another. Many disruptors break up existing value chains, break them down into their smallest components and put them together in a new way. They only require a minimum of value-added steps in the overall process and therefore manage with little capital investment. If the user base grows, network effects, which e.g. increase the network benefit in proportion to the square of the number of participants (cf. Metcalfe's law), initiate [13, p. 19].

Many of these aspects come to light in concrete business model patterns. The **Mass Customisation** pattern, for example, describes off-the-shelf individuality based on modularised product architectures. The immense wealth of variants is fed by the combinatorics of modules, which are standardised, in order to achieve cost levels comparable to those of mass production. Customers experience an I-do-it-myself effect through the selection process and feel more emotionally attached to the product and the company. Mass customisation has a particularly sales-increasing effect in areas in which customers appreciate individualised solutions and in which value creation processes can be intelligently automated at the same time [12, p. 233ff.].

The platform approach can be found in the **Two-Sided Market** business model pattern, which brings together two different user groups on the platform of a third party. The success of a platform depends on whether it succeeds in exploiting the indirect network effects, i.e. in achieving an increase in benefits for both sides by increasing the number of participants on the other side. To do this, the platform start-up must first solve the chicken-and-egg question, make the platform attractive to one or both user groups by means of suitable incentives and thus help it to spread quickly [12, p. 334ff.].

The **Subscription** pattern is like a subscription, where users purchase services at a pre-arranged frequency and for the agreed duration, which they pay for in advance or at regular intervals. Customers typically benefit from price discounts as they guarantee predictable revenue streams to providers in return. In addition, users benefit from a shortened purchasing period, continuous availability and reduced procurement risks [12, p. 316ff.].

6.4   Matching IT and Business Model DNA

6.4.1   Business Model DNA

Originally, the term **DNA** comes from biology and refers to the carriers of genetic information. It is essential that complex structures can be formed and described from a few basic building blocks. The basic idea of DNA is therefore to break down the elements of a more complex object into its core elements and thus to explain them more simply and, if necessary, to design them. The term DNA itself is also used inflationarily in management literature in different contexts to describe values, goals, strategies, competitive advantages, value propositions, etc., as it associates that with this term, the essence of a company can be described comparatively simply. At the same time, the different uses of the term contribute to confusion (e.g., King [28]).

The concept of **business model DNA**, as described by Böhm et al., follows an empirical approach [29, p. 1006ff.]. Böhm et al. classified about 180 companies (start-ups) using data mining methods. Among them were 31 failed ventures in addition to many successful ones. Twelve clusters of business models could be identified. The business models of a cluster have a similar business model DNA, i.e. they apply the patterns of business models according to Gassmann et al. in a certain characteristic combination. A single pattern may or may not be applied, resulting in a vector of 55 boolean elements that ultimately represents the business model DNA. Additionally, growth and success prospects could be identified and predicted with a probability of over 80%. This method is also applicable to other companies that have not been analysed, which helps to answer the research question that has been largely unanswered so far, namely which factors constitute a successful and sustainable business start-up. Table 6.1 shows an overview of the clusters and the business model patterns behind them, whereby a cluster combines between two and four business model patterns.

In practice, it makes sense to work out the basic elements of the business model in the company in order to critically rethink and further develop the components of the business model as part of a **business model innovation**. If novel IT technologies or components from various IT impact areas can be assigned to these basic elements, this will result in opportunities to address the digital transformation necessary at all levels in a more targeted manner [30]. Business models have thus become

Table 6.1 Business model DNA and business model patterns

Cluster (DNA)	Business model pattern 1	Business model pattern 2	Business model pattern 3	Business model pattern 4
Freemium platform	Freemium	Platform		
Experience Crowd Users	Experience Selling	Crowdsourcing	Leverage Customer Data	
Long Tail Subscribers	Longtail	Subscription		
Affiliate Markets	Aikido	Affiliation	Platform	
Mass Customising Orchestrators	Mass Customisation	Layer Player	Orchestrator	Two-sided Market
Innovative platforms	Aikido	Two-sided Market	Orchestrator	Revenue Sharing
E-Commercer	E-commerce	Direct selling		
E-Commerce Affiliates	E-commerce	Affiliation	The Long Tail	
Add-on layers	Add-on	Layer Player	Subscription	
Crowdsourcing Platforms	Aikido	Crowdsourcing	Customer Loyalty	Platform
Customised layers	Subscription	Mass customisation		
Hidden Revenue Markets	Hidden Revenue	Two-sided Market	Affiliation	The Long Tail

The Platform pattern includes one or more of the Orchestrator, Two-Sided Market or Long Tail patterns

the central research subject of information systems [31, p. 55ff.]. Business models can be used for analysis and classification, but from a practical point of view above all as a "recipe for creative managers" [32, p. 156].

Böhm et al. identified the clusters shown in Table 6.1 and determined the different prospects of success in terms of growth and probability of survival, albeit with limited significance. Almost all clusters contained the **pattern of digitalisation**, which demonstrates the importance of digitalisation in general, leading to the creation of many start-ups on the one hand and revealing the need for transformation of existing companies on the other hand. Otherwise, the patterns do **not show an equal distribution**. On the contrary, many patterns from the catalogue of Gassmann et al. hardly occur. However, this does not mean that the patterns are not relevant.

The clusters differ greatly in terms of **growth and survival prospects**. For the e-commerce cluster, for example, difficulties in market entry are described due to market saturation and high price competition. One to two decades earlier, the situation was certainly different. It therefore seems questionable whether the effects will last. This example points out that the start-up-based clusters are more of a **snapshot** in time and the investigation with some time lag could lead to highly divergent results. Moreover, the creative process of identifying business opportunities and cleverly combining different business model patterns within the team is left out of such retrograde studies. The importance of the team as a social unit also has a significant impact on the likelihood of success [33]. We therefore see the value of the Business Model DNA rather as a tool to roughly classify business models on a level above the pattern level and to use them as a promising starting point for entrepreneurial approaches.

6.4.2   Matching Process

If information systems want to make a significant contribution to the further development of business models, they must provide a **method** and a **process model** that evaluates technologies and IT developments in terms of whether they support a specific business model pattern or even enable it in the first place. Benefit assessments of specific elements from the aforementioned IT impact areas are indeed useful. However, technologies and the associated opportunities are developing and changing so rapidly that this assessment has to be done again and again and even results described here have a short half-life. Therefore, the method must be generic and at the same time simple, so that the process can be applied as well as possible by practitioners.

Process models and methods are now being developed to support the digital transformation in companies. In addition to the methodology of Gassmann et al., one example is the **Digitrans Method Framework** [34], which borrows methodologically from design thinking. Digitrans divides the procedure into the two main phases of innovation and transformation, which can also be iterated through, and complements numerous other popular methods and tools. The first phase – innovation – is divided into two elements: While the analysis process focuses on ideas based on the current state, the design process addresses the selection of possible solutions and the creation and evaluation of prototypes. This phase also includes the task of selecting appropriate innovative technologies for a particular business model or business model pattern, which we discussed in this paper. The result of the innovation phase is an expanded or even new business model that the company introduces in the subsequent transformation phase. **Business Model Building** includes checklists that are helpful for the development of business model innovations [35].

For the above-mentioned IT impact areas and selected innovative IT technologies, we explain the results and provide indications of where **patterns** and **technologies** fit together. They would be a first step towards enriching, for example, the pattern maps recommended by Gassmann et al. [12, p. 46ff.]. In order to be able to use new technologies in business models, those tackling digital transformation must first be familiar with the technologies, then understand and be able to assess them [36, p. 47ff.]. Since it can be assumed that there are deficits here, a matching of IT impact areas and their components and the business model patterns is valuable. The matching thus attempts to provide answers to the questions posed by Nagl and Bozem in their checklists for business idea development and for the development of the service and product offering: "Which trends and technologies make the realisation of the business idea possible in the first place? Which trends and technologies threaten the business idea? What technologies are required for product and service creation?" [35, p. 31, 34].

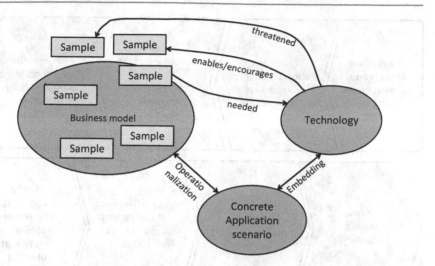

Fig. 6.2 Different perspectives on assessing the relationships between patterns/business models and technologies

Finally, the following questions are recommended as a starting point for evaluating concrete technologies and concepts for use in the respective business model:
- Which trends and technologies make the use of business model patterns possible, significantly easier or more cost-effective?
- Which technologies and concepts threaten individual business model patterns or entire business models?
- Which technologies and concepts are required for the realisation of a certain product or service creation?
- After embedding the technologies and concepts, what does the detailed value chain for creating or providing the product or service look like? [cf. 35, p. 37].

The questions illustrate the consideration of the topic from two different perspectives (see Fig. 6.2). Technologies can threaten and/or enable patterns. Conversely, the application of individual patterns may require and presuppose the use of certain technologies. Just as a business model is formed from several patterns (it may even use one pattern only partially), the operationalisation of the business model requires the use of that technology(ies) in a specific application scenario. In this context, it is important to address these issues early on in order to identify the potential promptly and exploit it in the market in the short term: "You have to act proactively before new entrants come into the market" [37]. The potential of a technology takes different forms. While some patterns can be implemented more efficiently, others develop disruptive forces [38, p. 214ff.].

The matching process proposed here (cf. Fig. 6.3) can be applied bidirectionally:
- For business model patterns already in use, companies can use certain technologies to enhance the benefits of pattern use. If a company intends to use a business model pattern, matching provides an indication of which technologies and IT impact areas should be considered for implementation.

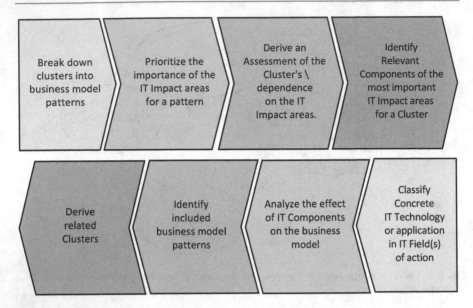

Fig. 6.3 Matching process

- Conversely, if an IT technology is available quickly and inexpensively, for example because it is already in use for other purposes or in other areas of the company or because partners can provide it, the current business model can be enriched by a promising pattern. Since IT technologies can also jeopardise business model patterns, their widespread availability means a concrete danger for the company, which it must perceive at an early stage in order to react appropriately.

6.4.3   Allocation of DNAs to IT Impact Areas

Table 6.2 summarises the assignment of the Business Model DNA clusters, their patterns and the importance of the IT impact areas, prioritises the IT impact areas for the effectiveness and success of the pattern and summarises the pattern evaluation for each cluster. As an example, we explain a possible reading from the pattern/business model perspective for three clusters. It should be noted that these are certainly subjective assessments and that other evaluations are possible depending on the concrete characteristics of the cluster or the focused business model under consideration.

The **E-Commercer** cluster combines the **E-Commerce** and **Direct Selling** patterns. Products or services are offered via the Internet and possibly also delivered or provided. The initially rather conservative pattern in combination with direct selling proves to be difficult in the above-mentioned study due to market saturation. Unless the products or services have a unique selling proposition, at least the e-commerce

Table 6.2 Importance of IT impact areas for business model patterns and clusters

Cluster	Pattern	Digital data	Computer technologies/ Networking	Innovative applications	Digital customer Access
Freemium Platform	Freemium	+	o	+	+
	Platform	++	++	+	++
	Total	++	+	+	++
Experience Crowd Users	Experience selling	+	+	+	+
	Crowdsourcing	o	o	o	+
	Leverage customer Data	++	++	+	++
	Total	+	+	o	++
Long Tail subscribers	The Long Tail	++	+	++	++
	Subscription	o	o	+	++
	Total	+	o	++	++
Affiliate Markets	Aikido	+	o	+	++
	Affiliation	+	o	+	++
	Platform	++	++	+	++
	Total	++	o	+	++
Mass Customising Orchestrators	Mass Customisation	++	+	+	++
	Layer Player	o	o	++	+
	Orchestrator	o	++	+	o
	Two-sided Market	++	++	+	+
	Total	+	++	+	+
Innovative Platforms	Aikido	+	o	+	++
	Two-sided Market	++	++	+	+
	Orchestrator	o	+	+	+
	Revenue Sharing	o	o	+	o
	Total	+	+	+	+
E-Commercer	E-Commerce	+	o	o	+
	Direct Selling	++	o	+	++
	Total	++	o	o	++
E-Commerce Affiliates	E-commerce	+	o	o	+
	Affiliation	+	o	+	++
	The Long Tail	++	+	++	++
	Total	+	o	+	++
Add-on Layers	Add-on	+	++	++	+
	Layer Player	o	o	++	+
	Subscription	o	o	+	++
	Total	o	o	++	+
Crowdsourcing Platforms	Aikido	+	o	+	++
	Crowdsourcing	o	o	o	+
	Customer Loyalty	++	+	+	+
	Platform	++	++	+	++
	Total	+	+	+	++
Customised Layers	Subscription	+	o	+	++
	Mass Customisation	++	+	+	++
	Total	++	o	+	++

(continued)

Table 6.2 (continued)

Cluster	Pattern	Digital data	Computer technologies/ Networking	Innovative applications	Digital customer Access
Hidden Revenue Markets	Hidden Revenue	++	++	+	o
	Two-sided Market	++	++	+	+
	Affiliation	+	o	+	++
	The Long Tail	++	+	++	++
	Total	++	+	+	+

process itself must function very well. The lasting loyalty of the customer to the company becomes a distinguishing feature. For this, corresponding digital customer access, comprehensive customer data collection and evaluations of customer profiles are crucial for proactively recognising sensitivities and changes in interests.

The **Hidden Revenue Markets** cluster dominantly combines the **Hidden Revenue** pattern with the **Two-Sided Market** pattern. For one of the sides involved, the offer is usually available free of charge, while the other side has to pay for its use. The **Long Tail** pattern implies a high number of transactions with different products, since the market participant only generates sufficient revenue overall through a high volume of small-scale sales. It turns out that across all patterns involved, all IT impact areas are affected, i.e. the cluster requires the comprehensive consideration of all IT opportunities. Long Tail requires detailed knowledge of user expectations, so digital customer access is essential. Efficient processing succeeds on the basis of comprehensive digitisation and automation (IT impact area DV technology/networking). The impact area of innovative applications gives the "Long Tail Subscribers" an edge over the competition.

The **Crowdsourcing Platforms** cluster is based on the platform idea, which can be expressed in different patterns (**Orchestrator, Two-sided Market, Long Tail**) or combinations of these patterns. The members of the crowdsourcing community are to be bound as closely as possible to the platform. To leverage the **Customer Loyalty** pattern, comprehensive digital customer access and profiling are crucial. The effect of unconventionally exploiting perceived weaknesses and adversarial strengths in the pattern **Aikido** can be strengthened by innovative applications and comprehensive digital customer access.

Looking further at the other platform, several **tendencies** emerge overall: The focus of many clusters is on the broadest possible user base through the provision of a platform. The companies provide the integrated offers and added value less themselves than through partners. Innovative service offers arise from the combination of different offer components, so that the ideal customer service is part of the core competence, which in turn requires comprehensive digitisation and profiling. The creation of such profiles is based on broad customer access and customer participation [37]. Innovative business models are less the result of new products or technologies and more of customer-related services: "We believe there is a major insight: digital transformation is not just about products and technology. In a connected world, where most physical products are already commodities, and people can quickly search for competitors on the Internet, market advantage should come from changing the business model, adapting it to new digital clients demanding customized services rather than new physical products" [39].

6.4.4   Exemplary Matching Between IT Impact Areas and Business Model Patterns

This section looks at the relationships between patterns and business models on the one hand and IT technologies and impact areas on the other hand, as shown in Figs. 6.2 and 6.3, from the perspective of the specific technology and provides information on how patterns or pattern combinations work (for details on the individual business model patterns see [12]). The topics listed should be seen as exemplary. They show that developments often threaten or enable several patterns.

6.4.4.1 Chatbots
Chatbots are conversational communication systems that typically involve a user communicating with a technical system via text messages formulated in natural language. Chatbots try to combine the simplicity of an online search with the personal feeling of a human-to-human conversation. Speech and text recognition have become mature for meaningful use. However, the technology is not yet firmly established in the market, as the providers of the basic technologies are still subject to strong changes and the maturity level of the partners in the chatbot ecosystem is rather low [26].

Chatbots are well suited to complement digital customer access and therefore influence all patterns that touch the customer access impact area. Customer dialogue automation tailors the customer dialogue to serve customers within the Long Tail pattern. The dialogue can use the information gained to insert advertising or for other approaches in the sense of **Hidden Revenue**, to re-populate the **Affiliate** pattern or for **Direct Selling** and **Cross Selling**. The targeted collection of customer data promotes the **Leverage Customer Data** pattern. If the chatbot is developed as a qualified service channel, it can be used as a building block in the **Add-on** pattern.

Chatbots are primarily a relieving supplement to existing customer and service channels, but the channels may also be cannibalised. Currently, companies should weigh the early stage of the technology, the immature ecosystem and the lack of experience against the advantages of an early adopter when using the technology in concrete application scenarios (see Fig. 6.2).

6.4.4.2 Blockchain
The (spreading) basic technology Blockchain, known in the context of cryptocurrencies, especially Bitcoin, allows through the intelligent combination of long-established technologies such as encryption and peer-to-peer networks the elimination of intermediaries, which yet have played their role as trusted partner for transactions as a business model, which was costly and time-consuming [40].

The distributed and trustworthy data storage of blockchains thus affects all business models and patterns that are based on cooperation between different partners. Due to the trustworthy traceability, blockchain offers the possibility to create value also through dynamically changing and newly added partners. This results in simplifying possibilities for the **Orchestrator** and **Auction** patterns, for example. For services provided via crowdsourcing, it could be possible to allocate revenues to the individual sub-services in line with performance, which promotes **Platforms** for **Crowdsourcing**, e.g. from the above-mentioned Crowdsourcing Platforms cluster. The same applies to **Crowdfunding** and the associated platforms. In general, there are further positive influences on all business models that use the Digitalisation pattern. Users of the **Fractionalised Ownership** pattern benefit from simplified processing and billing procedures through the use of a blockchain, as do patterns that focus less on the sale of products and more on benefit-based billing, such as the **Rent Instead of Buy, Performance-based Contracting** or **Pay per Use** patterns.

The more far-reaching idea of smart contracts, which provides for the automatic, "programmed" execution of contracts, supports the accelerated execution of business processes. Smart contracts map contracts digitally and check them automatically. Likewise, they can handle the negotiation or execution of a contract. Contract clauses can thus be partially executed or enforced themselves, which promises the contracting parties greater security compared to traditional contract law and at the same time reduces transaction costs [24].

At the same time, blockchain technology generally threatens **Platform-Based** business models whose strong market positioning is based on their services as a trusted intermediary. In the future, these platform companies will therefore have to focus even more strongly on the benefits for their customers, as the pure intermediary characteristic and the **Lock-In** pattern frequently practiced with it will become obsolete as a result of blockchain. Companies in the financial industry are experiencing this change particularly clearly, as their business model is primarily based on digitised data and relatively easily digitised services [41, p. 912 ff.]. Financial services companies are therefore coming under pressure from so-called FinTechs, which are embracing the special opportunities offered by new technologies and thus exploiting the pattern of **Layer Players**.

Even if many aspects are still open with regard to the useful areas of application and the efficient operation of blockchains, it makes sense to deal with the effects on one's own business model, as the developments affect many business model patterns. In addition to the question of the efficiency of one's own processes, the new technology also offers entirely new possibilities on the one hand and harbours potential threats on the other.

6.4.4.3 3D Printing

3D printing processes build a three-dimensional product additively, i.e. step by step, from one or more materials via an additive process. There are usually four phases in the development of 3D printing. After 3D printing produced only prototypes (rapid prototyping) in the early days, tools (rapid tooling) emerged as the process matured and at low cost. Towards the end of the first decade of this millennium, the costs had fallen so much and the quality and possibilities of the material had increased to such an extent that 3D printing could also directly produce end products (direct manufacturing). At this point, at the latest, 3D printing became a possible component of business models. The next step in the spread of 3D printing technology is the production of parts directly on site of the user or end consumer (home fabrication). This ultimately digitises the distribution of physical products to the end user completely, provided that the end user has the equipment and materials available to produce the physical product on site [38, p. 214 ff.].

Massive effects up to disruptive character on business models result at the latest from the third development phase, the end product manufacturing (direct manufacturing). Obviously, 3D printers can lead to shifts in the value chain. Individuality in the sense of **Mass Customisation** can be achieved at controllable costs. The exploitation of customer proximity in the **Direct Selling** pattern reinforces the potential of this pattern. While the well-known economies of scale apply to traditional production, 3D printing also offers opportunities to serve niches, which corresponds directly to the **Long Tail** pattern [39]. Via **platforms** that use **crowdsourcing**, customers can contribute their own ideas as 3D models (CAD) in the sense of the **User Designed** pattern. In a **multi-sided market**, both suppliers of models, specialised 3D printing service providers and the buyers of the end products benefit. With high-end and still cost-intensive 3D printers, there is potential to apply the pattern **Layer Player**. If the technology becomes more widespread and end users also have 3D printers at their disposal, users could print product extensions locally in the sense of the **Add-on** pattern and make use of the **Self-Service** pattern. This integrates customers more strongly into the value chain in the sense of the **From Push-to-Pull** pattern, possibly up to an **Open Business Model**. If the protection of intellectual property gains in importance, there are possible applications for the **License** pattern. With the goal of establishing a deep customer relationship, 3D printing can also serve the **Customer Loyalty** pattern.

3D printing generally threatens all business models in which other market participants simplify or accelerate production processes and thus potentially substitute parts of the value chain. The **Integrator** pattern, for example, is affected.

6.5 Conclusion

In the age of digital transformation, companies must rethink their business models and adapt them to the new challenges. This process must be supported in a structured manner. One approach is provided by the Business Model DNA, which, based on empirical studies, divides successful business models from practice into clusters of business model patterns. It shows that many business model patterns are closely related to IT innovations and are promoted by developments in the IT sector. On the other hand, new IT technologies or applications threaten existing business models, render the roles of diverse market participants redundant and favour the market entry of newcomers from outside the industry. Analysing the relationship between IT components and impact areas on the one hand and business model patterns as well as pattern clusters on the other hand can enable companies to visualise and understand the interdependencies between both areas and support their business models appropriately. A Chinese proverb says: When the wind of change blows, some build walls and others build windmills. In this sense, the matching between IT technologies and business model patterns should help companies to optimally support their business models through the use of suitable IT components and help them to succeed and, on the other hand, to make the best possible use of IT innovations for themselves and include them in an innovation process.

References

1. Lemke C, Brenner W, Kirchner K (2017) Einführung in die Wirtschaftsinformatik, Bd 2. Gestalten des digitalen Zeitalters, Heidelberg
2. Müller SC, Böhm M, Schröer M, Bahkirev A, Baiasu B-C, Krcmar H, Welpe IM (2016) Geschäftsmodelle in der digitalen Wirtschaft, Vollstudie, Studien zum deutschen Innovationssystem, Expertenkommission Forschung und Innovation (EFI) – Commission of Experts for Research and Innovation, No. 13-2016, Berlin. ISSN 1613-4338
3. Bauernhansl T (2017) Die Vierte Industrielle Revolution – Der Weg in ein wertschaffendes Produktionsparadigma. In: Vogel-Heuser B, Bauernhansel T, ten Hompel M (Hrsg) Handbuch Industrie 4.0, Bd 4. Allgemeine Grundlagen, Berlin, S 1–32
4. Bundesministerium für Bildung und Forschung, Zukunftsprojekt Industrie 4.0. https://www.bmbf.de/de/zukunftsprojekt-industrie-4-0-848.html. Accessed 26 Feb 2018
5. Kreutzer RT, Neugebauer T, Pattloch A (2017) Digital business leadership. Springer, Wiesbaden
6. Rikfin J (2014) Die Null Grenzkosten Gesellschaft. Fischer, Frankfurt am Main
7. Parker GG, Van Alstyne MW, Choudary SP (2017) Die Plattform-Revolution. mitp, Frechen
8. Rogers DL (2017) Digitale Transformation: Das Playbook. mitp, Frechen
9. Schallmo D (2013) Geschäftsmodelle erfolgreich entwickeln und implementieren. Springer, Wiesbaden
10. Osterwalder A, Pigneur Y (2011) Business model generation. Campus, Frankfurt am Main
11. Schallmo D, Rusnjak A (2017) Roadmap zur Digitalen Transformation von Geschäftsmodellen. In: Schallmo D et al (Hrsg) Digitale Transformation von Geschäftsmodellen. Springer Gabler, Wiesbaden, S 1–32
12. Gassmann O et al (2013) Geschäftsmodelle entwickeln. Hanser, München
13. Bloching B et al (Roland Berger Strategy Consultants) (2015) Die digitale Transformation der Industrie, Studie im Auftrag des BDI. https://bdi.eu/media/user_upload/Digitale_Transformation.pdf. Accessed 08 Sept 2018
14. Châlons C, Dufft N (2016) Die Rolle der IT als Enabler für Digitalisierung. In: Abolhassan F (Hrsg) Was treibt die Digitalisierung? Springer, Wiesbaden, S 27–39
15. Mayer-Schönberger V, Cukier K (2013) Big Data – Die Revolution, die unser Leben verändern wird, 2. Aufl. Redline, München
16. Plattner H, Zeier A (2012) In-Memory Data Management: ein Wendepunkt für Unternehmensanwendungen. Springer, Wiesbaden
17. Plattner H (2013) Lehrbuch in-memory data management. Springer, Wiesbaden
18. Freiknecht J (2014) Big Data in der Praxis. Hanser, München
19. Giel L (2013) Veracity – Sinnhaftigkeit und Vertrauenswürdigkeit von Big Data als Kernherausforderung im Informationszeitalter. http://blog.eoda.de/2013/10/10/veracity-sinnhaftigkeit-und-vertrauenswuerdigkeit-von-bigdata-als-kernherausforderung-im-informationszeitalter/. Accessed 31 Jan 2018

20. Tiemeyer E (2017) IT-Management: Einordnung, Handlungsfelder, Rollenkonzepte. In: Tiemeyer E (Hrsg) Handbuch IT-Management, 6. Aufl. Hanser, München
21. Schmitt J-H (2013) Social media. Springer, Wiesbaden
22. Wikipedia (2017) Wearable computing. https://de.wikipedia.org/wiki/Wearable_Computing. Accessed 31 Jan 2018
23. van der Aalst W (2016) Process mining: data science in action, 2. Aufl. Springer, Heidelberg
24. Schlatt V et al (2016) Projektgruppe Wirtschaftsinformatik des Fraunhofer-Instituts für Angewandte Informationstechnik FIT. Grundlagen, Anwendungen und Potenziale, Blockchain. https://www.fit.fraunhofer.de/content/dam/fit/de/documents/Blockchain_WhitePaper_Grundlagen-Anwendungen-Potentiale.pdf. Accessed 31 Jan 2018
25. Stieglitz S (2017) Enterprise Gamification – Vorgehen und Anwendung. In: Strahringer S, Leyh C (Hrsg) Gamification und Serious Games. Wiesbaden, S 3–14
26. Gabler Wirtschaftslexikon, Chatbot. http://wirtschaftslexikon.gabler.de/Definition/chatbot.html. Accessed 26 Feb 2018
27. Kollmann T (2016) E-Business, 6. Aufl. Springer, Wiesbaden
28. King R (2017) Business model canvas: a good tool with bad instructions? https://de.slideshare.net/RodKing/a-business-dna-map-of-the-business-model-canvas. Accessed 26 Feb 2018
29. Böhm M, Weking J, Fortunat F, Müller S, Welpe I, Krcmar H (2017) The business model DNA: towards an spproach for predicting business model success. In: Leimeister JM, Brenner W (Hrsg) proceedings der 13. Internationalen Tagung Wirtschaftsinformatik (WI 2017), St. Gallen, S 1006–1020. https://www.wi2017.ch/images/tagungsband_wi_2017.pdf. Accessed 08 sept 2018
30. Roth-Dietrich G, Gröschel M (2018) Digitale Transformation: Herausforderung für das Geschäftsmodell und Rolle der IT. In: Lang M (Hrsg) IT-management: best practices für CIOs. de Gruyter, Berlin, S 141–166
31. Veit D, Clemons E, Benlian A et al (2014) Geschäftsmodelle: eine Forschungsagenda für die Wirtschaftsinformatik. Wirtschaftsinformatik 56(1):55–64. https://doi.org/10.1007/s11576-013-0400-4
32. Baden-Fuller C, Morgan MS (2010) Business models as models. Long Range Plan 43(2–3):156–171. https://doi.org/10.1016/j.lrp.2010.02.005. ISSN 0024-6301. http://www.sciencedirect.com/science/article/pii/S0024630110000117. Accessed 26 Feb 2018
33. Spiegel O, Abbassi P, Zylka MP, Schlagwein D, Fischbach K, Schoder D (2016) Business model development, founders' social capital and the success of early stage internet start-ups: a mixed-method study. Bd. 26, 5. Aufl., S 421–449. http://onlinelibrary.wiley.com/doi/10.1111/isj.12073/full. Accessed 26 Feb 2018
34. Digitrans Method Framework. http://www.interreg-danube.eu/approved-projects/digitrans/section/digitrans-method-framework. Accessed 26 Feb 2018
35. Nagl A, Bozem K (2018) Geschäftsmodelle 4.0 – Business Model Building mit Checklisten und Fallbeispielen. Springer, Berlin/Heidelberg. http://www.springer.com/de/book/9783658188412. Accessed 26 Feb 2018
36. Schlotmann R (2018) Digitalisierung auf mittelständisch – Die Methode "Digitales Wirkungsmanagement". Springer, Berlin/Heidelberg, S 47–50. https://doi.org/10.1007/978-3-662-55737-2
37. BMI Lab, BMI and digital transformation, 08.05.2017. https://www.bmilab.com/blog/2017/3/28/bmi-and-digital-transformation-1. Accessed 26 Feb 2018
38. Rayna T, Striukova L (2016) From rapid prototyping to home fabrication: how 3D printing is changing business model innovation. Technol Forecast Soc Chang 102:214–224. https://doi.org/10.1016/j.techfore.2015.07.023. ISSN 0040-1625
39. BMI Lab How does digital transformation and business model innovation interlink, 28.07.2017. https://www.bmilab.com/blog/2017/7/28/how-does-digital-transformation-and-business-model-innovation-interlink. Accessed 26 Feb 2018

40. Giese P, Kops M, Wagenknecht S, de Boer D, Preuss M (BTC-ECHO) (2016) Die Blockchain Bibel: DNA einer revolutionären Technologie. CreateSpace Independent Publishing Platform, Kleve
41. Holotiuk F, Pisani F, Moormann J (2017) The impact of blockchain technology on business models in the payments industry. In: Leimeister JM, Brenner W (Hrsg) Proceedings der 13. Internationalen, Tagung Wirtschaftsinformatik (WI 2017), St. Gallen, S 912–926. https://www.wi2017.ch/images/tagungsband_wi_2017.pdf. Accessed 08 Sept 2018

Part IV

New Approaches in Process and Project Management

Process Digitalization Through Robotic Process Automation

Christian Czarnecki and Gunnar Auth

Abstract

In the context of digital transformation, innovative technologies, such as the Internet of Things and cloud computing, are seen as drivers for far-reaching changes in organizations and business models. Among these technologies, Robotic Process Automation (RPA) is an approach to process automation in which manual activities are learned and automated by so-called software robots. These robots emulate the inputs on the presentation layer, so that no changes to existing application systems are necessary for automating processes. The idea is to transform existing process execution from manual to digital, which differentiates RPA from traditional Business Process Management (BPM) approaches, where process-driven adjustments are required at the business logic level. In recent years, RPA has been intensively discussed in research and practice. Various RPA solutions are available on the market as software products. Especially for operational processes with repetitive processing steps in different application systems, good results have been documented using RPA, such as the automation of 35% of the back office processes at Telefonica. Due to the comparatively low implementation effort combined with a high automation potential, there is an increasing interest in RPA in practice (e.g., banks, telecommunications, energy supply). This chapter discusses RPA as an innovative approach to process digitalization and gives concrete recommendations for actions in practice. After an introduction to general architectures of RPA systems, application scenarios are discussed in respect of their automation potentials but also limita-

C. Czarnecki (✉)
FH Aachen University of Applied Sciences, Aachen, Germany
e-mail: Czarnecki@fh-aachen.de

G. Auth
Meissen University of Applied Sciences, Meissen, Germany
e-mail: gunnar.auth@hsf.sachsen.de

tions. Specific aspects of a structured selection procedure in the face of a growing market for RPA products are highlighted and complemented by a concise market overview. The use of RPA in practice is illustrated by means of three concrete application examples.

7.1 Basics of Process Digitalization

The digitalization of markets and value chains and the associated *digital transformation* have been discussed extensively in research and practice [1–3]. Innovative technologies and applications, such as the *Internet of Things*, *artificial intelligence* (AI), *cloud computing* and *social media*, are seen as enablers for fundamental changes in the business world, society, and private life [4, 5]. There is still no common definition of the terms *digitalization* and *digital transformation* [6], and the terminology and the distinction to existing approaches are also quite debatable [7]. It can be considered as a consensus that the objective of digital transformation is the change of business models and organizations through innovative technologies [8–11]. Frequently cited examples are companies such as Google, Facebook, Uber and Airbnb, which are challenging traditional business models [2].

Even though disruptive, digital technologies are seen as drivers, digital transformation is less a technical issue than a combination of strategic, organizational, and cultural challenges [12, 13]. This results in the need to adapt both concrete processes [14] and business process management approaches [15] to the requirements of digitalization, which is summarized under the term *process digitalization* [6, 7, 16–18]. The *Digital Maturity & Transformation Report* [19] – an empirical study with 452 companies – sees process digitalization as one of nine dimensions of digital transformation and defines it as the alignment of all processes to digital structures with as much automation as possible. The goal is the flexible and rapid adaptation of processes to new technologies in support of digital business models (see Fig. 7.1). Even though the terms process *digitalization* and *process automation* can be understood synonymously in many aspects, the process-related realization of digital transformation in particular involves a large number of specific challenges, such as new collaboration models and innovation partnerships [5], anchoring network organizations and digital ecosystems [2], customer centricity and a consistent focus on customer expectations [20], as well as leadership approaches oriented toward collaboration and agility [21].

Adapting processes to technological progress is not a new idea, but a core topic of the information systems discipline, the importance of which has been discussed for decades from cost, quality, and innovation perspectives [22, 23]. While the process defines the creation of the business outcome through activities, an application system encompasses the information processing and can either (1) take care of the whole process execution or (2) support humans in its execution [24, 25]. The first case represents automation of the complete process, while in the second case individual sub-processes are automated. The basic benefit aspects of automation are cost savings, higher availability, shorter lead times, and higher reliability as well as

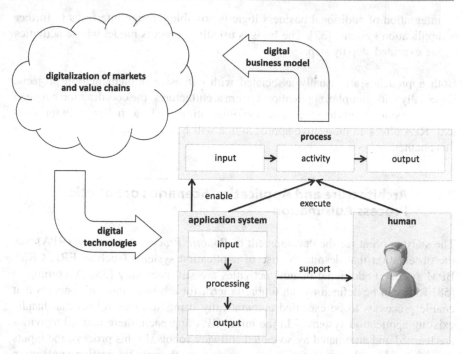

Fig. 7.1 Relationship between digital transformation and process digitalization

transparency [26]. In addition, certain processes are only made possible by application systems. This innovation potential from the interrelation of processes and technology was already discussed in the 1990s in the context of business process reengineering, among others [22, 27]. Nevertheless, in practice it has received less attention than efficiency potentials [28].

Basically, two approaches exist for the automation of processes, which will be referred to as *traditional approaches to process automation* in the following:

- The *implementation of processes by application systems*, such as enterprise resource planning (ERP) or customer relationship management (CRM) systems: since there is usually a difference between the existing processes and the available functionalities of the application system [29], this often requires either adaptations of the application systems to requirements of existing processes or adaptations of the processs to existing system functionalities. Based on traditional approaches of business process management, extensive models of the current and future state are created in this context [30, 31], which are then implemented both technically and organizationally.
- *Automation through business process management systems* (BPMS): depending on basic characteristics of an organization's value chain, BPMS may be implemented as *ad-hoc workflow systems, production workflow systems* or *case handling systems* [32]. The process models are executed step-by-step, whereby the

integration of additional business logic is possible through interfaces to further application systems [32]. The basis is usually a process model whose activities are executed step by step.

Both approaches are usually associated with extensive implementation projects. Especially with complex application system architectures, the coordination between business requirements and technical implementation can be a challenge. In this context, RPA offers an innovative approach that will be explained in the remainder of this chapter.

7.2   Architecture and Application Scenarios of Robotic Process Automation

The starting point for the development of *Robotic Process Automation* (RPA) was the observation that despite the use of application systems (such as ERP, CRM, BPM systems) additional manual activities are still necessary [33]. According to [58] RPA can be defined as "an umbrella term for a broad range of concepts that enable processes to be executed automatically using software robots that handle existing application systems." In the initial RPA approach, these manual activities are learned and automated by so-called software robots. In this process, the inputs are emulated on the presentation layer so that no changes to existing application systems are necessary.

Even though the term is based on tangible robots, such as those used as industrial robots in the automation of production processes [34] or for interaction in service processes [35], RPA is based exclusively on software systems. Just as tangible robots can perform human actions, in RPA manual activities are performed by software robots [36, 37]. Here, the software robot acts exactly like the human whose activity it automates. Thus, interaction with application systems is typically implemented through user interfaces. Existing operational application systems remain unchanged. This distinguishes RPA from traditional approaches to process automation (see Sect. 7.1), which usually require either technical or organizational adaptations.

Even if the concrete characteristics and functionalities of the available standard software for RPA (see Sect. 7.3) differ [38, 55], they are based on the architecture shown in Fig. 7.2. The basic principle is the automation of user input, which is technically implemented with existing approaches such as screen scraping[1] [39], macros [40], and scripting [41]. The core part of an RPA system can be structured into input sensors, intelligence center, and output actuators [56]. The intelligence center can vary from simple rule-based decisions to advanced concepts such as machine learning (ML), which is currently discussed using the term *cognitive RPA* [55, 57, 66].

RPA offers a wide range of functions for automating complete processes. An important aspect is that the basic implementation of RPA does not require advanced

---

[1]A method of reading text from computer screens, such as web pages.

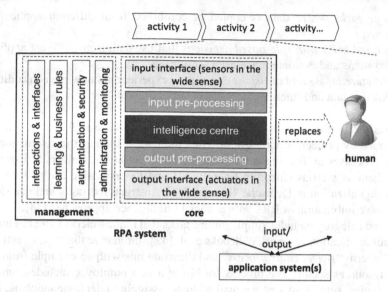

Fig. 7.2 Basic architecture of RPA [58]

programming knowledge [42]. Thus, the implementation can be realized mainly by the business side with no or reduced support by specialists of the IT department. The RPA system learns either by following rules or observing manual activities. Since the software robot communicates with underlying systems via the presentation layer, it requires a user account to login to each involved application system. Thus, from a business logic perspective, there are different software robots – as instances of the RPA system – that are each logged into the system with their own user IDs. In this respect, the number of client requests that can be processed on the server side forms a restriction for the scalability of an RPA system [36]. In addition, the management of access data is a security-relevant issue.

Compared to traditional approaches of process automation, RPA requires less implementation effort, since the RPA system does not require any adaptations to existing application systems. The resulting high profitability has been documented by different project examples, with return on investment (ROI) figures ranging from 200% to 800% [42]. Due to the easy integration of RPA into existing application systems, automation projects can be implemented by the business side. The coordination between technical framework conditions and business requirements that is necessary with traditional approaches to process automation is no longer required. This flexibility and speed is particularly advantageous with regard to the challenges of digital transformation. It should be noted, however, that the advantages described refer exclusively to the automation of manual activities in actual processes. The redesign of processes is not a goal here and would only be possible within a narrow set of conditions. The focus is on simple and repetitive activities in which different, non-integrated application systems are operated [36].

The possible applications of RPA depend on the complexity of the processes to be automated. A distinction can be made between the following degrees of complexity [37]:

1. *Routine tasks* where data is copied or combined from different application systems;
2. *Structured tasks with rule-based decisions* that use data from different application systems and evaluate it against a set of rules;
3. *Unstructured tasks and decisions* that require experiential knowledge in addition to existing data and rules.

While for the first two levels of complexity the successful use of RPA systems is documented by project examples in different industries, such as the automation of 15 core processes at Telefonica O2 [43], the RPA use at the University Hospital Birmingham as well as Gazprom Energy [42] and the extensive use of RPA for process digitalization at Deutsche Telekom [44], unstructured tasks and decisions require the combination of RPA with artificial intelligence approaches [33].

The first category includes simple routine tasks that require clerks to make entries in various application systems. Willcocks et al. [42] summarize this type of activity under the term *"swivel chair process"* and illustrate this with an example from the human resources sector: The process for hiring a new employee includes, among other activties, setting up a new e-mail address, assigning telephone numbers, setting up logins, creating a company ID card, and printing business cards. This often involves manually copying the relevant data into different application systems. Provided that a routine task is describable, automation can be performed by a software robot that takes over the previously manual entries [33]. Another criterion that makes sense from an economic point of view is a corresponding frequency of process execution. In the above example, the software robot logs on to the administration system and creates a suitable e-mail address derived from the first and last name of the new employee. The software robot then merges this email address with other data (e.g., phone number) to fill out and submit the appropriate order form for the business cards. In this logic, the software robot could take over all the previous manual routine tasks for hiring a new employee. Assuming the company hires a few thousand new employees each year, this would result in a substantial reduction in workload [42].

Basically, this category of routine tasks includes all repetitive, structured activities that require the use of different, non-integrated application systems [36]. These simple, manual activities can be located both in support processes, such as the creation of new users in IT administration, as well as in the core value creation, such as the forwarding of an order from the call center to production. Typical tasks that can be performed by RPA systems are, for example [33]:

- registration in existing application systems,
- fill out input masks,
- extract data,
- execution of transactions in ERP systems,
- perform calculations.

Rule-based decisions can be seen as an extension of simple routine tasks. An example of this is a business trip request in which decisions are made (e.g., selection of the cheapest flight) and data is consolidated (e.g., determination of the total price of the trip) on the basis of clear rules of the travel policy (e.g., flight in business class from 8 h flight duration, otherwise economy class) [33]. In principle, RPA can be used to automate all structured processes whose decisions can be described by clear business rules. By initially differentiating between standard cases that can be automated and special cases with manual activities, possible application scenarios can be further expanded (Sect. 7.4.3). Exemplary use cases are the processing of credit inquiries, needs-based order processing, and the classification of technical faults. Tasks taken over by RPA systems in this context include [33]:

- combine and evaluate data from different sources,
- create reports,
- open and process emails,
- rule-based execution of transactions in ERP systems.

Most documented applications of RPA can be seen as a mixture of simple routine tasks and tasks with rule-based decisions [42, 43]. Today (as of the end of 2021), first solutions for combining RPA with ML approaches are available and used in practice [61]. This is expected to provide further opportunities for automating unstructured tasks and decisions, such as identifying problems in direct dialogue with the customer or deriving strategic recommendations for action from sales data [33]. Furthermore, the architectural integration of RPA becomes more advanced [58, 62], which enables further functionalities, such as, automation on the data layer or communication between different software robots. Further topics that are currently discussed are, for example, the interrelation between RPA and process mining [63], the governance and management of RPA projects [64], and the combination of RPA and natural language processing [65].

The individual application scenarios depending on process and decision complexity are summarized in Table 7.1.

Table 7.1 Overview of RPA application scenarios

Process complexity	Decision complexity	Implementation effort	Example
Simple routine tasks	No decisions	Low	Create new users in different systems
Structured tasks	Rule-based decisions	Low	Processing of credit inquiries
Unstructured tasks	Experience required	High	Natural language dialogue in customer service

7.3   Selection of Standard Software for RPA

For the implementation of RPA, (standard) software systems are available on the market, which are referred to as RPA systems in the following. They differ considerably in structure and functionality. The following characteristics can be summarized as common features [36, 42]:

- The implementation of processes in RPA systems is done through rule-based configuration or observation, which is also known as training of the RPA system.
- Automation is based on the imitation of existing, manually executed processes.
- The RPA system is integrated with existing application systems mainly via user interfaces. Data exchange interfaces and APIs are also supported but require more advanced software development skills.

In addition to standard software products, there is also a range of specialized RPA services that are offered as a supplement to a specific RPA product, independently of a specific product, or in combination with proprietary software components of the service provider. Examples of such offerings include *Cognitive Robotics Automation Consulting* from *Atos*, the *Automation Suite* from *Conduent*, or so-called *robotics sourcing* from *Weissenberg Solutions*. Finally, the providers of classic BPM systems have also recognized the potential of RPA and are increasingly integrating corresponding extensions into their BPM products (e.g., *Scheer BPaaS*). However, product-service combinations and extended BPM products will not be considered further in the following; the focus in this article is exclusively on specific RPA systems.

The ten products listed in Table 7.2 were selected as examples from three commercial market studies [45–47]. These products are represented in all three studies[2] and are classified there as leading due to their scope of performance and degree of distribution.

While for the year 2017, Forrester [46] stated the number of RPA systems available on the market at 38 it has been growing to 146 until today [60]. Due to the number of products offered and the large differences between them, the selection of a suitable RPA system for a specific company or application scenario is not trivial. A systematic approach based on a criterion-based evaluation, as is also common for the selection of other standard software categories (e.g., ERP, CRM) [48–50], can protect against wrong decisions [59].

In such an approach, the value of available RPA systems (the objects of evaluation) is determined on the basis of the fulfilment or non-fulfilment of predefined, uniform comparison criteria. Both the definition of the criteria and the assessment of the degree of fulfilment of the evaluation objects are determined by the sponsor's evaluation objectives. These in turn result from the later application goals of the RPA system to be selected, for example, in a specific company. The evaluation

---

[2] With the exception of *Pega platform*, which is not represented in the 2016 Everest study. Instead, the provider *Thoughtonomy* was listed which was acquired by Blue Prism in 2019.

Table 7.2 Selected RPA systems (alphabetically by provider)

Provider	Product	Web page
Automation anywhere	Automation anywhere RPA workspace	https://www.automationanywhere.com/products/rpa-workspace
Blue Prism	Blue Prism Version 7.1	https://www.blueprism.com/de/products/intelligent-rpa-automation
Kofax	Kofax RPA 11.3	https://www.kofax.com/products/rpa
Nintex (Originally Kryon systems before acquisition by Nintex in 2022)	Nintex RPA	https://www.nintex.com/process-automation/robotic-process-automation
NICE	NICE robotic automation	https://www.nice.com/rpa/robotic-automation
Pegasystems	Pega platform	https://www.pega.com/products/platform
Redwood robotics	Redwood robotics	https://www.redwood.com/business-process-automation
Microsoft (Originally Softomotive before acquisition by Microsoft in 2020)	Power automate	https://powerautomate.microsoft.com/de-de/robotic-process-automation
UiPath	UiPath platform	www.uipath.com/product
WorkFusion	WorkFusion platform	https://www.workfusion.com/workfusion-enterprise

criteria are derived from the characteristics of the evaluation object. The morphological box shown in Table 7.3 supports the analysis and problem-oriented decomposition of the evaluation object with regard to the previous explanations of RPA systems.

RPA technology is basically industry and application neutral. Hence, it can be used for suitable processes from any application domain. Nevertheless, in order to differentiate themselves from competitors, suppliers sometimes emphasize certain industries in which, from the supplier's point of view, there is particular potential for the use of their product or in which focal points can be identified among the respective customers (industry focus). In a similar way, certain application areas are highlighted in the operational area, for example, through predefined processes (application focus), with regard to the type of automation tasks (automation focus) or the location of typical target systems in the operational application landscape (target system focus). In the training procedure, a basic distinction can be made between rule specification and observation of manual process execution, both usually supported by graphical process models. Great future potential for RPA is seen in AI capabilities. However, commercial systems are still in the early stages of development here and generously use the AI term as a label for processes and technologies from the fields of business intelligence and data analytics. The development here is aimed at self-learning software robots that exhibit great robustness and flexibility in the face of process dynamics and possess autonomous decision-making capabilities.

Table 7.3 Defining characteristics of RPA systems

Features	Profiles					
Industry focus	Without	Banks/insurances	Telecommunications	Health	Energy	Other
Application focus	Without	Customer interaction	Finances/payments	Purchasing/procurement	IT	Other
Automation focus	Without	Routine tasks	Structured tasks	Unstructured tasks		
Target system focus	Without	Desktop	Web	Back-end		
Training procedure	Rule specification	Observation				
AI skills	Without	Text/data/process mining	Problem identification	Problem solving	Learning/self-adaptation	Other
User interface integration	Screen	Speech processing	Chat bot			

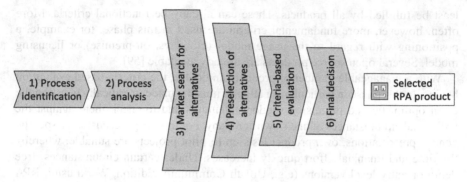

Fig. 7.3 Procedure for selecting RPA software

7.3.1 Procedure

With a systematic approach, the effort required for the selection decision can be kept within an appropriate, plannable dimension. In addition, the quality of the selection decision is also improved by critically reviewing vendor information on the respective products and supplementing it as required with further information for evaluating the decision alternatives [49, 51, 59]. Finally, a systematic approach also increases the transparency, comprehensibility and objectivity of the selection decision. Figure 7.3 shows a phase-oriented procedure for selecting an RPA system (based on [51, 52, 59]):

The procedure starts with the identification of appropriate processes with the most promising automation potential according to the benefit expectations for RPA and the associated deployment goals from a business perspective. It is advisable to take a comprehensive view that, in addition to the obligatory increase in productivity, also takes into account the potential of process automation for increasing sales and improving the customer experience. Gartner [47] refers to this as the development of an enterprise automation roadmap.

The process analysis examines the automation potentials from a functional and information technology perspective. The findings can be used to derive uniform criteria for evaluating the standard products, for which weighting should also be carried out on the basis of the defined objectives. When conducting the market search for RPA solution alternatives, the first step is to identify as many candidates as possible for the actual selection process. By researching Internet resources, trade publications, white papers/technical reports, etc., a corresponding list can be quickly compiled. If necessary, this can be supplemented by visits to trade fairs and exchanges with competitors, partners, suppliers, etc.

From the basic list of all RPA systems in question, a short list is now created by means of preselection. For this purpose, exclusion criteria are defined that must at least be fulfilled by all products. These can already be functional criteria. More often, however, more fundamental criteria are used in this phase, for example, a positioning with regard to the usage model (cloud vs. on-premise) or licensing model. Several open source products are already available [59].

With a manageable number of product candidates, the criteria-based evaluation begins. In this phase in particular, an attempt must be made to critically question the often optimistic and promising vendor statements and to check them against the individual circumstances of one's own company. For this purpose, customer-specific vendor presentations, own product tests up to pilot projects are suitable, whereby the time and financial effort quickly increases. Under certain circumstances, free demo or entry-level versions (e.g., UiPath Community Edition, WorkFusion RPA Express) can also be used for this purpose.

Ideally, the evaluation results in a clear ranking of the candidates, so that the decision is limited to a confirmation of the first-placed candidate. If the result of the evaluation is less clear, in-depth product analyses as well as additional price negotiations with the suppliers can contribute to clarification.

7.3.2 Selection Criteria

As is generally the case when selecting standard software, the basic criteria for a comparison of RPA systems are their cost-effectiveness and target fulfillment from the company's point of view. These criteria must be operationalized for RPA systems in a company-specific manner. In the non-functional area, general experiences and methods for the selection of standard business software can be used. With regard to quality criteria, the ISO standards for software products of the 250xx family (Systems and Software Quality Requirements and Evaluation – SQuaRE) provide a recognized basis. In addition to the product characteristics, the role of the vendor in the introduction, use, and further development of the system should also be included in the evaluation, especially in the case of RPA. For example, customer orientation, implementation competence (e.g., references), employee competence as well as availability, and corporate development of the vendor can be considered.

Finally, functional criteria should be defined for the evaluation of task-related goal fulfillment from the company's point of view; these criteria can be derived from use cases described in the course of the requirements analysis. Functional criteria should also be based on the typical functional scope of the products offered in the areas of robot development, training and deployment, robot control, system management, reporting, analytics, and data protection as well as security [46]. In the area of process automation, functionalities are often offered that serve to fill out input masks, execute functions in ERP systems, perform calculations, and open and process e-mails [33]. A comprehensive criteria catalog for RPA based on a multivocal literature review can be found in [59].

7.4   Application Examples

The use of RPA has been documented in a wide range of studies [33, 42–44, 53], although the focus varies from financial key figures to quotes from project participants to the presentation of transformation programs. In this chapter, process digitalization through RPA is presented using three project examples at the level of specific activities and application systems involved. Example 1 (Sect. 7.4.1) presents a proactive incident management during thunderstorms, where RPA integrates the processing in different application systems. Example 2 (Sect. 7.4.2) shows the automation of a service allocation, in which a variety of manual entries are necessary despite an existing workflow management system. Example 3 (Sect. 7.4.3) illustrates the handling of returns, whereby a distinction must be made between standard and special cases. In the standard case, automation through RPA is possible. The application examples are based on real projects, for which data was primarily collected through own research activities and observations. The presentation is anonymized and summarized.

7.4.1   Example 1: Proactive Fault Management during Thunderstorms

The subject of this application example is a leading telecommunications company [44]. During thunderstorms, there is an increased risk that the network infrastructure will fail and that communication services (e.g., telephony) will not be available to the customer. A three-step process was developed to proactively respond to such disruptions:

1. Proactive *communication of the customer before the thunderstorm*: The necessary data is available as weather forecasts. An evaluation and allocation of the affected customers is necessary to inform them via short message (SMS).
2. *Fault analysis and reset of affected network infrastructure*: After the thunderstorm, affected devices of the network infrastructure are to be identified by an analysis. An attempt is made to solve the fault by resetting these devices. At the same time, the customer is informed by SMS.
3. *Check the network infrastructure and, if necessary, send a service technician to solve the fault*: After the reset, the network infrastructure is checked again. If the fault is still present, a service technician is informed and assigned to solve the fault. In this case, the customer is informed by SMS.

Application systems are available for the respective process steps. Weather forecasts and geographical allocation of network areas are available in databases that can be evaluated via analysis tools. Access to customer data and customer communication are possible via a CRM system. Analyses and resets of network infrastructure devices are feasible via Operation Support Systems (OSS) diagnostic tools [54]. Scheduling and dispatching of service technicians is covered in a workforce

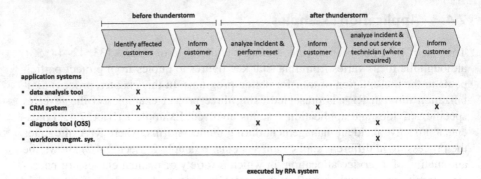

Fig. 7.4 Project example: Proactive fault management during thunderstorms

management system. However, these individual systems are not integrated, requiring manual copying of inputs and outputs. This is exactly what has been taken over by an RPA system. The relationship between activities, application systems, and RPA is summarized in Fig. 7.4.

7.4.2 Example 2: Activity Allocation for Technical Services

The subject of this application example is a company that provides technical services (e.g., remote maintenance) to private customers. For this purpose, different rates can be booked, each of which contains a certain scope of services. The services are provided in different competence levels via a call center. The employees are supported by a workflow management system, which enables, among other activities, a work list per employee, the assignment of agents, and due dates monitoring. The individual interactions with the customer are realized via order bookings (so-called tickets). During service provision, it may be necessary to charge for additional services. This can occur at any point in the process and at any competence level. This additional service allocation is mapped in the existing workflow management system as follows:

1. A new order is created for billing. This requires the manual entry of the customer and telephone number.
2. In addition, manual entries are necessary in the order, which are always the same for this case.
3. As options for billing, a distinction can be made between flat-rate and minute-based billing. In the latter case, the minutes to be billed must be entered manually.
4. The ticket is forwarded to the billing system, whereby the order number must be manually noted in the central order system.

Despite the use of a workflow management system, manual entries are necessary, which is due to the fact that clearing is treated as an additional order. In addition, the

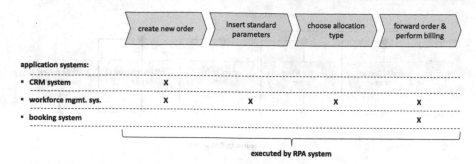

Fig. 7.5 Project example: Activity allocation for technical services

process is prone to errors, as traceability requires that all data has been entered correctly. An average process time of 7 minutes was determined for approximately 900 cases per month. In this use case, different application systems have to be operated as well as a high percentage of repetitive standard entries have to be performed. The improvement through the use of an RPA system is shown in Fig. 7.5.

7.4.3 Example 3: Handling of Returns

The subject of this use case is a retail company that, among other activities, ships goods. This use case deals with the booking of returned goods, so-called returns. The company works with an integrated CRM system that is used to process all operative customer interactions. Different steps are required to handle returns:

1. Identify and call customers;
2. Display order history, identify and call up respective order of the order number;
3. Check individual items of the order with the return for completeness;
4. Create a return order and link it to the items in the original order;
5. Complete standard entries in the returns order;
6. Complete the returns order and trigger the update.

The entire process is mapped in the CRM system, but requires a large number of manual entries in various input masks. If there is a complete return of an order with correct customer number and order number, the manual activities are exclusively repetitive standard entries. Only in special cases (e.g., order cannot be assigned) are further manual searches necessary. All standard cases can be automated by an RPA system. In this respect, a distinction must be made in the individual process steps. While special cases are forwarded for manual processing, the RPA system handles standard cases automatically. This relationship is shown in Fig. 7.6.

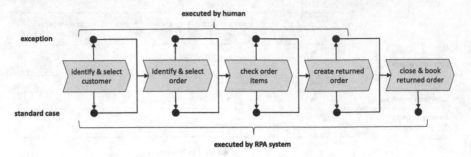

Fig. 7.6 Project example: Booking of returns

7.5   Summary and Outlook

In addition to traditional approaches to process automation, RPA is an innovative approach that is based on the emulation of user input when operating application systems. The process automation is realized by so-called software robots that inter-act with application systems mainly via their user interfaces. An adaptation of pro-gram code, interfaces, or data structures of existing application systems is therefore not necessary. The use of data exchange interfaces and APIs is also supported but requires the respective skills. The initial RPA approach does not optimize the auto-mated processes by adapting the process flow. This means that, compared to tradi-tional approaches to process automation, lower implementation costs and shorter implementation times can be assumed. From the company's point of view, the expected benefits of RPA focus on productivity gains, as they are also aimed for in automation with physical robots, such as, higher availability, shorter throughput times as well as higher reliability and transparency. The feasibility of these poten-tials has been demonstrated by a large number of application examples in different industries.

Low-variance routine processes with the highest possible transaction volume are primarily suitable for the application of RPA. In addition, tasks with a decision-making component can also be automated if suitable rules can be described for decision-making. Finally, the automation of unstructured tasks and decisions through RPA is increasingly being sought, for which, in addition to existing data and rules, the introduction of empirical knowledge is also required.

Despite the novelty of the RPA concept, a considerable number of standard soft-ware products for the implementation of software robots is already available on the market. However, the overall offering is characterized by significant differences in the structure and functionality of the solutions. In order to select a suitable product for the individual requirements of one's own company from the various alternatives, a systematic, criteria-based procedure is recommended, as described in this article.

Great potential for the future development of RPA can be seen in the combina-tion with AI methods and processes. The aim is to improve the self-learning and decision-making capabilities of software robots, which in turn will open up more dynamic and complex fields of application. In view of the current increase in the number of providers and solutions, however, a consolidation of the market is to be expected in the medium term, which would reduce the number of solutions on offer again. The extent to which the RPA approach will succeed in establishing itself permanently independently of classic BPM providers will also play a role here.

References

1. Cole T (2017) Digitale Transformation: warum die deutsche Wirtschaft gerade die digitale Zukunft verschläft und was jetzt getan werden muss! Verlag Franz Vahlen, München
2. Kreutzer R, Neugebauer T, Pattloch A (2017) Digital business leadership: digitale transformation – Geschäftsmodell-innovation – agile organisation – change-management. Springer, Wiesbaden
3. Mertens P, Bodendorf F, König W et al (2017) Digitale Transformation von Unternehmen. In: Grundzüge der Wirtschaftsinformatik. Springer, Berlin/Heidelberg, pp 189–204
4. Fitzgerald M, Kruschwitz N, Bonnet D, Welch M (2013) Embracing digital technology. MIT Sloan Manag Rev 55(2):1–12
5. Urbach N, Ahlemann F (2017) Die IT-Organisation im Wandel: Implikationen der Digitalisierung für das IT-Management. HMD Praxis der Wirtschaftsinformatik 54:300–312. https://doi.org/10.1365/s40702-017-0313-6
6. Schallmo D (2016) Jetzt digital transformieren: so gelingt die erfolgreiche digitale Transformation Ihres Geschäftsmodells. Springer, Wiesbaden
7. Legner C, Eymann T, Hess T et al (2017) Digitalization: opportunity and challenge for the business and information systems engineering community. Bus Inf Syst Eng 59:301–308. https://doi.org/10.1007/s12599-017-0484-2
8. Gimpel H, Röglinger M (2015) Digital transformation: changes and chances – insights based on an empirical study. Fraunhofer Institute for Applied Information Technology, Bayreuth
9. Hartl E, Hess T (2017) The role of cultural values for digital transformation: insights from a Delphi Study. In: Proceedings of the 23rd Americas Conference on Information Systems (AMCIS 2017), Boston, Massachusetts, USA, August 10–12
10. Henriette E, Feki M, Boughzala I (2015) The shape of digital transformation: a systematic literature review. In: Proceedings of Mediterranean Conference on Information Systems (MCIS)
11. Morakanyane R, Grace AA, O'Reilly P (2017) Conceptualizing digital transformation in business organizations: a systematic review of literature. In: BLED 2017 proceedings
12. Bensberg F, Buscher G (2016) Digitale Transformation und IT-Zukunftsthemen im Spiegel des Arbeitsmarkts für IT-Berater – Ergebnisse einer explorativen Stellenanzeigenanalyse. In: Tagungsband zur Multikonferenz Wirtschaftsinformatik (MKWI) 2016. Technische Universität Ilmenau, Ilmenau, S 1007–1018
13. Jung R, Lehrer C (2017) Guidelines for education in business and information systems engineering at tertiary institutions. Bus Inf Syst Eng 59:189–203. https://doi.org/10.1007/s12599-017-0473-5
14. Denner M-S, Püschel LC, Röglinger M (2017) How to exploit the digitalization potential of business processes. Bus Inf Syst Eng. https://doi.org/10.1007/s12599-017-0509-x
15. Roeglinger M, König U, Kerpedzhiev G, Rosemann M (2017) Business process management in the digital age. BPTrends. https://doi.org/10.13140/RG.2.2.12087.42408
16. Dünnebeil S, Kaletsch A, Jedamzik S et al (2011) Prozessdigitalisierung durch Mehrwertanwendungen der eGK am Beispiel der elektronischen Überweisung. perspegKtive 2011, Darmstadt
17. Manz S (2018) Digitale Transformation im Banking – lessons learned. In: Brühl V, Dorschel J (Hrsg) Praxishandbuch digital banking. Springer, Wiesbaden, S 161–187

18. Mayr R (2017) Rationalisierungspotenzial durch Prozessdigitalisierung am Beispiel der kaufmännischen Aufgaben und Meldepflichten. In: Hildebrandt A, Landhäußer W (Hrsg) CSR und Digitalisierung. Springer, Berlin/Heidelberg, S 279–294
19. Berghaus S, Back A, Kaltenrieder B (2017) Digital maturity & transformation report 2017. Institut für Wirtschaftsinformatik/Universität St. Gallen, St. Gallen
20. Hauk J, Czarnecki C, Dietze C (2018) Prozessorientierte Messung der Customer Experience am Beispiel der Telekommunikationsindustrie. In: Rusnjak A, Schallmo DRA (Hrsg) Customer Experience im Zeitalter des Kunden. Springer Fachmedien Wiesbaden, Wiesbaden, S 195–216
21. Petry T (Hrsg) (2016) Digital Leadership: erfolgreiches Führen in Zeiten der Digital Economy, 1. Aufl. Freiburg/München/Stuttgart, Haufe Gruppe
22. Hammer M, Champy J (1994) Reengineering the corporation: a manifesto for business revolution. HarperBusiness, New York
23. Porter ME (2004) Competitive advantage. Free, New York/London
24. Alpar P, Alt R, Bensberg F et al (2016) Anwendungsorientierte Wirtschaftsinformatik: strategische Planung, Entwicklung und Nutzung von Informationssystemen, 8., überarb. Aufl. Springer Vieweg, Wiesbaden
25. Laudon KC, Laudon JP, Schoder D (2010) Wirtschaftsinformatik: eine Einführung. Pearson Studium, München/Boston
26. Ferstl O, Sinz E (2018) Automatisierbarkeit von IS-Aufgaben. In: Gronau N, Becker J, Kliewer N et al (Hrsg) Enzyklopädie der Wirtschaftsinformatik – Online-Lexikon, Bd 10. GITO Verlag, Berlin
27. Davenport TH (1993) Process innovation: reengineering work through information technology. Harvard Business School Press, Boston
28. Kohlborn T, Mueller O, Poeppelbuss J, Roeglinger M (2014) Interview with Michael Rosemann on ambidextrous business process management. Bus Process Manag J 20:634–638. https://doi.org/10.1108/BPMJ-02-2014-0012
29. Fischer M, Heim D, Janiesch C, Winkelmann A (2017) Assessing process fit in ERP implementation projects: a methodological approach. In: Maedche A, vom Brocke J, Hevner A (Hrsg) Designing the digital transformation. Springer, Cham, S 3–20
30. Rosemann M, Schwegmann A, Delfmann P (2012) Vorbereitung der Prozessmodellierung. In: Becker J, Kugeler M, Rosemann M (Hrsg) Prozessmanagement, Bd 7. Springer, Berlin/Heidelberg, S 45–103
31. Speck M, Schnetgöke N (2012) Sollmodellierung und Prozessoptimierung. In: Becker J, Kugeler M, Rosemann M (Hrsg) Prozessmanagement, Bd 7. Springer, Berlin/Heidelberg, S 195–228
32. Dumas M, La Rosa M, Mendling J, Reijers HA (2013) Fundamentals of business process management. Springer, Berlin/Heidelberg
33. Scheer A-W (2017) Performancesteigerung durch Automatisierung von Geschäftsprozessen. AWS-Institut für digitale Produkte und Prozesse, Saarbrücken
34. Pires JN (2007) Industrial robots programming: building applications for the factories of the future. Springer, New York
35. Vincent J, Taipale S, Sapio B et al (2015) Social robots from a human perspective. Springer, Cham
36. Allweyer T (2016) Robotic Process Automation – Neue Perspektiven für die Prozessautomatisierung (in German only). http://www.kurze-prozesse.de/blog/wp-content/uploads/2016/11/Neue-Perspektiven-durch-Robotic-Process-Automation.pdf. Accessed 6 Dec 2021
37. Czarnecki C (2018) Robotergesteuerte Prozessautomatisierung. In: Gronau N, Becker J, Kliewer N et al (Hrsg) Enzyklopädie der Wirtschaftsinformatik – Online-Lexikon, Bd 10. GITO Verlag, Berlin
38. Schmitz B (2017) Robotic process automation: Leistungsübersicht über am Markt verfügbare Softwarelösungen. Hochschule für Telekommunikation Leipzig

39. Durand C (2009) Internationalizing mainframe applications through screen scraping. In: Aykin N (Hrsg) Internationalization. Design and global development. Springer, Berlin/Heidelberg, S 228–235
40. Sieberichs D, Krüger H-J (1993) Makros automatisieren die Arbeit. In: Vieweg Software-Trainer Microsoft Access für Windows. Vieweg+Teubner Verlag, Wiesbaden, S 303–313
41. Schwichtenberg H (2010) Windows Scripting: automatisierte Systemadministration mit dem Windows Script Host [5.8] und der Windows PowerShell [2.0], 6., ak. Aufl. Addison-Wesley, München
42. Willcocks L, Lacity M, Craig A (2015) The IT function and robotic process automation. The London School of Economics and Political Science. Outsourcing unit working research paper series, Paper 15/05, London
43. Lacity M, Willcocks LP, Craig A (2015a) Robotic process automation at Telefonica O2. The London School of Economics and Political Science, London
44. Schmitz M, Dietze C, Czarnecki C (2019) Enabling digital transformation through robotic process automation at Deutsche Telekom. In: Urbach N, Röglinger M (eds) Digitalization cases. Springer, Cham
45. Everest Global (2016) Robotic process automation (RPA) – technology vendor landscape with FIT matrix assessment. Everst Group, Dallas
46. Forrester Research (2017) The Forrester waveTM: robotic process automation, Q1 2017. Forrester Research, Cambridge
47. Gartner (2017) Market guide for robotic process automation software. Gartner, Stamford
48. Heinrich LJ (1999) Bedeutung von Evaluation und Evaluationsforschung in der Wirtschaftsinformatik. In: Heinrich LJ, Häntschel I (Hrsg) Evaluation und Evaluationsforschung in der Wirtschaftsinformatik: Handbuch für Praxis, Lehre und Forschung. Oldenbourg, München
49. Leimeister JM (2015) Einführung in die Wirtschaftsinformatik. Springer, Berlin/Heidelberg
50. Schallaböck M (1999) Evaluation von Standardsoftware-Produkten. In: Heinrich LJ, Häntschel I (Hrsg) Evaluation und Evaluationsforschung in der Wirtschaftsinformatik: Handbuch für Praxis, Lehre und Forschung. Oldenbourg, München
51. Gronau N (2018) Softwareauswahl. In: Gronau N, Becker J, Kliewer N et al (Hrsg) Enzyklopädie der Wirtschaftsinformatik – Online-Lexikon, Bd 10. GITO Verlag, Berlin
52. Bick M, Börkmann K (2009) A reference model for the evaluation of information systems for an integrated campus management. Santiago de Compostela
53. Lacity M, Willcocks LP, Craig A (2015b) Robotic process automation: mature capabilities in the energy sector. London School of Economics and Political Science, LSE Library
54. Czarnecki C, Dietze C (2017) Reference architecture for the telecommunications industry: transformation of strategy, organization, processes, data, and applications. Springer, Cham
55. Enriquez JG, Jimenez-Ramirez A, Dominguez-Mayo FJ, Garcia-Garcia JA (2020) Robotic process automation: a scientific and industrial systematic mapping study. IEEE Access 8:39113–39129. https://doi.org/10.1109/ACCESS.2020.2974934
56. Fettke P, Loos P (2019) "Strukturieren, Strukturieren, Strukturieren" in the era of robotic process automation. In: Bergener K, Räckers M, Stein A (eds) The art of structuring. Springer, Cham, pp 191–201
57. Houy C, Hamberg M, Fettke P (2019) Robotic process automation in public administrations. In: Räckers M, Halsbenning S, Rätz D et al (eds) Digitalisierung von Staat und Verwaltung. Gesellschaft für Informatik e.V, Bonn, pp 62–74
58. Czarnecki C, Fettke P (2021) Robotic process automation: positioning, structuring, and framing the work. In: Czarnecki C, Fettke P (eds) Robotic process automation: management, technology, applications. De Gruyter Oldenbourg, Berlin/Boston, pp 3–24. https://doi.org/10.1515/9783110676693-001
59. Bensberg F, Auth G, Czarnecki C (2021) Finding the perfect RPA match: a criteria-based selection method for RPA solutions. In: Czarnecki C, Fettke P (eds) Robotic process automation. De Gruyter, pp 47–76. https://doi.org/10.1515/9783110676693-003
60. Capterra (2021) Robotic Process Automation (RPA). https://www.capterra.com/robotic-process-automation-software/. Accessed 6 Dec 2021

61. Czarnecki C, Hong C-G, Schmitz M, Dietze C (2021) Enabling digital transformation through cognitive robotic process automation at deutsche telekom services Europe. In: Urbach N, Röglinger M, Kautz K, Alias RA, Saunders C, Wiener M (eds) Digitalization cases, Management for professionals, vol 2. Springer, Cham. https://doi.org/10.1007/978-3-030-80003-1_7
62. Auth G, Czarnecki C, Bensberg F (2019) Impact of Robotic Process Automation on Enterprise Architectures. In: 50 Jahre Gesellschaft für Informatik – Informatik für Gesellschaft (Workshop-Beiträge). Gesellschaft für Informatik e.V, Bonn, pp 59–65
63. Aalst W (2021) 12 Process mining and RPA: how to pick your automation battles? In: Czarnecki C, Fettke P (eds) Robotic process automation: management, technology, applications. De Gruyter Oldenbourg, Berlin/Boston, pp 223–240. https://doi.org/10.1515/9783110676693-012
64. Herm L, Janiesch C, Steinbach T, Wüllner D (2021) 2 Managing RPA implementation projects: a framework applied at SYSTHEMIS AG. In: Czarnecki C, Fettke P (eds) Robotic process automation: management, technology, applications. De Gruyter Oldenbourg, Berlin/Boston, pp 27–46. https://doi.org/10.1515/9783110676693-002
65. Aa H, Leopold H (2021) 10 Supporting RPA through natural language processing. In: Czarnecki C, Fettke P (eds) Robotic process automation: management, technology, applications. De Gruyter Oldenbourg, Berlin/Boston, pp 187–200. https://doi.org/10.1515/9783110676693-010
66. Sultanow E, Chircu A, Plath R, Friedmann D, Merscheid T, Sharma K (2021) 17 AI evolves IA: a practitioner view on artificial intelligence information architecture. In: Czarnecki C, Fettke P (eds) Robotic process automation: management, technology, applications. De Gruyter Oldenbourg, Berlin/Boston, pp 349–376. https://doi.org/10.1515/9783110676693-017

Output Management in the Insurance Industry: Transformation Towards a Future-Oriented Omnichannel Architecture

8

Stefan Unterbuchberger, Lucas Hubinger, and Thomas Rodewis

Abstract

This chapter deals with the question of how the transformation of output management in the insurance industry can succeed. Up to now, outgoing communication with customers and business partners has primarily taken place in paper form. The focus was on information artifacts that were assembled into documents. Regulatory requirements and the companies' understanding of communication shaped the requirements for the channel provided. This view is now considered outdated, as customer needs demand flexible provision of information: In the right form, via the desired channel and at the right time. Proprietary technologies do not meet these requirements or have limitations with regard to future viability. Formulated business requirements must therefore be translated into guard rails for the technical architecture. The following article leads through the analysis of the existing architecture, via the formulation of requirements, to the development and commissioning of the applications. The picture is rounded off by an outlook in the direction of further trends – entirely in the sense of an omnichannel strategy.

> Two things are necessary to our work: tireless perseverance and the willingness to throw away something in which you have put a lot of time and effort. (Albert Einstein (1879–1955))

S. Unterbuchberger (✉) · L. Hubinger · T. Rodewis
Versicherungskammer Bayern, Munich, Germany
e-mail: stefan.unterbuchberger@vkb.de; lucas.hubinger@vkb.de; thomas.rodewis@vkb.de

8.1   Motivation: Output Management as the Key to Successful Customer Communication

When we talk about the trend of "digitalization", we often mean advanced technological capabilities that enable companies to better respond to customer needs. "Better" is often interpreted as faster, more individualized, or more targeted.

In the insurance industry, however, the trend of "digitalization" means something even more banal: "Putting the customer first" also means accepting that customers do not differentiate between whether they are currently communicating with an insurance company or their preferred online delivery service. Why should the expected level of service be any different in terms of speed and convenience.

Or put even more directly: If an online delivery service manages to deliver physical goods to my doorstep within a few hours, why should I wait several days for an insurance policy?

The challenges for the insurance industry resulting from this banal-sounding question are manifold: Digital contact points that provide customers with all the services they need, from information and contract conclusion to contract amendment and termination, must be newly established or adapted to current requirements.

The business model of many service insurers is also based on a distinctive sales structure. Here, too, it is important to make the exchange of information as efficient as possible within the framework of the legal requirements. The options arising from digitalisation offer a variety of starting points here.

In the end, it is necessary to completely rethink the standard communication with the customer that has been tried and tested over decades. In the scenario described above, who would still want a standard paper invoice that delivers no personal added value?

In the following article, we address the particular challenges that an insurance company faces in this context.

8.1.1   Analysis of a Heterogeneous System Landscape

In large insurance companies, central IT systems often have a long life cycle. This applies to the core applications of inventory management as well as to cross-sectionally oriented systems, which also include the installations in the area of output management.

The model of the IT life cycle is defined by different phases from the realization of the application to the rollout and the phasing out of the application. In the concrete example, the phase of decline has already been reached (cf. Fig. 8.1). All major business units of the insurance lines (health, life and non-life insurance) used the existing output applications. Innovations that followed the requirements of the digital strategy could no longer be implemented at that time, or only at a cost that could hardly be justified from a business perspective.

The realization at this point led to the need for change also being understood in management. The order was therefore formulated to carry out a preliminary study

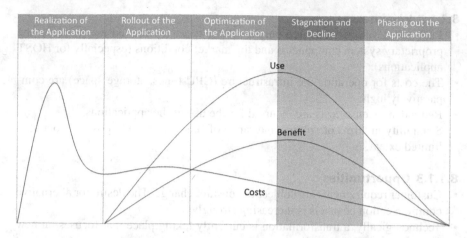

| Realization of the Application | Rollout of the Application | Optimization of the Application | Stagnation and Decline | Phasing out the Application |

Fig. 8.1 Phase model of software usage

to examine the current status of the output application landscape (development status, stability, fulfilment of user expectations) and its future viability. With regard to the result, there were no specifications. Both modernization of the existing software and complete replacement were conceivable options.

The result after completion of the preliminary study showed a very heterogeneous system landscape that had developed over many years. From a technical point of view, three output systems could be identified: In addition to a more modern variant, with its own format and structure language for specifying documents and business rules, these were also classic HOST applications, with a simple line-oriented document structure and a static layout with non-proportional font.

Differing technical requirements led to the existing output systems being integrated in different process contexts and infrastructures. This resulted in various application derivatives, each with its own migration requirements. In total, nine relevant (main) installations were documented.

In addition to the technical evaluation, further dimensions of the existing applications were elaborated based on a SWOT analysis [1]. The results can be divided into four segments: Strengths, Weaknesses, Opportunities and Threats.

The following main issues were identified:

8.1.1.1 Strengths
- The applications run very stable in operation and have a low error/failure rate.
- Technologically, the systems are well developed and have been tested in practice many times.
- Even large print volumes can be processed without problems within the defined service levels.
- Basic requirements regarding quality (e.g. print result and document layout) are met.

8.1.1.2 Weaknesses

- Required developer skills are only available to a very limited extent due to the proprietary system components and the market conditions (especially for HOST applications).
- The costs for operating the infrastructure (CPU times, storage space) are comparatively high.
- Redundant license costs are incurred for the use of the applications.
- Scalability in terms of volume and range of functions is only possible to a very limited extent.

8.1.1.3 Opportunities

- Customer requirements are subject to constant change. The desire for alternative communication channels is increasing strongly.
- Technologically, a transformation is currently taking place that focuses on new formats in the digital environment.
- Significant cost effects can be achieved with the consistent implementation of a future-oriented digital strategy.

8.1.1.4 Threats

- The development of digitalization shows disruptive effects in output management (the principle of classic paper processing is successively being displaced)
- The market demands new forms of communication in order to satisfy customer needs. The question of change thus takes on a strategic character.

8.1.2 Identification of Specific Needs

On the basis of the identified fields of action, a technical target picture was formulated: The output application should address existing strengths and compensate for identified deficits or weaknesses. The following objectives were derived from this:

8.1.2.1 Sustainability

The application shall support flexible and open formats. The output format is no longer limited to DIN A4, but should be able to be selected dynamically with regard to the selected dispatch channel and the specific requirements (so-called responsive approach).

8.1.2.2 Editorial Process

The maintenance of documents and associated shipment specifications should primarily be possible by specialists who do not have proven IT skills. The goal is to move the editing process as far forward as possible.

8.1.2.3 Process Support

If consignments and documents cannot already be determined automatically by business rules, corresponding workflows and tools must be provided for the clerks. These should optimally support the underlying business processes.

8.1.2.4 Format and Presentation

Documents should be provided in such a way that they meet the requirements of the recipients with regard to the desired presentation in connection with the respective end device. The formatting should not be limited to pure text, but should also allow the option of integrating other objects, such as graphics.

8.1.2.5 Shipping Channels

Ideally, the process should determine the correct channel – depending on customer preferences and the legal requirements for transmission. The clerk should be given the option to override if this is necessary for technical or process-related reasons.

8.1.3   Balance Between Self-Development and External Development

Corresponding to the technical specifications, fundamental architectural guidelines were defined. The basis for this was the requirement to process documents with all data in XML format. For the complete specification of the document output, XSL-T (XSL transformation) was to be used as part of the XSL language (Extensible Stylesheet Language). This language is supported by the World Wide Web Consoritum and is subject to W3C standards.[1]

The advantage of this standard is that it is highly compatible with existing applications. By dispensing with proprietary elements, individual components can be exchanged or new processes implemented. In addition, there is a consistent architecture that covers all aspects from data modeling to transformation and conversion into the required target format. The proximity to web standards facilitates the use of modern technologies, such as the integration of document content in web representations via the HTML format.

All framework conditions were formulated as requirements and served as a performance catalog for the tender of the software solution. It was clear at a relatively early stage of the conception that not all requirements could be covered by purchasing external software components. This was especially true for the area of shipment control.

---

[1] The World Wide Web Consortium (W3C) is an international community that aims to develop universally applicable web standards. Only through standardization is it possible to fully exploit the potential of web-based applications [2].

This component forms the process-related interface between the specialist system and the actual output application. The triggering business transaction in the backend system forms the trigger for determining a suitable shipment to one or more defined recipients. Ideally, this is done via a logical link between the business transactions and shipments or via appropriately defined business rules in the background, i.e. without intervention by the clerk.

Correspondingly defined key figures provide a reference value of more than 80% dark processing quota on average for the various specialist processes. This has a direct effect on the complexity, since a great deal of specific technical know-how must be packed into sets of rules. Ultimately, this is a large part of the communication logic in an insurance company, which also has special features for each line of business.

8.1.3.1 Example for Clarification

The business partners, such as customers or sales activities, are assigned certain characteristics using roles. In the health insurance line of business, the policyholder is stored as the actual contract partner. In addition, there are 1-n insured persons who can receive benefits within the framework of the existing contract. Depending on the business transaction, different roles (persons) are addressed in communication. In the case of contract processing, the policyholder is in the foreground, but in the case of benefits, the insured person is often in the foreground. The knowledge of the correct recipient is defined in the set of rules for shipment determination. In addition, there are requirements for the control of consignment copies, which are made available to the contract broker, for example.

The example gives an idea of the possibilities of combinatorics. In this way, various scenarios can be set up that link the most diverse roles (policyholder, insured person, assignment creditor, legal representative, intermediary, etc.) with corresponding business transactions in a complex matrix. The decision was therefore made to develop this part of the solution ourselves.

Figure 8.2 shows the basic structure of the output application. A central element is the dispatcher component. The previously determined consignments and documents are transferred to the dispatcher. The dispatcher controls the transformation and conversion into the required target formats, controls processes in case of errors and transfers the orders to the output control.

The task of the output control is to operate the different output channels in a closed loop. The closed loop processing ensures that all transferred dispatch jobs are reliably processed. If errors occur in the printing process, for example, the process is marked as open until successful processing and repeated until successful processing.

In the case of electronic transmission, a change of channel can be made as an alternative. If, for example, e-mail delivery fails due to an incorrect address, a substitute delivery is made by letter.

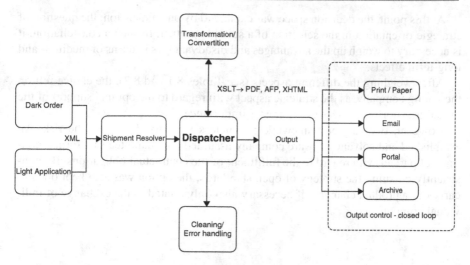

Fig. 8.2 Dispatcher

8.2   Planning of the Pilot Application

After determining the specific requirements and deciding which components should be developed in-house or purchased, the planning of the pilot application began. The content here was both the selection of the cooperation partner and the determination of a technical candidate.

8.2.1   Product Selection Factors

Following the preliminary work, the tender process was launched in the first round with 19 providers. The selection was based on a market analysis and a pre-selection of potential partners who generally offer solutions in the output environment.

For the next stage of selection, a structured list of questions was developed that contained weighted individual criteria as well as some exclusion factors. The feedback was consolidated and evaluated by the team's specialists. By weighting individual criteria, priorities could be worked out from a professional and technical point of view. The selection was refined via interviews, product presentations and test installations to such an extent that at the end of the process only two providers were left to choose from.

The essential core requirements in terms of functional scope and technical specifications were met by both companies. In terms of company characteristics, however, a young innovative company was in competition with an established provider that had already gone through a certain period of development.

At this point, the decision space was expanded by one dimension: the question of strategic orientation in the selection of a suitable partner. In such a constellation, it is necessary to weigh up the advantages and disadvantages in terms of medium- and long-term effects.

After weighing the different aspects (see Tables 8.1 and 8.2), the choice fell on the young company, as the strategic aspect with regard to the optimal support of the digital transformation was given greater importance.

However, two further framework parameters were fixed to limit the risk: An established and solvent software company assumed the guarantee as a formal contractual partner with regard to the fulfilment of the contractual obligations. By consistently pursuing the strategy of open standards, the option was also kept open to carry out a product change – if necessary also only related to the exchange of individual components.

Table 8.1 Young innovative company, low market maturity

Advantages	Disadvantages
High degree of innovation (adaptation to market trends)	Software product may be immature in some aspects
Willingness to consider individual customer requirements	Economic viability can only be guaranteed to a limited extent due to the lack of a customer base
Active co-design of the further development by the customer	Long-term risk in terms of lack of innovation in the absence of economic impetus
Stronger orientation towards technical standards, few proprietary solutions to maintain backward compatibility	

Table 8.2 Established company, high market maturity

Advantages	Disadvantages
The solution is in large parts mature and tested in practice	Customer requirements from the past have led to specific solutions within the open standards
Due to the already achieved market penetration, a constant further development can be assumed	The degree of innovation is high, but depends to a large extent on the requirements of existing customers
Customer wishes can be taken into account due to the size of the developer team	Individual further developments do not flow into the product standard, but are part of own extensions, which cause additional maintenance efforts
The framework conditions create greater planning certainty with a lower implementation risk	

8.2.2   Search for a Suitable Technical Implementation Candidate

In the next phase, the task was to define a technical candidate for testing, who would act as the client and later user within the framework of a PoC (Proof of Concept).

The migration of an output application is generally associated with high costs. Depending on the maturity of the application, the technical effort is balanced by the business effort. From a technical point of view, the conceptual preparatory work – especially the editorial implementation of each individual document – and the tests to be carried out are particularly significant.

For this reason, a number of criteria fields should be taken into account in advance when making a selection and decision:

- The candidate for implementation must support the project unconditionally. For success, it is important that there is a concrete professional interest and that appropriate resources are made available to the required extent.
- The project must be feasible within a reasonable time frame (within 1 year). Longer durations for initial projects make planning more difficult and risks hardly calculable. There is also the risk that, as the project progresses, it will be critically discussed and possibly stopped if no visible successes are achieved.
- The project must not be dimensioned too small in order to obtain sufficient findings for the viability of the solution and further migration steps. Particularly in the case of in-house developments, essential functions should be implemented and approved.
- In the case of overarching projects that affect all areas of the company, active stakeholder management should be pursued. The support of top management is essential in order to drive the project forward in the long term.

Taking these aspects into account, the choice fell on the area of real estate credit (granting loans for construction financing), which plays a special role in the insurance industry. The backend system for contract management is not as strongly interwoven with the technical infrastructure as the applications of the large insurance lines. The adjustments could therefore be limited to a narrowly defined area. Due to the multi-layered business processes, it was nevertheless possible to test all the essential requirements for an output system.

In addition to the connection to an existing HOST legacy application, the requirement was to implement complex shipment control and the option of light and dark processing. This offered the opportunity to develop the system to a level of maturity suitable as a basis for further migration projects.

Another argument arose from the aspect of risk management. The new application to be developed could be implemented in parallel to the existing solution without transferring the existing process to a fixed date. This fallback ensured the ability to work even in the event of technical problems.

8.3   Project Phase

In the course of the project planning, the question of the appropriate methodology was also clarified. Due to the framework conditions, the project was predestined for the use of agile methods. It was therefore decided to use the Scrum method for the development of the new components.

8.3.1   Methodology: Scrum and Waterfall Form One Unit

Two – seemingly – opposing approaches enjoy great popularity in corporate practice: Specifically, the Scrum model, as well as the waterfall model.

8.3.1.1 Scrum Model

The Scrum model originated in the software development environment, but is now also used in many other areas. It provides for an iterative, empirical and incremental approach to development projects (Fig. 8.3).

The Scrum Team is at the center of the Scrum process. This is subdivided into several roles; specifically into Product Owner, Scrum Master and Development Team. The tasks of the individual roles are clearly distributed:

- The product owner sets the functional requirements and prioritizes them.
- The Scrum Master makes sure that the methodology is followed and removes obstacles during the Scrum process.
- The development team develops the product. In particular, the self-determined work of the development team is characteristic of Scrum [3].

So-called sprints characterize dedicated time segments within the project, which have a maximum length of 4 weeks and pursue the goal of a product increment. This ensures that a high speed of results and the highest possible customer benefit are achieved by means of short feedback loops [3].

8.3.1.2 Waterfall Model

The waterfall model, on the other hand, consists of several individual, fixed phases. Each phase is dependent on the previous one, which means that it must be completed before the next one can begin. For this reason, the waterfall model often has a reputation for being cumbersome and lengthy. As a result, late visibility of the

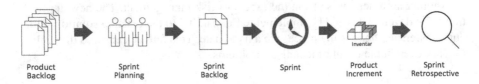

| Product
Backlog | Sprint
Planning | Sprint
Backlog | Sprint | Product
Increment | Sprint
Retrospective |

Fig. 8.3 Exemplary representation of the Scrum process

Table 8.3 Summary of the advantages and disadvantages of both methodologies

Scrum model	Advantages	Disadvantages
	Flexibility	Planning uncertainty
	Transparency	
	Alignment with customer needs	
Waterfall model		
	Clear definition of:	Late visibility of the result
	Girth	Rigid specifications
	Tense	Late detection of errors
	Cost	High conceptual effort

produced result follows, and along with it, delayed detection of errors. Changes to desired requirements are also often difficult to implement and involve considerable additional effort [4].

At this point, it is deliberately not intended to take a further in-depth look at the individual phases. Instead, the advantages and disadvantages of the model are briefly outlined, which were also discussed in the run-up to the project in order to select the appropriate methodology.

Table 8.3 shows quite clearly that in project management there is no "silver bullet" for making implementation projects as efficient as possible, since both methods presented have their advantages and disadvantages.

Precisely this discussion also led to the conclusion in the run-up to the implementation of the concrete use case that a combination of both models could make sense. Thus, both methodologies were used to exploit common synergy effects.

The dedicated development of the new output application was therefore carried out using the Scrum methodology; the actual integration of the output system into the existing system landscape, on the other hand, was implemented using classic line application development, which operated according to the waterfall principle.

This combination of methods resulted in the challenge of control and close interlocking. The normal development cycles are linked to release dates that are subordinate to company-wide planning. Corresponding result types could therefore not be made available at will. This problem continues in the integration and deployment in the test environments, as there are predefined time corridors here that are somewhat at odds with the Scrum requirements to provide a presentable and potentially testable artifact after each sprint.

The solution was to decouple agile development as far as possible. New components could be implemented autonomously and tested in their own test environments. This included the process from (simulated) commissioning to transformation and conversion. One advantage at this point was that the development team was recruited from members of one organizational unit, making it easier to realize a very close collaboration – apart from the methodological framework.

8.3.2   Ruby on Rails and Open Formats as Technical Guard Rails

In addition to the methodology, the decision had to be made on which technical basis the use case should be implemented. The choice fell on the open source web framework Ruby on Rails, or RoR for short. It is based on the Ruby programming language and can be distinguished by two basic principles: *"Don't repeat yourself"* and *"Convention over configuration"*.

The principle *"Don't repeat yourself"* pursues the goal of having to perform as few redundant development activities as possible. Repetitive code and repetitive work steps (e.g. generating class frameworks that differ only in a few lines of code) are largely avoided in the framework.

"Convention over configuration" requires developers to follow **conventions** for **naming** objects such as pages or functions instead of variable but complex configuration [5]. The result of the two principles is extremely fast efficient development with understandable code.

Why was RoR chosen? What are the main, concrete advantages of this framework?

RoR is geared towards the fast and agile development of modern web applications. At the heart of RoR is the Model View Controller. This pattern divides the programming logic into three different levels: The "Model" contains the actual business logic, for example actuarial calculations. The "Controller" takes user input and passes it on to the "Model", for example to generate HTML or JSON templates for outputting or displaying content as a view. These examples already show that many tools and functions are already included in the framework "out of the box".

Java EE, on the other hand, has a wide range of libraries, which opens up countless options for achieving the same result in different ways. On the one hand, this framework provides for almost inexhaustible code design possibilities – no problem that cannot be solved with Java. For developers, however, this creates a lot of detailed work in the implementation and identification of the optimal solution, which in the end costs time.

RoR offers easier access here with clearer structures. Many functions are predefined, as mentioned at the beginning. The path to implementation is much faster due to the guard rails of the framework. Accordingly, visible successes can be achieved after a short time, which in turn increases the motivation of the developers.

At this point, it should not go unmentioned that although RoR was very "hyped" in the community at the start of the project, this framework was not yet established in the insurance environment. The basis for Java EE was much broader, both in terms of available know-how carriers on the market and in relation to the use of the platform.

The dynamics of the RoR community compensated for this with broad support. The development team was able to contribute intensively here, so that development results of their own project also flowed into the community.

8.3.2.1 Example

In the course of development, a JDBC adaptor for DB2 on Z/OS was created. This enables the execution of corresponding SQL statements on the HOST.

RoR was chosen for the in-house developments in the shipment control environment due to the recognizable advantages in the implementation and the balanced risk management. This decision also fitted in well as a technological mosaic stone in the target picture of the innovation-driven strategy.

8.4 Trends and Success Factors for Further Transformation

As already stated at the beginning, documents in the insurance industry, but also in many other sectors of the economy, are based on known norms and standards. The structure of a business letter is described in great detail with the writing and design rules according to DIN 5008, among others [6]. The following points highlight various aspects of output processing and their relationship to digital transformation.

8.4.1 XML and XSL Form the Basis for Web-Oriented and Flexible Document Output

The definitions in the various DIN standards have their origin in the well-known source formats, such as DIN A4, which is used in many parts of the world, or the letter format, which is used in the USA and Canada.

In order to present information in a way that is suitable for recipients in the future, it is necessary to break away from these framework conditions. In the future, the DIN A4 format will only be one possible output variant, which will be assigned to one or more channels, for example paper dispatch.

If the channel changes, the preparation and presentation of the information must adapt to the new circumstances. This feature is known as Responsive Design from the web environment. The presentation of the website adapts to the device – whether mobile phone, tablet or notebook – and thus ensures the best possible usability by the user.

These characteristics must be transferred to output management. In the end, you have to separate the content – that is, the technical content – from the presentation. This is one of the design principles pursued with the new output application.

The core of these efforts is the use of XML and XSL as the basis for document specification. XML provides data in a hierarchically structured form that can be read by both humans and machines. For output management, the required parts of the data model are read from the backend systems and transferred via an appropriate interface.

SOAP web services were set up for the connection of other systems (for example, the partner application) and for calling the output system by other users (using systems). These are orchestrated via the ESB (Enterprise Service Bus) and secured via Datapower. The communication within the output components (e.g. browser to backend) runs via REST calls. In the future, this variant will be preferred for the connection of interfaces.

At this stage, the XML document already has the essential metadata for later output. This includes shipping information such as address data of the recipient, values to be output as individual attributes or iterating lists. Attributes for later rule control are also already included.

What is still missing are the parameters for the transformation. These are supplemented by XSLT instructions. These are on the one hand text, i.e. the linguistic content, and on the other hand stylesheets, which contain formatting information.

Document-related rule sets can be implemented using XPath expressions. This includes simple business rules based on IF-THEN-ELSE structures, but also more complex expressions and nested rules.

Example of a rule that evaluates a risk object indicator and a service key:

```
/Output order/Allg/Header/Risk object = '00014' and (for $x in //
Service   accounting//Note   return   substring($x,   1,   4)) =
('1426','1434','1435','1436')
```

Documents defined in this way can be read in via XSLT processors, which generate the desired output format. Modern web browsers already have XSLT processors integrated. They are thus able to display such documents.

XSL-FO (Extensible Stylesheet Language-Formatting Objects) is used for professional processing and a CI-compliant layout (corporate identity). This application from the XML environment provides the necessary elements and attributes for display. These include margins, page dimensions, page sequences, numbering, frames, spacing, columns, blocks, paragraphs, lists, tables, sentence formats, hyphenation and graphic elements such as lines or images.

Looking at the overall process of output generation, the sequence shown in Fig. 8.4 emerges.

The starting point is the XML document, which is transformed into an XSL-FO file using an XSLT stylesheet. This structured FO tree can be converted into a wide variety of output formats using a suitable converter (cf. FO processor).

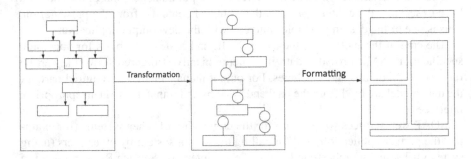

Fig. 8.4 Schematic representation of the overall output generation process

In addition to the well-known PDF format (Portable Document Format), the AFP (Advanced Function Presentation) format for transactional printing or XHTML (Extensible Hypertext Markup Language or extensible HTML) in our example are relevant here.

8.4.2 AFP and PDF, Two Competing Approaches

Which formats are important in the context of existing or future output channels? Even if paper output is no longer the focus in the long term, it still covers the majority of outgoing text-based communication today.

The AFP format has long been the standard in the transaction printing environment. This format was developed by IBM in order to be able to process large print data streams as efficiently and layout-faithfully as possible. The printers in the professional environment have corresponding processors to generate raster formats from the data. The pages generated in this way contain, in principle, an image of the document, resolved into fine pixels, which can be produced in this way.

However, the format is completely unsuitable for sharing or digital use, as it does not meet any of the requirements formulated in the digital strategy.

The PDF format has developed into an alternative in this context and is now established as the standard in many places. Developed by Adobe in 1993, the aim of the format was to enable cross-platform exchange. The aim was to ensure that the display and output was as identical as possible on all devices.

This requirement and the addition of further features (for example, the embedding of video files) are somewhat at odds with the requirements of transaction printing. Here, a lean format is needed that provides the necessary information in the most resource-efficient way possible.

To take this into account, the PDF/VT subform has emerged from the PDF standard. The addition VT (Volume Transactional Output) or also VDP (Variable Data Printing) already allows conclusions to be drawn about the intended use.

With the help of this standard, developed in 2010, the bridging between two essential output channels is to be achieved: The documents are usable in the field of mass production as well as on the end devices.

The advantages are obvious. At this point, the process only needs to be optimized for one output format. Using appropriate formatters or converters, the required substandard can be generated without losing any of the document's essential properties.

In our example, the PDF format was used consistently – for example in the context of archiving. Since the processes in the context of output processing have not yet been completely converted and the processing at the printers is dependent on the preprocessing of the data, an intermediate step was added in the first stage: The documents already available in PDF format are still converted to AFP format in order to be able to use the existing processing path for physical printing unchanged.

8.4.3   Output Channels of the Future: Omnichannel Communication

Does this meet the future requirements of an omnichannel architecture? No! This status basically represents the status quo in the area of output management. Up to now, it has been sufficient to optimize paper dispatch and support the electronic route in parallel as a derivative. Electronic delivery focuses primarily on e-mail dispatch and provision via portals.

However, customers have a completely different set of expectations. Mobile devices are becoming increasingly important in everyday life. The simplification of processes that the customer experiences at this point is also transferred to the expectations in output management.

Information should be accessible on any device at any time and any place. In this context, proprietary applications (such as PDF readers) only play a subordinate role. Restrictions to certain operating systems or platforms are dissolving. The elimination of paper also means that the rigid DIN framework mentioned at the beginning no longer plays a role. Formats and media become arbitrary.

The chosen architecture offers a basis here to meet these requirements. The PDF format is only one variant to accompany the transition period. The output of XHTML opens up new possibilities for presenting information. The content can thus be provided with basic instructions in order to display the content in a browser-based presentation, for example. A responsive approach provides the necessary dynamics to serve a wide variety of devices.

An example illustrates the need:

8.4.3.1 Example
The benefit process in health insurance has already changed in the direction of digitalization in the area of the access channel. Today, it can basically be described as a market standard that benefit vouchers can be recorded and submitted electronically via corresponding apps.

The follow-up processes were often still conventionally designed. After benefit processing, a benefit letter was usually sent to the customer containing information about the amount of the reimbursement.

From the customer's point of view, there is a media break here. If the amount submitted is reimbursed in full, no extensive letter is usually required, but rather information about the processing and the imminent payment is sufficient.

This information should now be transmitted via the channel desired by the customer, which is also suitable for this defined business transaction for procedural and legal reasons. This can be in the form of an SMS, as an e-mail, in the context of social media or as a note in the service app used at the beginning.

For output management, the challenge here is to prepare the information in a way that is suitable for the channel. While a normal letter with different sections, such as a tabular list of the individual receipts, is required in the case of a comprehensive invoice, an SMS only contains a short confirmation text.

This is where consignment control comes into play. In addition to taking the correct recipient role into account, the consignment matching the business transaction and channel must be determined with the associated documents on a rule-based basis. If the rule is resolved, only a text file would be generated in the case of the SMS, which contains the mobile number as the "address" in addition to the channel.

This flexibility is what is meant by the term omnichannel in output communication. When initiating corresponding projects, care must be taken to ensure that the prerequisites for this are consistently incorporated into the design of the applications and the corresponding architecture decisions.

8.4.4 Automation of Processes: From Output to Input

With all the above-mentioned aspects of output processing, it is important to remember that communication is a bidirectional process. Either the dialogue is initiated by the customer or the customer responds to the information received. This process can be summarized under the term input capable output.

Our project has also dealt with this question in detail. The spectrum is wide at this point. Therefore, first a selection of the considerations and solution packages:

- In the course of the implementation, the possibility to use existing PDF forms was implemented. In many companies, extensive libraries exist – usually already as static or writable PDF documents. Refactoring is extremely time-consuming for forms, since a static layout with a lot of detailed information must be implemented. Classic output management systems, however, are designed more for formatting dynamic text content.

If input fields have already been created, they can be filled via the defined XML data streams. The customer then receives a document electronically that has been preconfigured with the known data. The fields that can be edited on the screen are retained in this process, so they can still be used to edit the data on the screen.

If the recipient uses this option, then a document is generated whose content can be read out via corresponding OCR processes with a high recognition rate. Defined subsequent processes can be supplied with values by the subject data extraction and ideally run in the dark.

- Another option results from the provision of digital forms. For this purpose, the content is integrated in a web-based representation. The captured data is not only forwarded as readable information, but also stored in the background and transferred to the backend systems for further processing.

8.4.5 White-Labeling as Support for Flexible Distribution Channels

A completely different aspect results from the topic of white-labeling. It is not only in the insurance sector that there is a trend towards product providers and sales brands not necessarily being identical. For output management, this results in the requirement that a kind of "sales cover" is ultimately put over documents. This can include layout features such as logos, but also legal information about the company, which usually appears in so-called footers.

When designing the output application, we therefore took great care to separate two elements from each other: On the one hand, there is a master layout that contains definitions of the brand or a client and, on the other hand, the actual document behind which the technical content is hidden.

In the later process, these separate logical units are brought together via rules. In this way, a process with the associated documents can be used for a wide variety of brands. This has a lasting effect on maintenance efforts and thus ultimately also on costs.

8.4.6 Good Style Is More Than Just Spelling

In addition to the media-appropriate preparation of content, other factors are necessary in order to address customers according to their needs.

One factor that is considered highly relevant in output management is the design of the language – in addition to correct spelling, which is taken for granted, the comprehensibility of the texts is another point. In the insurance environment, however, this is often cumbersome and characterised by a multitude of technical terms. This is in the nature of things, as insurance itself is always immaterial, complex and abstract.

In terms of customer orientation, however, it is essential to formulate documents in such a way that the customer also understands what I want to convey to him as a company. The correct design of the "corporate language" and its comprehensibility therefore play a further central role in output management alongside spelling and form.

8.4.6.1 Example

Various methods can be used to examine the comprehensibility of texts. One of the best-known methods is the so-called **Hohenheim Comprehensibility Index**, which calculates an index value from individual scale values – the text is thus given a score that can range from 0 (= low comprehensibility) to 20 (= high comprehensibility). For letters used for customer communication, a value of at least 14 is recommended [7].

Relevant text parameters that are used to calculate the index are, for example:

- Average sentence length in words
- Average word length in letters
- Proportion of words with more than 6 letters

- Percentage of sentences with more than 12 words
- Percentage of sentences with more than 20 words
- Negative formulations
- Filler words and abbreviations

Other proven means such as verbs instead of nouns, the avoidance of foreign words as well as the use of positive incentives characterize "good" letters.

How can companies quickly and easily examine the comprehensibility of written documents in practice? **TextLab** is an exemplary software based on the Hohenheim Comprehensibility Index. The text analysis programme is constantly being further developed by linguists and communication scientists and offers the user concrete suggestions for improvement and valuable tips for optimising the text: Is the message to the customer polite, too abstract, too distant or too technical? In addition, the *corporate* language can be anchored in the output by integrating corporate *wording* and defined terminologies [8].

This means that, in addition to flexible output formats and real-time output, there is now also a customer-oriented preparation in terms of content. Next, we will look at how clerk processes can be optimized within the framework of output management.

8.4.7 Simplification in Case Processing Through Intelligent Rules and a Stronger Document Orientation

The keyword costs also finds a completely different reference in output management. In addition to the familiar factors such as operating costs (infrastructure, licenses, maintenance, etc.) and shipping-related costs (primarily postage), process costs also play a decisive role. This applies at least to industries with a high proportion of manual clerk processes.

Automation has become increasingly prevalent in the insurance industry. At least for simple products, the policy is usually issued in the application process in the dark – i.e. without any interaction with the clerk. The associated mailings and documents are also generated and sent automatically.

The situation is different for processing-intensive transactions with a high degree of individuality. This is particularly the case with complex products or difficult issues (for example, in benefits or claims processing).

The degree of manual editing is fluid and ranges from the composition of a document with the help of predefined text modules to completely free formulation. The latter case can currently only be supported to a limited extent technically. The only thing that can help here are optimal tools that meet as many text editing requirements as possible.

In all other cases, technology can make a very good contribution to efficiency. A central question here is which philosophy of document design is being followed. There are two extreme forms of this:

- The highest possible degree of reusability – embedded in complex sets of rules and high dependencies of text modules and documents.
- A document-oriented approach in which redundant text modules are deliberately accepted.

From the analysis and practical experience of the past, the design principle was derived to choose an approach that is as document-oriented as possible. There are several advantages associated with this principle:

- In the process, clerks always first select a transmission or a document. For the clerk, the document is the natural representative of the information to be sent.
- Selecting from a large number of text modules within a document quickly becomes confusing and takes time. Selecting from a maximum of five text modules, on the other hand, is very efficient.
- In the editing process, the use of text module references also very quickly leads to dependencies and high costs (see next section). A document that is as complete as possible in itself allows for a focus and is thus also more efficient – especially against the background that the editors are usually technical or legal colleagues.

8.4.8 From the Idea to the Production-Ready Document: Editorial Processes Optimized

In addition to the clerk processes, the editing process for creating documents is an important lever for optimization. In the insurance industry, content is usually defined by specialists and lawyers. However, the customizing of output applications – i.e. the maintenance of mailings, documents, text modules and business rules – is reserved for technical specialists due to their complexity. The systems have evolved so that trained IT specialists are not required. Nevertheless, the job requires a certain level of technical understanding and continuous involvement with the subject.

However, in times of digitalization and high dynamics, this is in contradiction to the requirements. It is hard to imagine that the new and innovative product launch is not distributed in parallel on all communication channels. Therefore, this process is also part of the digital transformation.

One approach to solving this problem is an intelligent mixture of different process models. A separate workflow was developed for static text content. The editors are usually familiar with the common text processing systems. Therefore, templates were defined in Word that can be edited in a net display (print area without margins).

This provides the specialists with all the tools they need to formulate the content quickly and efficiently. Especially functions such as change tracking are very helpful for extensive and comprehensive coordination.

These document templates are then converted into various end formats via automated processes. Currently, PDF documents and AFP documents are output. PDF documents can be used directly, for example to fill info databases or to enable a download on the homepage.

The AFP documents are stored as resources in the output repository. During processing, these resources are embedded in previously defined envelope documents that contain format information such as page margins, similar to the master templates. This creates complete documents that can be processed.

For dynamically generated documents, a transfer of the subject matter cannot be avoided. The editor must define the content, but also the conditions under which values are to be output or variable text modules are to be printed. Here, the dilemma already formulated in the previous section becomes apparent. Too much complexity at this point leads to considerable effort. The simpler the document is structured, the easier the functional specification and ultimately also the test at the end of the development.

In order to make the documentation as efficient as possible, editing templates were designed that correspond to the technically designed document in a simplified form. Editors can thus formulate their changes for customizing.

However, the aim of the application is to further facilitate access. For example, simple changes that only relate to individual texts can be made by the specialist editors themselves in future.

8.4.9　Documents Become Colourful: Also in Paper

The final section is dedicated to the topic of color in output management. As part of the digital transformation, the design and physical production of documents have been fundamentally reformed. In addition to the use of objects that can be dynamically controlled, such as trademarks, signatures or text, options for finishing (including the application of a micro-perforation) were also implemented.

The new output system already supports these processes in the design, as it is possible to visually specify in the document where and according to which rules, for example, a graphic is to be output. In the processing stage, print data is then generated that contains all objects and color information.

The digital version corresponds to the physical result. Regardless of the channel chosen, the customer receives documents that meet all the essential requirements of the CI (corporate identity). From the point of view of strengthening the brand's external impact, this is an important factor.

In order to implement this in production, the existing laser printers were replaced by state-of-the-art inkjet systems. The colour information from the print data stream can thus be printed in CYMK colour space in very good quality. The profiles for compliance with the colour specifications are supplied with the print data or generated directly at the printer by the colour management system.

The selection of a suitable paper grade is decisive for the quality of the printouts and the fulfilment of the colour specifications. Optimum interaction between hardware and consumables was achieved over several test iterations. The result is so good that for the normal customer a difference to the offset version is hardly noticeable. This is remarkable in that the specifications call for color tones from the HKS spectrum[2] that are not always easy to implement even in offset production.

In addition to the qualitative effects described, there were also effects on processes and their efficiency. Transactional printing used to be geared towards the processing of pre-printed business papers. The preprinted letterheads had to be stocked in a wide variety of forms and fed into the processing chain in the process. Since the capacity of the paper trays was limited, this resulted in a comparatively high personnel requirement. In addition, this repeatedly led to disruptions or errors in the processing.

Significant improvements have been achieved here with this new technology. The paper is fed into the printing process via a roll. One roll corresponds to approx. 75,000 sheets in DIN A4 format. The processes for paper loading or changeover can thus be significantly reduced.

The complete print data is then transferred to the spool[3] in the process. In addition to controlling processing, this process is also responsible for color management. An example: If applications in the CMYK color space supply maximum values,[4] which corresponds to the color black, this information is converted into real black (use of the key color). This can significantly reduce toner consumption.

However, a problem arose in the process due to the fact that not all applications had been migrated to the new output system at the time of the technical changeover. Therefore, both complete documents with all color information were delivered, but also documents that actually require a pre-printed business letterhead.

The solution at this point was to implement an additional virtual tray. For this purpose, the tray control, which actually serves the correct feeding of the pre-printed letterheads, was retained. The identifier of the preprinted sheet to be used, which is supplied in the tray control, was mapped with a corresponding image of the letterhead. For production, the print data is merged with the images so that the documents are available in a processable form.

The printed pages produced in this way are rolled up again and then processed further on the inserting machine. First, they are cut to the final format (currently DIN A4). Depending on the subsequent envelope size, all the sheets belonging to a mailing are folded in half (one or two folds). The mail package is supplemented with inserts as required and automatically packed into envelopes.

---

[2] The HKS colour spectrum comprises 88 basic colours and 3520 spot colours for various types of paper (art paper, uncoated paper, newsprint and continuous paper). This reference is established via the additions K, N, Z and E. The colour code HKS 43 K anchored in the CI thus states that the reference corresponds to a blue tone on an art paper.

[3] The spooling process is essentially used to buffer the transmitted print jobs. The method is derived from English and means *simultaneous peripheral operations online* [9].

[4] The CMYK color model is a subtractive color model that forms the technical basis for modern four-color printing. The abbreviation CMYK stands for the three color components cyan, magenta, yellow and the black component key. The target color is defined by the mixing ratio of the individual components. The possible values for each color are between 0% and 100%. Colors from other tables can be converted accordingly. For example, the color HKS 13 (red) corresponds to the values C 0, M 100, Y 95 and K 0.

In a further step, the control system was expanded so that subgroups in the mailings (a group of contiguous individual pages) can be provided with an indicator for stapling. This allows machine stapling in the processing procedure. The already enveloped mailings can still be individually printed in colour at the end. The inserting system has been extended by a corresponding inkjet module to apply text or graphics in the process.

The last point in the process chain concerns dispatch control. The individual items produced are prepared in postal boxes and handed over to the shipping service provider. In the course of optimization, additional partners were added. The control system was therefore extended to split the mail volume. For this purpose, a geocoder was integrated into the application for postage optimization and dispatch preparation. This module allows control according to geodata in order to separate the mailings according to postal codes, for example. Via a corresponding extension of the mailbox processing, different mail deliveries can be realized in a partially automated way.

In terms of business management, the outlined investments in the transformation of processing led to considerable savings effects. In addition to lower personnel deployment, material costs were also significantly reduced. This effect is supplemented by significantly greater flexibility in the control and implementation of functional requirements. The use of neutral paper rolls also results in a positive environmental balance, as fewer prefabricated sheets of paper have to be destroyed in the event of technical changes.

8.5   Outlook

We have seen what challenges await insurance companies in the context of making output management more flexible and what methods and technologies can be used to create solutions here.

In relation to the trend of "digitalization" described in the introduction, this is only one stage on the way to meeting customer expectations. Communication on every channel, combined with the possibility of changing the channel flexibly and independently of time, will be an important element. It almost goes without saying that the information will be prepared and presented in a way that is appropriate for the channel.

This expectation is supplemented by the requirement that all parties involved have transparency at all times about the progress of the underlying transaction and the associated content. Specifically, communication via quickly accessible channels, such as e-mail or WhatsApp, misses its target if the customer does not receive the identical information when calling the service center or his agent. The term omnichannel management therefore takes on another dimension, which can be described as the synchronicity of information.

Once these challenges have been mastered, further evolutionary stages can be integrated into the output process much more easily. From the customer's point of view, we are looking forward to these developments: Personalized videos that explain insurance needs and scope of benefits in a way that is appropriate for the target audience, personalized messages that really explain a premium adjustment, and much more.

References

1. Homburg C (2000) Quantitative Betriebswirtschaftslehre: Entscheidungsunterstützung durch Modelle. Gabler, Wiesbaden
2. W3C (2018). https://www.w3.org/. Accessed 25 Feb 2018
3. Preußig J (2015) Agiles Projektmanagement: Scrum, use cases. Task Boards, Haufe-Lexware/ Freiburg
4. Ruf W, Fittkau T (2008) Ganzheitliches IT-Projektmanagement: Wissen, Praxis, Anwendungen. Oldenbourg Wissenschaftsverlag, München
5. Williams J (2007) Rails solutions: ruby on rails made easy. Springer, New York
6. Grün K (2013) Der Geschäftsbrief. Gestaltung von Schriftstücken nach DIN 5008, DIN 5009 u. a. Beuth, Berlin/Wien/Zürich
7. Bredel U, Maaß C (2016) Leichte Sprache. Duden, Berlin
8. Dunkl M (2015) Corporate Code: Wege zu einer klaren und unverwechselbaren Unternehmenssprache. Springer, Wiesbaden
9. Werner J (1979) Betriebswirtschaftliche Datenverarbeitung, Systeme, Strukturen, Methoden, Verfahren, Entscheidungshilfen. Gabler, Wiesbaden

Vision and Maturity Model for Digitized Project Management

9

Holger Timinger and Christian Seel

Abstract

Project management software has been a standard tool in projects for years. Current software solutions focus primarily on planning and progress control in projects as well as communication between project stakeholders.

However, digitization enables further advanced applications, e.g. through machine learning. This makes it possible to better support decisions in projects or to automate activities of project managers. Two examples are the tailoring of the project management method and automated scenario planning.

Accordingly, this paper draws the vision of a digitized project management, which in particular uses machine learning methods and goes far beyond the currently widespread use of digital tools. In order to make this vision tangible and to show ways to achieve it, the maturity model M2DIP is presented. This maturity model enables both the determination of one's own position and the derivation of a development path for digitalized project management.

9.1   Digitalisation in Project Management

9.1.1   Introduction

The term digitalization has not yet been uniformly defined. Often, it is understood to mean the transformation and representation of information and communication or the digital modification of instruments, devices and vehicles, as well as the digital revolution as a social process [1].

H. Timinger (✉) · C. Seel (Deceased)
Landshut Unversity of Applied Sciences, Landshut, Germany
e-mail: holger.timinger@haw-landshut.de

© The Author(s), under exclusive license to Springer Fachmedien Wiesbaden
GmbH, part of Springer Nature 2024
T. Barton et al. (eds.), *Digitalization in companies*,
https://doi.org/10.1007/978-3-658-39094-5_9

145

In terms of project management, digitalization focuses primarily on the conversion and presentation of project-relevant information through software tools. For example, these display project plans or show the current status of the project. Project management software itself has changed significantly in recent years. In the 1990s and early 2000s, project management software was often limited to the creation of Gantt charts. Many programs were single-user solutions. Later, database and server-supported programs were added, which enabled cross-project resource planning. In the meantime, there is a clear trend towards software-as-a-service (SaaS) solutions that run completely in the web browser on the user side and no longer require local installation.

With the proliferation of SaaS solutions, planning functionality has been supplemented and sometimes even replaced by collaboration functionality. The manufacturers of project management software have recognized that the best plans are of no use if they are not understood by the employees or if problems arose during the course of the project not due to a lack of planning, but due to insufficient communication. Collaboration software today offers features for communication, data storage, and shared synchronous and asynchronous editing of documents. Project team members are automatically reminded of upcoming deadlines from the schedule and resource managers are informed about resource overload.

However, project management software does not have to be limited to the digitization of documents and plans and the communication of stakeholders in the project. In the future, artificial intelligence or, more precisely, machine learning approaches could also increasingly automate planning tasks or decision support functions and support the tailoring of the project management method itself through software.

An example of a digital approach to tailoring the project management method is the hybrid project management model (HyProMM) [2]. HyProMM is an approach based on an adaptive reference model. This model, which is implemented in software, is automatically adapted to the respective project, the employees and the customer based on parameters such as project complexity, team size or experience of the team. The structured processing of completed projects and the use of machine learning methods such as Deep Learning or Case-based Reasoning (CBR) are particularly promising for such approaches. In this way, a tailoring of the process model and project management methods can take place in the future that is based less on the subjective experiences and preferences of individual persons, but rather systematically incorporates completed projects into a knowledge base and uses this as the basis for a constantly improving tailoring.

This example illustrates that advanced methods of digitization such as machine learning enable new functionalities and scenarios for project management tools. In order to enable a systematic further development of project management tools, the aim of this paper is to show the current state and potential future development of digitalization in project management by means of a maturity model.

For this paper, the following research questions arise:

1. Which functionalities of project management tools are made possible by digitalization?
2. How can the state of digitalization in project management be captured in the form of a maturity model?
3. What implications arise for companies from a less than maximum maturity level and what measures can they derive from this?

9.1.2   Research Methodology and Structure

In order to answer these three research questions, the research method used will first be outlined. The research method used depends directly on the objective of the research questions [3]. Since this paper aims to develop a vision and, above all, a maturity model of digitalization in project management, the research questions can be addressed using the tools of design science [4]. In their memorandum on design-oriented business informatics, Österle et al. [5] postulate that design-oriented work must satisfy the following principles:

- *Abstraction*: An artifact must be applicable to a class of problems.
- *Originality*: An artifact must make an innovative contribution to the published body of knowledge.
- *Rationale*: An artifact must be justified in a comprehensible way and be validatable.
- *Benefit*: An artifact must be able to generate a benefit for the stakeholders today or in the future.

Therefore, these four principles are to be detailed and verified for the present contribution. A vision and a maturity model for digitalization in project management can be applied to all projects, which satisfies the principle of abstraction. Since neither exists yet, the contribution can also be considered original. The most far-reaching implications for the further procedure arise from the principle of justification and the principle of benefit, as both are directly reflected in the further structure.

In order to obtain a comprehensible rationale for a maturity model for digitalization in project management, the morphology of maturity models is presented in Sect. 9.2. In addition, the state of the science is highlighted in this section.

In the following Sect. 9.3, a vision of digitalized project management is outlined. Based on this vision, the maturity model M2DIP is developed in Sect. 9.4. In order to demonstrate the benefits of the model, Sect. 9.5 shows the implications of the maturity model for companies and provides examples of the application of the maturity model.

9.2   Maturity Models in Project Management

9.2.1   Aim and Purpose of Maturity Models

Maturity models enable organizations to evaluate properties, structures and processes on the basis of defined characteristics. The characteristics are assigned maturity levels that allow an evaluation of the respective characteristic. Based on the assessments, the own performance can be evaluated or compared with other organizations. Maturity models can be used for one's own further development of characteristics, structures and processes. In addition, the use of maturity models can be helpful in cross-organizational collaboration. For example, companies can demand certain maturity levels from their subcontractors in order to ensure compliance with their own requirements during the collaboration.

The name maturity implies that the maturity of properties, structures and processes is specified in degrees, i.e. measurable levels. Many established maturity models use four to five levels. The lowest level usually corresponds to the complete absence of a characteristic. The highest level corresponds to the complete fulfillment of a characteristic. The overall maturity level results from the aggregation of several characteristics.

The levels of maturity models build on each other. The next higher level of a maturity model can only be attained if the characteristics of the lower levels are fulfilled and, in addition, the characteristics of the targeted level that go beyond them are fulfilled. For example, an organization may have completely fulfilled the requirements for level 1 of a maturity model and already fulfilled many, but not all, of the requirements for level 2. Nevertheless, the organization is thus still assessed at level 1. Only when all requirements of the next higher level are fulfilled, the transition to this level is accomplished.

9.2.2   Common Maturity Models

One of the most common maturity models is the Capability Maturity Model Integration (CMMI), which is coordinated by the CMMI Institute [6]. The origins of CMMI date back to 1979 when Crosby published the Quality Management Maturity Grid [7]. The Quality Management Maturity Grid was intended to help organizations advance their quality management practices. In 1993, the Capability Maturity Model was published, which evolved into the Capability Maturity Model Integration (CMMI) in 2000 [8]. Initially, the CMMI focused on development organizations with the goal of improving their enterprise-wide processes. In 2010, version 1.3 of the CMMI was released. Since then, there have been specific models for procurement, development, and service organizations.

CMMI uses five maturity levels. The lowest level 1 is called "initial". Organizations at this level work with chaotic workflows. In level 2 "managed", guidelines must exist and followed for relevant processes within the company. In level 3 "defined", work processes are described with the help of standards, procedural instructions, tools and methods. In level 4 "quantitatively managed", the organisation uses quantitative indicators and targets as well as statistical procedures to manage the work processes. In level 5 "process optimization", the quantitative metrics known at level 4 are used for continuous process improvement. For each level, CMMI defines process areas for which the model is to be applied. These include, for example, configuration management, measurement and analysis, project planning and risk management. The higher the maturity level, the more process areas must be considered.

CMMI is a rather comprehensive maturity model. In addition, there are now many industry or area-specific maturity models. Other maturity models related to project management are the Organizational Project Management Maturity Model (OPM3) of the Project Management Institute [9] or the Organizational Competence Baseline (OCB) of the International Project Management Association (IPMA) [9]. Both enable the classification of one's own project orientation into the international standards of the respective project management organization. In 2002, Crawford presented the Project Management Maturity Model (PMMM), a maturity model with the five levels "Consistent Language", "Procedures and Standards", "Consistent Methodology", "Benchmarking" and "Continuous Improvement" [10].

For some time now, there have also been efforts to establish maturity models with reference to digitalization. A scoring model exists for medium-sized companies that allows companies to classify themselves in categories between "digital beginner" and "digital expert" [11]. The Federal Ministry for Economic Affairs and Energy publishes a checklist to help companies assess the relevance of Industrie 4.0 [12]. Neu-Ulm University, together with Minnosphere, has presented an online analysis tool to determine the digital maturity level [13]. Telekom offers a self-evaluation that provides a digitalization index to classify one's own level of digitalization [14].

These and other maturity models are still quite new and have yet to prove themselves. In addition, some are directly linked to services provided by consulting or other companies with products that promote digitalization. The independence and objectivity of the results is not always clear to the evaluating organizations.

Currently, there is no maturity model that focuses on the digitalization of project management. Although some of the models mentioned above include project management in their holistic approach, they remain too imprecise as far as the digitalization of project management is concerned to allow concrete strengths and weaknesses to be analyzed and groundbreaking strategies to be derived from the maturity assessment.

9.2.3 Structure of Maturity Models

Maturity models can be structured as a simple checklist. However, it is common that characteristics or capability levels are defined for the individual maturity levels, which must be fulfilled to a certain degree in order to correspond to the corresponding maturity level. This typical structure is illustrated in Fig. 9.1.

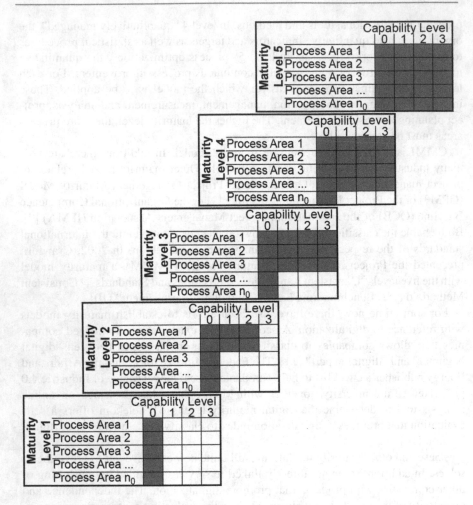

Fig. 9.1 Typical structure of maturity models

9.3 Vision of Digitalised Project Management

9.3.1 State of the Art

Focusing on and limiting to the functionality of project management software does not go far enough in terms of digitalization. In the following, the vision of digitalized project management will be outlined, on the basis of which a maturity model for digitalized project management will be created.

It is interesting that with the emergence of agile process models, analog, haptic planning tools such as metaplan cards, pin boards and whiteboards are becoming more important. Many project teams consider working with such materials more motivating, clearer and more communicative. This examples illustrates, that digitalized project management is neither good and desirable per se nor bad and avoidable per se. In certain constellations, digitalization can help to carry out projects more efficiently and effectively and to better develop one's own project management. Digitalization can play to its strengths particularly in so-called standard projects and to some extent in potential projects. According to Boos and Heitger, the focus here is on technical and content-related work ([15], see Fig. 9.2). However, acceptance and pioneer projects can also benefit from digitalization as it helps them to cope with social complexity.

The starting point for the vision of digitalized project management is the hybrid project management model HyProMM ([16], see Fig. 9.3).

HyProMM organizes the essential tasks of project management along the project life cycle and supplements higher-level leadership aspects and supporting continuous tasks. The project life cycle is divided into the phases I-Initialization, D-Definition, P-Planning, S-Steering/Control and A-Accomplishment/Completion, whereby each phase can also be conducted several times. Each element of the model can have different instantiations. For example, the element P.1 Planning Content can be used using different processes (first view of the model), methods and tools (second view) and involving different roles (third view) in a project. For example, one of the following instantiations of methods can be used to plan the content of a project

- informal to-do list,
- work breakdown structure or
- product backlog

involving one or more of the following roles

- project manager
- project staff
- client

A detailed description of the model and its elements can be found in [17]. Based on the model, the vision of digitalized project management can now be derived.

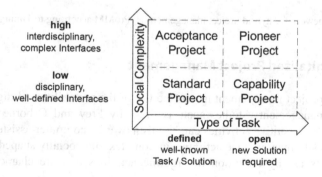

Fig. 9.2 Project types according to Boos and Heitger

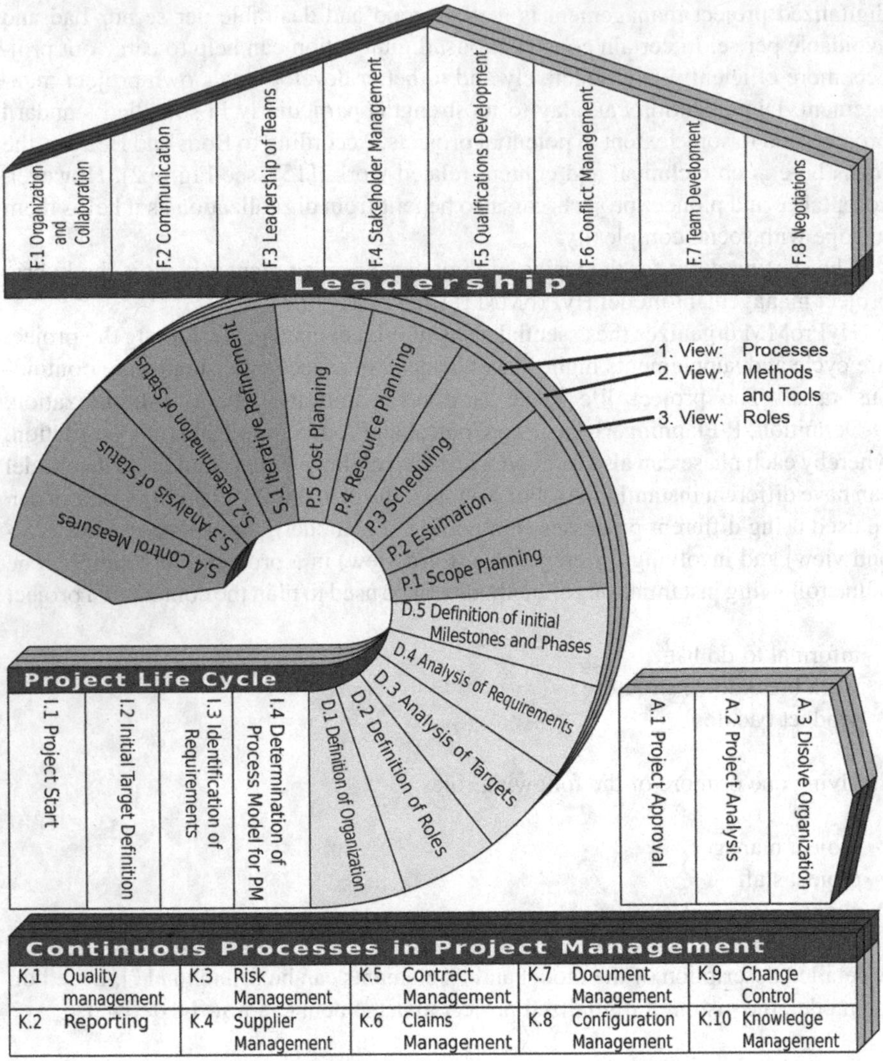
Leadership
F.1 Organization and Collaboration
F.2 Communication
F.3 Leadership of Teams
F.4 Stakeholder Management
F.5 Qualifications Development
F.6 Conflict Management
F.7 Team Development
F.8 Negotiations
1. View: Processes
2. View: Methods and Tools
3. View: Roles
S.4 Control Measures
S.3 Analysis of Status
S.2 Determination of Status
S.1 Iterative Refinement
P.5 Cost Planning
P.4 Resource Planning
P.3 Scheduling
P.2 Estimation
P.1 Scope Planning
D.5 Definition of initial Milestones and Phases
D.4 Analysis of Requirements
D.3 Analysis of Targets
D.2 Definition of Roles
D.1 Definition of Organization
Project Life Cycle
I.1 Project Start
I.2 Initial Target Definition
I.3 Identification of Requirements
I.4 Determination of Process Model for PM
A.1 Project Approval
A.2 Project Analysis
A.3 Disolve Organization
Continuous Processes in Project Management
K.1 Quality management
K.2 Reporting
K.3 Risk Management
K.4 Supplier Management
K.5 Contract Management
K.6 Claims Management
K.7 Document Management
K.8 Configuration Management
K.9 Change Control
K.10 Knowledge Management

Fig. 9.3 Framework for hybrid project management HyProMM according to Timinger and Seel

9.3.2 Digitalized Project Management

Digitalized project management means the use of the possibilities of digitalization in project management. Studies such as those by Frey and Osborne show that administrative, repetitive activities can be taken over by computer-assisted automation more easily than creative activities in complex and socially shaped situations [18]. Projects are by definition not routine activities and are characterized by collaboration between people. However, even here there are aspects that can benefit from digital workflows. The vision of digitalized project management can be illustrated in a two-dimensional space (see Fig. 9.4).

Along the project life cycle, from project initialization to successful completion, the elements of HyProMM can be digitalized to different degrees. Digitalization includes the use of digital media, but goes far beyond that. Networked planning, control and collaboration tools can change the nature of project management and teamwork. Resource balancing tasks between projects and organizational units of the line organization can be automated. Case-based reasoning or machine learning based on predictive models or artificial neural networks enable systematic learning from experiences of past projects and the development of digital project assistants for automated planning, control and scenario creation.

A broad scenario for digitalized project management along this project life cycle may look like as follows: During the clarification phase of the project as part of the **initialization phase**, the project goals are developed between the client and the contractor and defined in a project assignment. Collaboration takes place via a digital and mobile collaboration platform. The specifications are provided electronically, evaluated automatically by the software and a quotation is created. To do this, the software uses experience about effort and costs from past projects. The software recognizes unclear requirements and gaps and in turn automatically requests the client and contractor to provide the corresponding information.

The information which was (partially) automated collected is used together with HyProMM to select a suitable process model for project execution and to perform tailoring [2]. The process model can either be configured in a purely traditional way, for example using the waterfall model, or in an agile way, for example using Scrum. Hybrid processs models are also possible and are chosen according to the existing framework. Based on the selected and tailored process model, the project management software used for planning, collaboration and control is automatically configured so that it fits the selected process.

In the **definition phase**, milestones are derived on the basis of the client's requirements and the appropriate team members are automatically selected from the resources with specific competencies available in the company. A collaboration platform is available for cooperation within the team. Clients and suppliers are

Fig. 9.4 Two-dimensional space for building the vision of digitalized project management

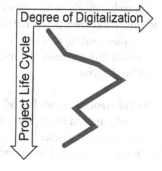

included via designated areas, e.g. for the clear demonstration of interim results, for online and video conferences, joint document processing and data storage, etc.

In the **planning phase**, the detailed planning of the project takes place. Based on the specified requirements, the knowledge from past projects and the selected traditional, agile or hybrid process model, the software creates corresponding planning documents. If information is missing or if the software detects inconsistencies, the user is requested to provide the relevant information.

The experience of past projects, the automatically analyzed requirements and the plans already created are also used for risk management. Conversely, the identified risks are used to update the planning and to derive an appropriate contingency and management reserve.

The reporting system is set up in such a way that important key figures are collected and reported automatically. Workflow-based software is used for document management, change management, contract management and claim management.

In the **control phase**, the software automatically detects deviations from the agreed targets. Inconsistencies in plans, risks and other documents are identified. From this information, the software develops alternative scenarios and presents them clearly. To integrate the customer, reviews and retrospectives are integrated into the status assessment and findings from these are automatically incorporated into the plans. Based on the scenarios, costs, resources and priorities, control measures are also automatically proposed and initiated if necessary.

As needed, the process model is adjusted automatically. If it becomes apparent during project execution that the customer needs to be more involved or, conversely, that the customer does not want to be involved, appropriate adjustments are made to the process model.

In the **final phase**, the project approval is documented, corresponding reports and protocols are created automatically and the project is analyzed on the basis of the agreed targets. During the entire project lifecycle, empirical values have already been collected, processed and used for machine learning of the software. This includes experience from the analysis of the specifications, the risks and their countermeasures, the effort- and cost-related target and actual values as well as the success of control measures. The information is used by the digitalized self-learning project management system to automatically improve the approach of future projects.

In this scenario, project managers do not become needless. However, they receive – similar to assisted driving – a system that uses past experience much more comprehensively than before and relieves from administrative tasks. In terms of agility, more time is left for people, collaboration with the customer and the creation of an outstanding result.

From this scenario, the following main fields for digitalized project management can be derived:

Digital process models and tailoring: These enable the automated selection and configuration of traditional, agile and hybrid process models and their automated tailoring. The selection and tailoring are based on criteria that are derived from the project assignment and the general conditions for processing.

Document management and workflows: All project documents are managed electronically and created, reviewed and processed in a workflow-driven manner. This includes other processes such as change management and contract management.

Planning: Project planning of deadlines, resources and costs is done with software that is networked with software of other projects and units of the line organization if required.

Controlling and reporting: The progress of the project is determined using defined targets in an electronic system. This system creates corresponding project reports from the determined key figures and forwards them to the relevant stakeholders.

Control: The system automatically determines recommendations for project control on the basis of determined key figures, available resources and other framework conditions.

Internal collaboration: There are electronic tools for project-internal collaboration, such as forums, joint document prepration, video conferencing systems, screen sharing etc.

External collaboration: Electronic tools exist for collaboration with entities external to the project, such as the client and suppliers.

Closing: An automated project closing with document archiving, post-calculation, project analysis, experience backup and knowledge transfer takes place.

9.4 Maturity Model for Digitalized Project Management M2DIP

Based on the considerations of the previous chapters, the maturity model for digitalized project management M2DIP (*Maturity* Model for Digital Integration in Project Management) will now be developed and presented. The maturity model consists of five maturity levels. To achieve a maturity level, defined degrees of digitalization must be demonstrated in different areas of project management. The maturity levels (ML) and their meaning are:

Maturity level 1 – initial: Projects hardly use digital tools to process the project object or these tools are used uncoordinated and not systematically.

Maturity level 2 – isolated: Projects use digital tools as a so-called isolated solution. Digital tools are used for defined areas of project management, but they are not cross-linked or integrated.

Maturity level 3 – integrated: Projects use integrated digital tools or digital tools that are cross-linked to each other. This means that data is only held once and can be used in all defined areas of project management.

Maturity level 4 – learning: Projects use integrated digital tools or digital tools that are cross-linked to each other. These tools automatically collect data in the sense of knowledge and experience retention and allow their later retrieval.

Maturity level 5 – autonomous: Projects use learning integrated or cross-linked digital tools. These are able to make their own decisions or propose decision templates in the defined areas of project management.

The scope of the defined areas of project management increases from maturity level 2 to maturity level 5, i.e. fewer areas need to be digitally supported for maturity level 2 than for maturity level 5. The extent to which an area is digitalized is indicated by its degree of digitalization (DG). There are four levels of digitalization (DG0 to DG4):

Digitalization level 0 – incomplete: No systematic use of digital tools. Individuals use software sporadically.

Digitalization level 1 – isolated: Defined digital tools are used as isolated stand-alone solutions without networking.

Digitalization level 2 – integrated: The digital tools used are cross-linked and access a common database.

Digitalization level 3 – learning: The digital tools used collect and archive data that can be used again in later projects.

Digitalization level 4 – autonomous: The digital tools can independently create decision templates and make decisions based on the current situation and collected data.

An overview of M2DIP with important areas of project management and the levels of digitisation required to reach a certain level of maturity is shown in Fig. 9.5.

To illustrate this, an example from the M2DIP maturity model will be explained: A company that has the **maturity level 2 – isolated** for digitalized project management must have at least the **digitalization level 1 – isolated in** the areas of document management, planning, and internal collaboration for all sub-areas, for example digital templates, scheduling, etc. If it wants to achieve **maturity level 3 – integrated**, it must also digitalize the areas of external collaboration, workflows, controlling and reporting, and financial statements. In all areas, the **digitalization level 2 – integrated** must be achieved. This means that the digital tools are networked with each other and access common data.

No additional areas are added to achieve **maturity level 4 – learning**. However, all areas that were relevant for **maturity level 3 – integrated** must now analyze the collected data, archive it, and make it available for new projects.

At **maturity level 5 – autonomous**, these archived experiences must be evaluated and used for the automated further development of the digital tools. This corresponds to **digitalization level 4 – autonomous**. Furthermore, the data must be used for the automated generation of project scenarios and for decision templates. In addition, digital process models and tailoring are added as new areas. Based on relevant key figures and characteristics of the project, a suitable process model is automatically configured and adapted to the project. The adaptation can change if new constellations arise during the course of the project, such as additional customers, new suppliers, etc.

Areas of Project Management	DG1 isolated	DG2 integrated	DG3 learning	DG4 autonomous
Document Project Management	**ML 2**	**ML 3**	**ML 4**	**ML 5**
cloud-based document archive	ML 2	ML 3	ML 4	ML 5
digital templates	ML 2	ML 3	ML 4	ML 5
...	ML 2	ML 3	ML 4	ML 5
Planning	**ML 2**	**ML 3**	**ML 4**	**ML 5**
Scope Planning	ML 2	ML 3	ML 4	ML 5
Scheduling	ML 2	ML 3	ML 4	ML 5
Resource Planning	ML 2	ML 3	ML 4	ML 5
Cost Planning	ML 2	ML 3	ML 4	ML 5
...	ML 2	ML 3	ML 4	ML 5
Internal Collaboration	**ML 2**	**ML 3**	**ML 4**	**ML 5**
E-Mail Lists	ML 2	ML 3	ML 4	ML 5
Chats	ML 2	ML 3	ML 4	ML 5
Video Conferencing and Screen-Sharing	ML 2	ML 3	ML 4	ML 5
Forum / Wiki	ML 2	ML 3	ML 4	ML 5
synchronous and asynchronous editing of documents	ML 2	ML 3	ML 4	ML 5
...	ML 2	ML 3	ML 4	ML 5
External Collaboration	**ML 3**	**ML 3**	**ML 4**	**ML 5**
Chats	ML 3	ML 3	ML 4	ML 5
Video Conferencing and Screen-Sharing	ML 3	ML 3	ML 4	ML 5
Forum / Wiki	ML 3	ML 3	ML 4	ML 5
synchronous and asynchronous editing of documents	ML 3	ML 3	ML 4	ML 5
Digital platforms for bids and assignments	ML 3	ML 3	ML 4	ML 5
digital market places	ML 3	ML 3	ML 4	ML 5
digital rights management for approvals	ML 3	ML 3	ML 4	ML 5
digital interfaces, e.g. with respect to change control	ML 3	ML 3	ML 4	ML 5
...	ML 3	ML 3	ML 4	ML 5
Workflows	**ML 3**	**ML 3**	**ML 4**	**ML 5**
digital signatures	ML 3	ML 3	ML 4	ML 5
workflow-based document approval	ML 3	ML 3	ML 4	ML 5
workflow-based change control	ML 3	ML 3	ML 4	ML 5
workflow-based configuration management	ML 3	ML 3	ML 4	ML 5
workflow-based contract management	ML 3	ML 3	ML 4	ML 5
workflow-based supplier management	ML 3	ML 3	ML 4	ML 5
...	ML 3	ML 3	ML 4	ML 5
Controlling and Reporting	**ML 3**	**ML 3**	**ML 4**	**ML 5**
Kennzahlenerfassung	ML 3	ML 3	ML 4	ML 5
Kennzahlenanalyse	ML 3	ML 3	ML 4	ML 5
Berichtserstellung	ML 3	ML 3	ML 4	ML 5
...	ML 3	ML 3	ML 4	ML 5
Project Approval and Closure	**ML 3**	**ML 3**	**ML 4**	**ML 5**
Archiving	ML 3	ML 3	ML 4	ML 5
Post-Calculation	ML 3	ML 3	ML 4	ML 5
Project Analysis	ML 3	ML 3	ML 4	ML 5
Leassons Learned	ML 3	ML 3	ML 4	ML 5
Knowledge Transfer	ML 3	ML 3	ML 4	ML 5
...	ML 3	ML 3	ML 4	ML 5
Scenario Planning	**ML 5**	**ML 5**	**ML 5**	**ML 5**
Automized Scenario Planning	ML 5	ML 5	ML 5	ML 5
Recommender Systems	ML 5	ML 5	ML 5	ML 5
...	ML 5	ML 5	ML 5	ML 5
Digital Process Models and Tailoring	**ML 5**	**ML 5**	**ML 5**	**ML 5**
Automized Selection of Process Models	ML 5	ML 5	ML 5	ML 5
Automized Tailoring at Project Start	ML 5	ML 5	ML 5	ML 5
Continuous Tailoring	ML 5	ML 5	ML 5	ML 5
...	ML 5	ML 5	ML 5	ML 5

Fig. 9.5 Maturity model for digitalized project management M2DIP

9.5   Implications of the Maturity Model in the Company

The M2DIP maturity model has implications for project management users and digital project management product vendors.

For users in companies, M2DIP serves as a basis for the digitalization of project management. It allows the assessment of the current state of digitalization and shows possibilities for further development via the individual areas and digitalization stages.

At the same time, every company is free not to fully digitalize all areas. The goal is not to achieve the highest possible level of maturity, but an optimal level of digitalization. The diversity of projects, framework conditions and stakeholders means that there is no single optimal level of digitalization for every situation and every company. Instead, each company should develop and implement a digitalization strategy for project management for itself. M2DIP provides impulses as to where digital tools and processes can be useful. It covers the range from no digital tools and processes at all to (almost) autonomous projects that are planned and controlled at least partially automatically.

Even with digitalized project management, a sound understanding of project management is important for everyone involved. For this purpose, the Capability Maturity Model Integration and the Project Management Maturity Model are maturity models that help in the further development of project management in the company. There are also a large number of standards that can be used for successful project management.

Work packages or tasks are usually processed by employees in a project. Digitalized project management requires that their results can be recorded digitally, for example in the form of key figures (effort estimates, actual costs, etc.) and documents (specifications, design drawings, parts lists, etc.). Employees must consequently be sufficiently qualified to understand the effects of their interaction with the digital tool.

Agile transformation puts people and interactions between people at the center to increase flexibility and innovation. Digitalization can promote innovation and create free spaces for interactions between people by taking over certain activities from digital tools.

Interfaces between man and machine are consequently an important success factor for the success of the digital transformation in project management. The interface and data processing enable new project management products that go far beyond the functionality of tools in widespread use today. Machine learning still offers a lot of potential here. Overall, the M2DIP maturity model offers manufacturers of digital tools a basis for classifying their existing products and identifying and implementing potential for further development.

9.6   Summary and Outlook

In this paper, the vision of digitalized project management was drawn and the maturity model M2DIP for digitalized project management was presented.

It has been shown that digitalization in project management does not end with bar charts created with software or with the use of digital collaboration platforms. Digitalization enables much more: The importance of knowledge management in projects has been pointed out for a long time. Nevertheless, in practice it is usually the case that, for reasons of time and cost, it is better to start with the next project than to secure and pass on knowledge and experience. Digitization and machine learning offer new opportunities to collect and evaluate information, to use it in the digital tool itself and to pass it on to relevant stakeholders. The digital project assistant plans possible project scenarios and creates decision templates with updated plans and resulting risks.

People will not become needless, but will be given more freedom for activities that can currently only be performed inadequately by digital systems. Examples include creative tasks, leadership and customer care.

Project management software has already changed a lot in the past few years. A few years ago, project management software was synonymous with a computer program for creating bar charts. Today, programs are often cross-linked or directly web-based and can manage resources across projects and serve as a communication platform. Many project management programs today prefer to call themselves collaboration software to indicate functionality beyond scheduling. Often, such software can also deal with task boards and kanban boards. Some software can even manage hybrid projects and handle traditional Gantt charts and agile task boards equally well.

The integration of individual functions will continue to increase and with it the possibility of accessing common data. These can be evaluated and used to further develop project management processes and improve planning and project control. The digital project assistant becomes possible.

References

1. Bendel O Definition "Digitalisierung". In: Gabler Wirtschaftslexikon Springer, Wiesbaden
2. Timinger H, Seel C (2017) Ein adaptives Vorgehensmodell für hybrides Projektmanagement. In: Barton T, Herrmann F, Meister VG et al (Hrsg) Prozesse, Technologie, Anwendungen, Systeme und Management 2017: Angewandte Forschung in der Wirtschaftsinformatik, 1. Aufl. mana-Buch, Heide/Holst, S 20–29
3. Seel C (2010) Reverse Method Engineering: Methode und Softwareunterstützung zur Konstruktion und Adaption semiformaler Informationsmodellierungstechniken. Wirtschaftsinformatik – Theorie und Anwendung, Bd 20. Logos, Berlin
4. Hevner AR, March ST, Park J et al (2004) Design science in information systems research. MIS Q 28(1):75–105
5. Österle H, Becker J, Frank U et al (2010) Memorandum zur gestaltungsorientierten Wirtschaftsinformatik. Schmalenbachs Z Betriebswirtsch Forsch 62(6):664–672
6. CMMI (2018) CMMI Institute. http://cmmiinstitute.com//. Accessed on 08.01.2018

7. Crosby PB (1979) Quality is free: the art of making quality certain. McGraw-Hill, New York
8. Software Engineering Institute (2011) CMMI für Entwicklung, Version 1.3. https://www.sei.cmu.edu/library/assets/whitepapers/10tr033de_v11.pdf/. Accessed on 08.01.2018
9. Matassa P (2006) Grow up already! – An OPM3® primer. In: Paper presented at PMI Global Contress 2006 – North America. Project Management Institute, Seattle
10. Crawford JK (2007) Project management maturity model. Center for business practices, 2. Aufl. Auerbach, Boca Raton
11. Hauke F, Thomas T (2014) Mittelstand im Wandel – Wie ein Unternehmen seinen digitalen Reifegrad ermitteln kann. BSP Business School, Berlin
12. BMWi (2018) Checkliste: Kommt Industrie 4.0 für unser Unternehmen in Frage? https://www.existenzgruender.de/SharedDocs/Downloads/DE/Checklisten-Uebersichten/Checkliste-Industrie-4-0.html/. Accessed on 08.01.2018
13. HNU (2018) Analysetool digitaler Reifegrad. http://reifegradanalyse.hs-neu-ulm.de//. Accessed on 08.01.2018
14. Telekom (2018) Digitalisierungsindex. https://benchmark.digitalisierungsindex.de//. Accessed on 08.01.2018
15. Boos F, Heitger B (1996) Kunst oder Technik? Der Projektmanager als sozialer Architekt. In: Balck H (Hrsg) Networking und Projektorientierung: Gestaltung des Wandels in Unternehmen und Märkten. Springer, Berlin/Heidelberg, S 165–182
16. Timinger H (2016) Seel C (2016) Ein Ordnungsrahmen für adaptives hybrides Projektmanagement. GPM-Magazin PMaktuell 4:55–61
17. Timinger H (2017) Modernes Projektmanagement: Mit traditionellem, agilem und hybridem Vorgehen zum Erfolg, 1. Aufl. Wiley-VCH, Weinheim
18. Frey CB, Osborne M (2013) The future of employment: how susceptible are jobs to computerisation? https://www.oxfordmartin.ox.ac.uk/publications/view/1314/. Accessed on 08.01.2018

Part V

Innovation in Product Development and Production

Systems Thinking in the Product Development Process 4.0

Martina Königbauer

Abstract

This chapter describes the obstacles many companies face on their way to implementing a PDP 4.0 – a product development process in the era of digitisation and Industry 4.0. The chapter highlights real-life experiences gained from providing consulting support for product development departments at German SMEs. Systems thinking contributes a great deal towards resolving the interdisciplinary issues that product developers face by making sure that a range of perspectives is taken into account before an during the process. Each challenge described is followed by a few sample questions, enabling readers to tackle these challenges using systems thinking. In this way, the chapter helps enhance readers' understanding of the topic, without the need to study the theory of systems thinking in greater depth. The discussion focuses on stage two of the PDP – the actual product development –, as the perspectives and approaches from systems thinking are particularly relevant as this stage. The chapter does not explicitly deal with what are usually referred to as stages one and three of the process, the generation of product ideas (1) and production and sales (3), although some of the "sample questions for systems thinking" listed may be helpful there as well.

10.1 Chosen Approach to Systems Thinking

There is a vast range of theories and schools dealing with systems thinking. For the purposes of this chapter, we have chosen approaches that are most helpful in defining system boundaries and visualizing systems, as that is what practitioners typically grapple with most in their work.

M. Königbauer (✉)
Faculty of Electrical Engineering, Technical University of Applied Sciences, Augsburg, Germany
e-mail: martina.koenigbauer@hs-augsburg.de

T. Barton et al. (eds.), *Digitalization in companies*,
https://doi.org/10.1007/978-3-658-39094-5_10

According to an old and very popular phrase generally attributed to Aristotle, "the whole is greater than the sum of its parts" [1]. Across the different scientific fields, "the whole" signifies a system. By definition, we are dealing with a system when its elements interact, resulting in qualities that the sum of its individual elements could not generate otherwise. So, in a systems analysis, it is always important to look not only at the individual elements but also at the connection between them (interrelations, interactions, information flows, etc.) [1, 2]. In some cases, individual system elements can be regarded as (sub)systems in themselves (Fig. 10.1).

In what follows, the term "systems" refers to products to be developed, product development projects, processes, organisations, and issues for which a solution or consensus is sought. "Elements" refers to organisations, technical departments, people involved, technologies used, approaches, and processes/workflows.

For the purposes of this chapter, the above definition of systems thinking is not comprehensive enough, however. In addition to the system's structural complexity (i.e., the number of elements and relationships), it is also important to consider its dynamics – i.e., the scope and frequency of changes to system elements [3] and to the relationships between them.

Günther Ossimitz includes these considerations in his definition of systems thinking, which comprises the following points:

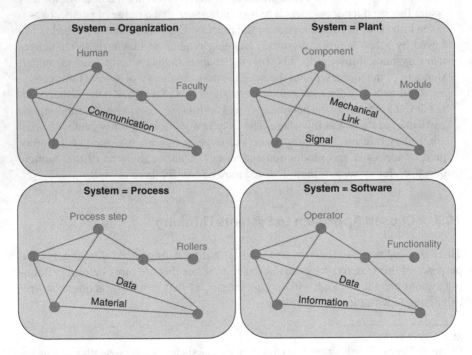

Fig. 10.1 Basic concepts of systems thinking

1. Networked thinking

Thinking in feedback loops, i.e., identifying and assessing direct and indirect effects, recognising feedback effects on causes, establishing and understanding cause-and-effect relationships, and considering connections [3, 4].

2. Dynamic thinking

Considering processes, i.e., a system's inherent dynamics, future development potential, and long-term impact. In addition, dynamic thinking includes the ability to identify, assess, and depict simultaneous processes, delays, periodic fluctuations, and linear, exponential, or logistic growth [3–5].

3. Thinking in models

Structured thinking and an awareness that perceived systems are simplified models of reality and, as such, subject to assumptions. As a consequence, the same system can be described using a variety of models, which are often based on different perspectives (e.g., a focus on structure, effect, or environment [2]). As a result, there is no such thing as one correct model [3, 4].

4. Acting in a Manner Compatible with the System

Understanding conditions of use as well as secondary and remote effects [4], i.e., making deliberate interventions in a system [3].

10.2 Focus and Evolution of This Chapter

The original intention of this chapter was to analyse the typical challenges of developing digital products, based on case examples, and to show how "networked thinking" – a sub-category of "systems thinking" – can help resolve these challenges and suggest solution options. The goal was to provide some some guidance to companies facing the dilemma of grappling with analogue problems while digitising their products or processes. Highlighting the aspect of "networked thinking" seemed essential in this context, as it is considered a key capability across industries.

In preparation for the chapter, interviews were conducted with companies that are perceived as pioneers of digitisation because they have successfully developed Internet-of-Things (IoT) and portal solutions for several years. In the first two interviews, however, a series of patterns emerged that – contrary to initial assumptions – can be considered typical of companies in early stages of digitisation. Confirming previous observations made in consulting projects with product development departments of SMEs, it became clear that these patterns prevented these companies from appropriately participating in digitisation or even keeping up with it.

As a result, the focus of this chapter shifted in that networked thinking is used to first identify existing obstacles to digitisation and to establishing a PDP 4.0, to then to offer a series of questions that can help companies reflect on their situation in a structured manner, Consultants may also find the questions useful for their work.

10.3   Definition of the Product Development Process 4.0 (PDP 4.0)

The title of this chapter is not meant to present the PDP 4.0 as the fourth in a series of PDPs; rather, "PDP 4.0" is to be understood as an umbrella term for product development processes applicable in the context of digitisation and Industry 4.0.

10.4   Using Systems Thinking to Define and Establish a PDP 4.0

10.4.1 The PDP 4.0 Matrix and Its Matrix Fields

In addition to being a blanket term for all product development processes compatible with Industry 4.0, the term "product development process 4.0" has also been chosen to make a clearer distinction: According to numerous readily accessible sources, product development 4.0 – or product development in Industry 4.0 – is an element of virtual or software-supported product development. Taking this a step further, the present chapter aims for a more differentiated perspective on the PDP 4.0 by including further topical aspects such as agile work. The following matrix can be useful as a basis for discussion in the context of a company's digital realignment.

Figure 10.2 shows possible manifestations of the PDP 4.0. Originally, the complete matrix comprised nine fields; however, since most SMEs today have incorporated some form of system support (such as CAD in hardware engineering), the

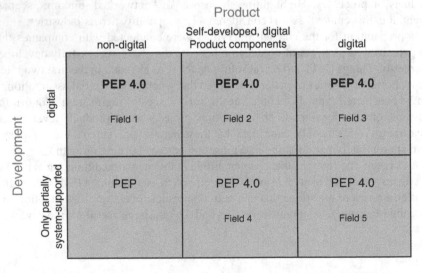

Fig. 10.2 Orientation matrix for the product development process 4.0 (own illustration)

three boxes depicting the non-digital development process – which is no longer relevant in most cases – have been omitted here.

The remaining six boxes result from different combinations of the following characteristics.

1. Non-digital products:
   This refers mostly to manufacturing companies offering purely mechanical solutions or non-digital services.
2. Digital product components developed in-house:
   Companies in this category typically face the challenge of combining proprietary hard- and software in one product, digital products with a service (e.g., consulting), or a non-digital product with digital advisory services. In a PDP 4.0, the digital part of the product is crucial for its market success. Not included in this variety of the PDP 4.0 are companies that buy digital products as complete systems and integrate them into their hardware without any proprietary software development. Such solutions belong in the non-digital products category above.
3. Digital products
   This refers to an intangible asset developed, marketed, and used by means of information technology; often, this type of offering is referred as "smart services" [6]. Examples include videos, e-learning, and advisory services (without human involvement) offered online as well as numerous other products such as digital news formats and magazines [7].
4. Partially system-supported development process:
   This characteristic desribes product development processes typically found at large corporations and SMEs. While system support is usually available in most departments involved in the PDP (in the form of PLM, ERP, supplier portals, etc.), 100% virtual collaboration is usually not feasible, e.g., because the configuration management for development-specific documents is performed manually and/or offline and/or decision documents must be compiled/calculated manually using data retrieved from different systems.
5. Digital development process:
   Examples include technology-based design and requirements engineering, virtual collaboration, augmented reality applications, the Internet of Things, and hand-held devices [8], all of which support mobile work.

Placing the PDP 4.0 in the orientation matrix helps determine what different forms of product development it includes; further nuances exist within each matrix field or box. For instance, the digital PDP 4.0 in box 3 could refer to a highly interconnected systems landscape that, triggered by interventions from the outside (e.g., data query by voice), displays the relevant data for a product in a user-specific form. At an even more sophisticated level, artificial intelligence could draw conclusions from existing data on products and processes and, on that basis, proactively suggest appropriate steps.

It should be noted here that although the rows and columns of the orientation matrix are organised from "non-digital" to "digital," the individual boxes do not imply a gradation in terms of digital maturity, let alone any type of evaluation in the sense of "better" or "worse."

Generally speaking, many companies today are still far from actively participating in digitisation, as they neither use Industry 4.0 solutions in their products or PDP nor aspire to do so.

That said, the terminology of digitisation is frequently used in product development functions, the vision being to fully digitise the product and/or process eventually. The temptation seems strong for product development units to give new software projects a name ending with "4.0" and announce digitisation across the organisation – whereas, in fact, projects of this kind often belong in matrix field 0 on the bottom left.

10.4.2 Using Systems Thinking to Find the Right Matrix Field

As a first step, a company can use the PDP 4.0 orientation matrix to work out a differentiated picture of its current state of digitisation and discuss which PDP 4.0 field seems to fit the company's goal best. The questions in Table 10.1 below incorporate the four aspects of systems thinking described in Sect. 10.1 to help determine what PDP 4.0 field a company can and should aim for.

Table 10.1 Sample questions for systems thinking about the PDP 4.0 fields

Networked thinking	Based on what event/(emergency) situation/vision do we seek to achieve a certain PDP 4.0 field, or shift to another one?
	Why do we want/need to add digital elements to these products?
	Is the targeted PDP 4.0 field we are aiming for really right for all our products?
	To which products do we want or need to add digital elements?
	Which products do we no longer need?
Dynamic thinking	Which products would we make worse if we added digital elements?
	What steps will we need to take to reach the PDP 4.0 field we are aiming for?
	Which field represents the next level of maturity for us in terms of business needs and strategy?
	What project, what type of customer, what market situation will represent a major challenge when we enter another PDP 4.0 field?
Thinking in models	Whom will we need to involve to achieve the PDP 4.0 field we aim for?
	What requirements will those involved in the change have to meet?
	What requirements will be added for those affected by the new PDP 4.0 field; what requirements will no longer be relevant?
	What will get better/worse/simpler/more difficult once we have reached the targeted PDP 4.0 field?
	What dimensions (people/technology/processes/methods/organisation) will we have to change, and in what ways, to successfully complete the steps towards the targeted PDP 4.0 field?
	Will it suffice to digitise the development process, or will we have to digitise products as well?
System-compatible action	If we do not act, what will happen to our products in the market?
	What capabilities do we have in the company that will help us take the next step towards digitisation in the short term?
	What capabilities will we need to acquire in order to achieve our target PDP 4.0 field in the medium term?

10.4.3 Product Development Process vs. PDP 4.0

Many small and medium-sized companies have spent years defining, documenting, and iteratively enhancing an overall product development process specifically tailored to their products. This typically holds true especially for the product development stage of the process per se (regardless of "4.0" characteristics). This established PDP often specifies very precisely what steps must be taken and what documents generated for which product components, by which department, and by what milestones, in order to make sure the product will be completed and available within a specified time frame. The benefits of a well-documented development process are self-evident, especially when similar products are generated repetitively:

- The project team can use it as a checklist for essential to-do's
- Having the process organised in a schedule facilitates the planning of new projects
- Required inputs and target outputs are clear for each step of the process
- It is also clear which version of which template must be used for documentation
- Responsibilities are clear
- So are the methods to be used.

The PDP 4.0 orientation matrix roughly indicates what kinds of changes companies need to make in products and the development process once they start thinking about digitisation. At this juncture, the benefits of a structured and well-documented PDP, as previously outlined, can turn into disadvantages – a challenge some companies are already facing. The following typical obstacles are observations from practice.

After years of adhering to an established PDP based on guidelines that do not allow even the slightest deviation, people tend not to question the necessity of existing documents and methods (to-do's), not even when considering completely new products or development processes. The resulting bureaucracy can be a key driver of complexity when entering a new PDP 4.0 field. As a result, the shift to that field is perceived as difficult and sometimes even avoided entirely.

What people need to realise, however, is that the timing of development steps under the existing PDP becomes obsolete with the development of each new product, as new development by definition implies venturing into new territory for which there are no tried-and-tested PDPs yet. Any attempt to plan and schedule the individual steps of a new product development according to existing process guidelines will require tremendous amounts of time and capacity. In practice, an almost pathological control mania on some projects causes people to focus on formalities rather than the product [9]. Even worse, projects are sometimes abandoned before they really get started.

When methods and creativity techniques in the existing PDP have so far been used to solve operational problems and create variations for existing products, it can make sense to apply new approaches for generating new product ideas. Examples of state-of-the-art techniques include Design Thinking and Agile Project Management. Although most product development departments are willing to try out these new methods, they will apply them only half-heartedly if managers define a narrow solution space or modify techniques to make them fit with the existing mindset (control, known products, etc.).

10.4.4 Using Systems Thinking to Shift to Another (PDP 4.0) Matrix Field

It should be noted that the goal is not to replace or dramatically change the existing PDP. In some cases, a few adjustments may suffice to enable the shift to another (new) PDP 4.0 field. The questions in Table 10.2 below help to find out whether and to what extent the existing – and well-documented – PDP continues to be applicable in the digital world, whether it needs to be adjusted, and, if so, specifically where and how.

10.4.5 Business Strategy vs. Digitisation Strategy

In the business strategy context, several unhelpful patterns can be observed in product development, as well as in related functions that are to be digitised.

Table 10.2 Sample questions for systems thinking about the PDP

Networked thinking	What is the purpose of the methods currently included in the PDP?
	When we introduce a new technology/software in product development, is it based on the existing PDP?
	Or do we need to adapt the current PDP to be able to use the new technology/software appropriately?
Dynamic thinking	How do we want to shape a learning process to ensure it will enable us to derive and gradually optimise the new PDP?
	How will we respond if we realise that the new 4.0 methods do not work for us?
Thinking in models	Do we need to move into a PDP 4.0 box or can our product development do without it?
	Which departments will be involved in the new PDP 4.0?
	Who should be able to use the new PDP 4.0?
	How detailed do we want the new PDP 4.0 to be?
	What parts of the PDP 4.0 do we need to describe, apart from stages or "gates"?
	Will we need to structure the new PDP 4.0 in consistent stages for all product components, or will it make more sense to describe it based on other criteria? Example: What is the latest order or completion date per component?
System-compatible action	What elements of the existing PCP do we want to keep as they are?
	Under what conditions will we apply the old versus the new PCP?

In companies where management is open to digitisation and eager to reap the benefits, the term is sometimes used very sweepingly, possibly for lack of knowing better. Apart from the use of terms such as "networked," "disruption," and "agility," there is often no effort to specify more clearly which technologies and perspectives will be used to accomplish which specific visions, strategies, and/or goals. Digitisation is often presented as the company's strategy rather than as a part of it. Employees are left with lots of open questions, as the reasons and purposes of digitisation – its benefits for the company – are not really clear. This may result in managers and employees figuring out their own meaning, then taking their own steps towards digitisation – i.e., optimising locally rather than working towards an integrated overall solution. Another possible effect is that employees perceive digitisation as an end in itself, which is evident from comments such as "Just another hype," "We'll surely come up with a problem for this solution," or "Ah, so we're trying to run with the big dogs again. Alright, let's continue to improve product XY and call it digitisation." In short, there is a risk that digitisation efforts are not accepted in the organisation – either because people consider them unnecessary or not feasible, or because they feel that "digitisation" is just a fancy label used for bringing the company up to speed.

In addition, there is a widespread fear that new technologies such as the Internet of Things (IoT) or artificial intelligence and the collecting of data will lead to people being monitored by means of data analysis or serve some other shady purpose. People conjure up disaster scenarios but fail to see opportunities for the company, often arguing that "We don't need that," and "We've been doing very well without." Even the option to upgrade existing products by adding services for which product data have to be collected and analysed (e.g., predictive maintenance [10]), will often raise eyebrows.

Irrespective of what management and staff think of digitisation and Industry 4.0, it is striking how often product development staff seem confused by what look like conflicting strategies. One illustrative example is the interplay of a new innovation strategy with the existing platform strategy (Fig. 10.3 [11]).

At creativity workshops in product development, it is often quite evident how much participants hold back when it comes to generating ideas, and how difficult it is for them to be creative beyond the limits of the platform strategy. This kind of internal block must be dissolved before people can start working on new product ideas or implement new work approaches.

Another unhelpful pattern typical of digitisation / Industry 4.0 projects is that people tend to focus on the information technology part of the transformation. This pattern is familiar to many consultants and managers from earlier software

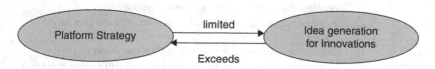

Fig. 10.3 Sphere of action for platform and innovation strategy

implementation projects, where the internal "marketing" of a new project would often focus on software-driven efficiency gains while failing to mention the need for changes to processes and methods. In digitisation projects, such changes can include new job profiles or forms of organisation.

10.4.6 Using Systems Thinking to Define a Digitisation Strategy

When working out a digitisation strategy, the questions listed in Table 10.3 below can be useful. While they are probably just one of several key elements, reflecting on them in depth helps identify and avoid major obstacles to digitisation.

10.4.7 Top-Down vs. Bottom-Up Agile Change

At many companies, the search for the right PDP 4.0 field – or the path to a field already chosen – is currently supported by procedural models from agile project management, or individual techniques from these models. Agile project management is highly attractive for some companies, as it enhances their customer focus and ensures a lot of flexibility in dealing with customers' change requests. The agile approach fits very well with digitisation projects, where customer centricity is also

Table 10.3 Sample questions for systems thinking about "strategies"

Networked thinking	Who are the people responsible for conflicting strategies?
	Who will benefit if a given strategy is implemented?
	What strategies are driven by economic necessity?
	What customer problem are we solving with this strategy?
	What new capabilities do we need in the team in order to implement the new strategies?
Dynamic thinking	From which strategy will the company benefit more in the short term?
	Which strategy promises positive effects in the longer term?
	What time horizon should we define for our strategy, and why?
	Is successful implementation of the strategy even possible?
Thinking in models	Which strategies seem to contradict each other?
	Which strategies support each other?
	Which strategies are neutral vis-à-vis each other?
	How should employees read potential contradictions within the strategy, and how should they deal with them?
	What is our business strategy? What is our digitisation strategy?
	In these strategies, have we addressed/considered all relevant dimensions (people/technology/processes/methods/organisation)?
	Do we even distinguish between business strategy and digitisation strategy?
System-compatible action	Under what conditions can we diverge from our strategy?
	Are there any strategies in the company that we will need to give up in order to implement the digitisation strategy?

a key component. That said, agile development or agile project management poses some major challenges for employees in product development functions.

Ideally, management has gathered some experience with agile project management, enabling them at least to roughly outline the value they expect agile approaches to add for the company. Ideally, they will actively support their introduction and application in the company, and act as role models for agile values [12].

In practice, however, the reverse – bottom-up "agilisation" – is also quite widespread: While management initiates the introduction of agile procedures in product development top-down, they actually expect staff to take the initiative in implementing agile changes. One possible reason might be superficial knowledge of agile practices, combined with the belief that agile approaches will make employees more efficient, faster, and more creative without requiring much time or effort. Many managers emphasize these expectations when facing numerous and/or complex projects. At the same time, what often happens is the bottom-up version of agile change, with managers demanding "compliance" from their people yet failing to live agile values themselves. In cases like these, employees are expected to use traditional project management metrics for their reports (such as resource utilisation or degree of completion), and simultaneously to perform their day-to-day duties using agile control tools (such as velocity and customer feedback). The result can be a conflict between two strategies, as described in Sect. 10.4.5.

The traditional approach requires tasks to be scheduled, so as to ensure people's capacity is optimally utilised and milestones are met – the agile approach, however, calls for a fast change of priorities when customer feedback on the latest partial delivery requires changes.

More recently, one attempt to solve this conflict has been to combine traditional and agile perspectives in a hybrid process model. However, if the underlying conflict is allowed to continue, there is a risk that the term "hybrid project management" will sooner or later meet with resistance: Employees will associate it with being left to their own devices when it comes to weighing strategic decisions (such as resource utilisation versus flexibility to comply with customers' expectations).

Another risk of bottom-up change is that people forget about the conditions required in order to work with approaches such as Scrum. One obvious example is a method for prioritising customer requirements in the order backlog. If the customer is available, priorities can be set jointly. If, however, orders are dropped into the backlog by sales, company management, or other internal units, there must be very clear-cut criteria for selecting the next order to be processed – otherwise, the development team will be the ones to decide on the order of processing, which can cause tremendous coordination efforts and disruptions in the department's work. The Scrum Guide [13] does not offer a specific solution for this, apart from the need to coordinate with the customer, so companies need to identify and implement a suitable evaluation method themselves.

At this point, another reference to the product development process is warranted: The PDP can be a hindrance for agile approaches if it is applied too rigidly or if, over the years, employees have grown used to following it very precisely. For instance, existing mechanisms such as a mandatory simultaneous transition from one product development stage to the next for all components of the product will hinder the iterative and incremental working style called for under agile approaches. In this case, it may happen that components that could technically be varied at a later stage are finalised at a set transition point, merely to ensure that all components will pass a certain bureaucratic approval process simultaneously.

Another factor that can get in the way of implementing agile working methods is when deviations from the PDP would previously be penalised. Quite understandably, fear of such sanctions will tend to prevent employees from applying agile behavior (such as taking responsibility and introducing customer-induced changes to the product) and keep them on the path so far perceived to be correct and safe. One indicator that a team has yet to overcome this obstacle is the following phrase typically found in very PDP-oriented organisations: "Other departments must be finished with X, before we can begin working on Y."

This leads us to the subject of "agile attitudes" (or "being agile"), which is particularly vexing in that it is often forgotten in change projects. "*Doing* agile" is relatively easy, as it can be trained using agile practices. What "*being* agile" means is not that obvious. Experience shows that employees who have only recently begun looking into agile development approaches will need some extra training to put the new thinking into practice, even under otherwise excellent conditions. Usually, traditional ways of thinking will continue to persist for quite a while, and "relapses" into the traditional way of thinking will occur over and over again.

The following is a visualisation of possible clues that an agile attitude (= being agile) has taken root, based on agile values (blue background, Fig. 10.4). In order for a consultant or manager to get people to commit to the agile attitude, a framework for further agile topics (e.g., sprint, time box, retrospective, agile roles, communication channels, etc.) could be developed jointly with managers and employees.

One final, equally topical issue is the transfer of agile ways of working to hardware development. Here, too, there is a full range of possible obstacles:

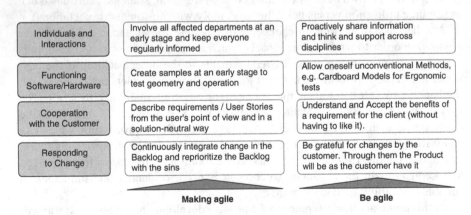

Fig. 10.4 Example of "Doing Agile" and "Being Agile"

- People reject agile practices, claiming they are incompatible with the hardware developed because components are too difficult to modifiy in the event of customer change requests.
- Software support for task management is tailored to software development, making it of limited use in hardware development.
- Some jobs are highly specialised (e.g., design, testing, specific components, logistics planning, etc.), limiting people's ability to support one another.
- The organisation is structured in technical departments, and floor space is assigned accordingly.
- User stories are slow to materialize because, when the customer's and the company's staff have a different understanding of quality, either the entire project is called off or the customer's people insist on basing the project on a list of very precise specifications, enabling them to document alleged quality flaws and get management approval to continue (a strategy to cover their backs).

10.4.8 Using Systems Thinking to Introduce Agility in Development

As in the previous tables, the list of questions in Table 10.4 below does not claim to be exhaustive. It does, however, include the key elements of the agile methodology (using Scrum as an example), which should help assess whether agile approaches might be useful in the course of the PDP 4.0. These elements include roles, artifacts (backlog), meetings (retrospective), and practices [13].

10.5 Applying Sample Questions from Systems Thinking

The sample questions listed represent a small selection of possible questions that can be used in strategy workshops as well as in process improvement or organisational development, be it in one's own company or at client organisations. The list can be extended and the questions varied ad libitum.

A very simple way to vary questions is by asking them from the perspective of the people or organisations affected by the problem:

Take, for instance, the question "What, specifically, does 'doing agile' and 'being agile' mean for us?" from Sect. 10.4.8 (own perspective). Variations could be:

- What does "doing agile" and "being agile" mean for department/person/supplier/ customer XY?
- What advice would the other department or person give us to help us "do and be agile"?

A further variation involves extending the perspective beyond the stakeholders to include the remaining elements of the system: processes, methods, technologies, and software tools. Here, the sample question on agile approaches can be varied using the "process" element as follows:

Table 10.4 Sample questions for systems thinking about agile approaches

Networked thinking	Which technical departments need to be involved in agile change to avoid local optimisation and ensure that a well-balanced solution can be obtained?
	Exactly which aspects of the agile approach appeal to us and what exactly do we want to achieve with them?
Dynamic thinking	What conditions need to be created in the company, or in product development, to ensure that agile practices can yield their benefits?
	Which components need to be defined early on in the development process (geometry, measurements, interfaces with other components)?
	Which components can be adapted in the course of product development?
	How will we integrate hardware and software components?
	What does the requirement profile for each new role look like?
	How long should a "sprint" be?
Thinking in models	Which of the data we have been collecting on work progress in product development do we want to continue to have access to in the future?
	Which of the methods of classical project management should we continue to apply, as they are working very well for us?
	Is the PDP still compatible with agile/hybrid approaches?
	In what aspects will we have to continue to apply the current PDP?
	At which points does the current PDP leave us degrees of freedom?
	What benefits of the classical and of the agile approach do we want to keep using in practice?
	Which agile practices fit with our company, and which do not?
	Which agile practices fit with the department, and which do not?
	How should the team to be organised to facilitate agile ways of working?
System-compatible action	What concerns are employees likely to have?
	What, specifically, does "doing agile" and "being agile" mean for us?
	Do we want to work with story points? (Not: Can we …)
	How do we want to live and exemplify agile values?
	How do we need to structure the backlog?
	What method do we want to use to keep updating the order of priorities in the backlog?
	How can we ensure that feedback from team retrospectives (lessons learned) will be put into practice??

- How does the current process help us do agile, and how does it allow us to be agile?
- How does the current process keep us from doing and being agile?
- What does the future process need to look like, for us to do and be agile?

The following are variatinos of the question for the "software tool" element:

- How does the software we use enhance our ability to do and be agile?
- How does the software we use limit our ability to do and be agile?
- What settings can we change in the software in order to improve our ability to do and be more agile?

All questions listed in Sects. 10.4.2, 10.4.4, 10.4.6, and 10.4.8 can be varied accordingly. By using the methods described here, companies looking for a suitable PDP 4.0 field, or wishing to determine their own approach to dealing with the problem areas described, can derive practical value from the diverse perspectives provided by systems thinking.

References

1. Kleve H (2005) Systemtheorie. Theoretische und methodische Fragmente zur Einführung in den systemischen Ansatz. Hochschulscript, Fachhochschule Potsdam
2. Haberfellner R, Daenzer WF (2002) Systems engineering. Methodik und praxis, Bd 11. Verlag Industrielle Organisation, Zürich
3. Denk R, Pfneissl T (eds) (2009) Komplexitätsmanagement. Linde international Fachbuch Wirtschaft, Linde, Wien
4. Ossimitz G (2000) Entwicklung systemischen Denkens. Theoretische Konzepte und empirische Untersuchungen. Klagenfurter Beiträge zur Didaktik der Mathematik, Bd 1. Profil, Klagenfurt
5. Strohschneider S (Hrsg) (2003) Entscheiden in kritischen Situationen. Schriftenreihe der Plattform Menschen in Komplexen Arbeitswelten e.V. Verlag für Polizeiwissenschaft, Frankfurt am Main
6. Stelzer D (2000) Digitale Güter und ihre Bedeutung in der Internet-Ökonomie. Das Wirtschaftsstudium (wisu) Zeitschrift für Ausbildung Prüfung Berufseinstieg und Fortbildung 29(6):835–842
7. Clement R, Schreiber D (2016) Internet-Ökonomie. Grundlagen und Fallbeispiele der vernetzten Wirtschaft, 3. Aufl. Springer Gabler, Berlin/Heidelberg
8. Handheld-Computer: Gewappnet für Industrie 4.0? I Rugged Devices. https://www.it-zoom.de/mobile-business/e/handhelds-gewappnet-fuer-industrie-40-17039//. Accessed on 01.03.2018
9. Mees J, Oefner-Py S, Sünnemann K-O (1993) Projektmanagement in neuen Dimensionen. Das Hologramm zum Erfolg. Edition Gabler's Magazin. Gabler, Wiesbaden, S 1
10. Vogel Business Media GmbH & Co. KG was ist predictive maintenance? Vogel Business Media GmbH & Co. KG. https://www.bigdata-insider.de/was-ist-predictive-maintenance-a-640755//. Accessed on 28.02.2018
11. Lindemann U (2016) Handbuch Produktentwicklung. Carl Hanser Verlag GmbH & Company KG, München
12. (2016) Manifest für Agile Softwareentwicklung. http://agilemanifesto.org/iso/de/manifesto.html/. Accessed on 28.02.2018
13. Schwaber K, Sutherland J. The scrum guide https://www.scrumguides.org/scrum-guide.html/

Manufacturing Execution Systems and Industry 4.0

11

Norbert Ketterer

Abstract

After business processes were integrated horizontally by ERP systems in recent decades and then vertically by other systems (such as SCM, CRM, PLM, SRM), the digitization of manufacturing has once again become the focus of attention in recent years as part of verticalization. In the German-language terminology, the buzzword "Industry 4.0" in particular has become established, in which "intelligent machines" independently coordinate manufacturing processes or "service robots" support people in assembly, for example (BMWI (2017) Dossier Industry 4.0: Digitale Transformation in der Industrie, Federal Ministry for Economic Affairs and Energy. https://www.bmwi.de/Redaktion/DE/Dossier/industrie-40. html/. Accessed on 04.12.2017). The aim of this automation is in particular individual products, i.e. one-offs, at a price and quality comparable to mass production.

The bridge from the ERP systems to these "intelligent machines" is built by "Manufacturing Execution Systems" (ME systems, production control systems), which can be available in various forms, from individually created single systems, for example solely for production data acquisition or solely for the quality management of specific processes of a company, to standardized and integrated overall solutions.

In this chapter, the functionality of ME systems is presented and differentiated from the functionalities of surrounding systems. As a concrete example, processes within the "SAP University Alliance Industry 4.0" landscape will be considered in particular; this landscape is made available to colleges and universities via the SAP Academic Alliance.

N. Ketterer (✉)
Hochschule Fulda, Fulda, Germany
e-mail: norbert.ketterer@cs.hs-fulda.de

179

11.1   Manufacturing Execution Systems

In contrast to ERP systems, Manufacturing Execution Systems (ME systems) are directly connected to production and operate in a more timely manner, often even in real time. Central aspects are the control of production and the integration of various functions from the production environment with the establishment of control loops for production control. A comprehensive description of ME systems can be found in Kletti [1] and [2] and also in Louis [3]. Müller [4] provides an interesting, comparative overview of various sources on the subject of "MES"; the various definitions and functionalities are also compared here [4, p. 17f., 20ff.].

Due to their real-time and reaction capability, ME systems represent an instrument for implementing control loops that can react efficiently to incoming events (such as malfunctions or rush orders) [2, p. 24f.], because they often collect the required data by directly connecting machines, measuring systems or semi-automatically via workers' terminals. Thus, a responsive, transparent and economic production can be realized. Important data to be recorded are [2, p. 25] deadlines, machine status, tool status, personnel availability, material buffer and batch data as well as quality and process data. ME systems can be divided into three task areas [2, p. 20], namely "production" (e.g. machine data, production control station, traceability), "personnel" (e.g. personnel time recording, personnel resource planning and incentive wage calculation) and "quality assurance" (e.g. production inspection, statistical process control and test equipment management).

Theoretically, production planning and CAD systems, but also PLM, CRM[1] and SCM systems can be connected to the ME system; the most obvious candidate here is, of course, the ERP system [2, p. 46], from which specifications such as production orders, but also other planning specifications (such as capacity plans) can be transferred. Additional data can also be transferred, for example with PLM reference – such as CAD data, NC programs or other documents that cover the information requirements of the production environment.

11.1.1 ME Systems and Standards

For details of the functions of ME systems, reference is made in particular to VDI Guideline 5600 and to MESA's c-MES model.

The VDI guideline 5600 is presented for example by Kletti [2, p. 27f.] and lists the following functionalities of an MES system – a broader view of MES than a pure manufacturing connection is shown – for example by an information or also energy management.

- Detailed planning and control
- Resource Management
- Materials Management

[1] CRM systems, such as for exchanging sales and service data with the ME system.

- Workforce Management
- Data acquisition and processing
- Performance analysis
- Quality Management
- Information Management
- Order Management
- Energy management

The c-MES model [5] of the MESA replaces the older MESA model, which consists of 11 functions and which is still often found in recent works. The latter model has a strong internal focus on manufacturing, while the c-MES model (Table 11.1) includes a strong collaborative aspect of MES functionality to better reflect trends in collaborative manufacturing than the older MESA model.

In the overall landscape of business application systems, MES can be classically classified following the ISA 95 model [6] as well as Louis [3, p. 14] as shown in Fig. 11.1; the ME system connects the overall business process level with the control level.

11.1.2 ME Systems and Industry 4.0

Industrie 4.0 centers around intelligent products and production units – the former know their properties and how they are manufactured [7, p. 42], the latter know their capabilities and they know whether they can perform a certain function. The goal is to achieve a strong customization of products; this customization should be possible down to a quantity of one [8, p. 18]. Despite this flexibility, the use of resources should of course keep up to the expected economic productivity.

Typical for the IT side of "Industry 4.0" is an aggregation of information in engineering and operation across different projects, plants and operators. However, data is not only aggregated, but also evaluated, for example by displaying correlations between them. The basis are "Cyber-Physical Systems" (CPS), which directly collect data, evaluate data, are interconnected and use globally available data and services and interact with the real world [7, p. 37]. In this context, CPSs are e.g. devices, buildings, production facilities [8, p. 14]. A number of authors are of the opinion that the classic automation pyramid from Fig. 11.1 will not remain in place – for example, by communicating directly via the CPS level and thus exchanging data without detours via higher levels (such as ERP). However, such a landscape does not automatically lead to a removal of MES responsibility; instead, new challenges arise for MES systems to organize these scenarios [2, p. 269ff.] – for example, through a stronger encapsulation of services and coordination of these.

The RAMI model [9, 10, p. 92ff.] attempts to represent the essential aspects of "Industry 4.0" as a framework – existing solutions can be classified in this – Fig. 11.2. The hierarchy levels describe the hierarchy of the factory, the shown architectural levels describe the IT representation of the physical things in layers, the last dimension describes the product life cycle. An ME system covers the

Table 11.1 c-MES functions according to MESA [5]. (Own representation)

c-MES function	Meaning	Examples of collaborative functions
Product tracking and genealogy	Recording of materials and current processing status; link to supplier lots, clear identification of the produced lot and thus easy traceability	Feedback to product designers and suppliers; transparent product information for customers; updating of default values in ERP&SCM systems; information for service systems/control of recalls
Resource allocation and status	Management of non-production resources, such as tools, documents, tanks, including their status	Integration with PLM functionality also in terms of feedback from production; connection with supply chain engineering/supply chain management, connection to maintenance systems and OEM customers
Performance analysis	Analytical view of all core functions of the MES as well as connected systems (PDM, ERP, SCM, CRM, etc.) via flexible dashboards/OLAP functions	A wide variety of functions can analyze the impact of manufacturing decisions, such as design-related, supply chain-related. HR can identify top performers or shifts and plants can be compared
Process management	Detailed specification of the process, in particular the operations & routings as well as additional information, such as documents; flexible (via attributes/business rules) definable operations and sequencing via business rules	Linking of detailed work plans with those of the ERP system; information on product design and work planning; information exchange with outsourcing partners; information for collaborative design partners
Data collection acquisition	Collection and storage of data from facilities; materials, people and systems for analysis purposes	Transfer of current process information to the PLM system as well as to detailed planning (e.g. in SCM); coupling of ERP (and SCM) for current cost/planning information; coupling of customers for information about order statuses
Quality management	Statistical process control/process quality management based on online and offline analyses; categorization of errors; notifications/alerts	Integration with work scheduling to account for defects; integration with purchasing to account for statistics; integration of design teams; integration of maintenance systems.
Labor management	User administration, user groups/qualifications	Tracking of qualifications/certifications for regulatory reasons with QM systems, defined access for business partners to the ME system
Dispatching production units	Management of the flow of production, production unit has to take place at workstation/operation. Recalculation of occupancy, potentially automated via business rules	Status of inventory and orders available for customers and suppliers, integration with SCE/SCM, inventory data available for other enterprise applications (e.g. ERP)

c-MES functions, their meaning and relationship to surrounding systems

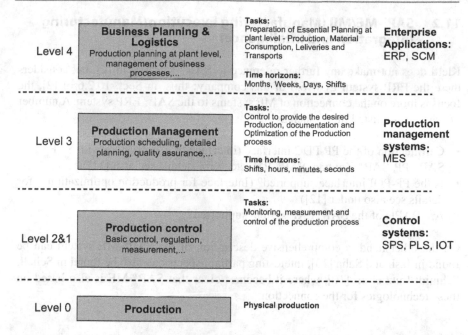

		Tasks:	
Level 4	**Business Planning & Logistics** Production planning at plant level, management of business processes,...	Preparation of Essential Planning at plant level - Production, Material Consumption, Leliveries and Transports **Time horizons:** Months, Weeks, Days, Shifts	**Enterprise Applications:** ERP, SCM
Level 3	**Production Management** Production scheduling, detailed planning, quality assurance,...	Control to provide the desired Production, documentation and Optimization of the Production process **Time horizons:** Shifts, hours, minutes, seconds	**Production management systems:** MES
Level 2&1	**Production control** Basic control, regulation, measurement,...	Monitoring, measurement and control of the production process	**Control systems:** SPS, PLS, IOT
Level 0	**Production**	Physical production	

Fig. 11.1 System hierarchy in the production environment. (Own representation based on [3, 6])

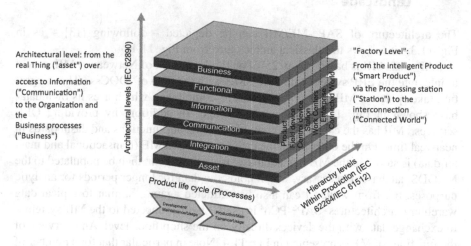

Fig. 11.2 RAMI model. (Own representation based on [9, 10, p. 92])

architectural level, even if the leading data system may be the ERP or PLM system; a digital representation of the real thing is still available. With regard to the process level, an ME system (together with an ERP/SCM system) covers the second part (production), whereas the first part would be found in a PLM system. With regard to the hierarchy levels, it should be noted that communication here is also no longer as hierarchical as shown in Fig. 11.1, but can take place across levels.

11.2   SAP°-ME/MII (Manufacturing Execution/Manufacturing Integration and Intelligence)

Kletti does not make any further reference to SAP®-ME/MII in [2], but considers there the ERP system ECC 6.0 of this company; thus, in Sect. 10.2.6 of [2], the focus is more on the connection of ME systems to the SAP® ERP system. A number of criterias are listed there, such as:

- Certification of the PP-PDC interface (interface of a subsystem with SAP®-HR, SAP®-PP, SAP®-Kanban, SAP®-PM, etc. – for details see also [11])
- Is the PP-POI interface supported? (Interface for production optimization – for details see also under [12])
- Are BAPIs of the SAP® ERP system supported?

On the other hand, a comprehensive description of the SAP®-ME system can be found in Jash and Saha [13], interesting partial aspects can also be found in Schell, Schmidt-Lutz et al. [10], where it becomes clear that SAP®-ME is also based on these technologies for the connection.

11.2.1 Architecture of SAP°-ME/MII and the Industry 4.0 Landscape

The architecture of SAP®-ME/MII can be depicted – following [13] – as in Fig. 11.3 – it follows the classical architecture from Fig. 11.1.

SAP®-ME/MII is based [13, p. 25ff.] on the Java stack of Netweaver, MII is used to integrate the ERP system with SAP®-ME with the help of IDOCss.[2] The integration takes place in MII within the "MEINT" component, which uses its own database shown in Fig. 11.3 for message storage. In addition, by providing OEE services,[3] MII has the capability to provide monitoring functions and dashboards in near-real time. On the other hand, the data generated in ME (transactional and master data) is stored in the MEWIP database; from this, it can then be populated to the MEODS database if necessary, which holds the data for longer periods for analytic purposes, but from which it can also be extracted again – similar to typical data warehouse architectures. SAP®-PCo[4] is used – here connected to the MII system – to exchange data with the devices directly on the shop floor level. An overview of the functions of ME is presented in Fig. 11.4. Note in particular that for a number of functions it is easy to relate to the c-MES model – for example, between "Product Tracking & Genealogy" and "Genealogy/Tracking", "Performance Analysis" and the "Reporting" blocks, and "Historical Data (ODS)" and "Process Management"

---

[2] IDoc (Intermediate Document) is an SAP® standard format for electronic message exchange.

[3] OEE = Overall Equipment Effectiveness, general term but also exists as a component in MII.

[4] PCo stands for "Plant Connectivity" [14] – a component for connecting manufacturer-specific production level systems, such as PLC or DCS, to an SAP® system.

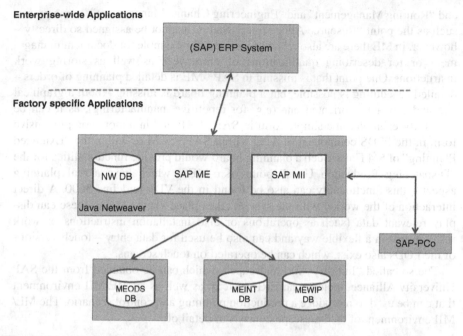

Fig. 11.3 Architecture of SAP®-ME/MII. (Own representation based on [13, p. 26]. With kind permission of Rheinwerk-Verlag)

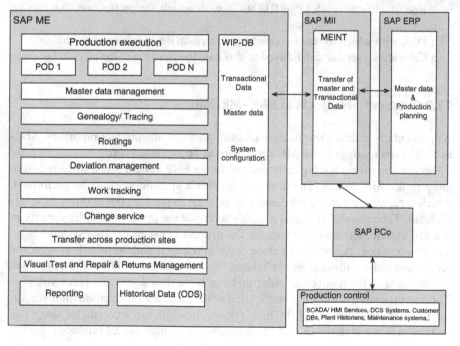

Fig. 11.4 Functional overview of ME including essential components of MII& PCo. (Own representation based on [13, p. 24]. With kind permission of Rheinwerk-Verlag)

and "Routing Management" and "Engineering Change Management". Some points, such as the point "Resource Allocation & Status" cannot be assigned so directly – however, in ME there are also related functions, for example for document management or for describing qualifications of employees as well as storing work instructions. One point that is missing in SAP®-ME is detailed planning of orders – detailed scheduling is possible, but a planning board is missing – both a graphical one and a quantity-oriented one (e.g. for repetitive manufacturing), as it can be found, for example, in a simple form in SAP®-ERP, and in a more comprehensive form in the PPDS component of APO within SAP®-SCM or within the "Extended Planning" of S/4 Hana. Such a planning board would provide functionalities for the "Dispatching Production Units" point of c-MES, which have a real planning aspect – this functionality can also be found in the VDI guideline 5600. A direct interaction of the worker with the system takes place via the PODs, these can display relevant data (such as operations or also installation instructions or work instructions) in a flexible way and can also be used for data entry – touch versions of the PODs also exist, which can be operated on touch screens.

The so-called "Industry 4.0 Landscape", which can be obtained from the SAP University Alliance, includes an ERP system, as well as an ME/MII environment that can be used to reproduce a production planning and control scenario. The ME/MII environment of the landscape consists in detail of:

- an MII system that connects the ME system with the ERP system
- an ME system
- a line monitor (from SAP®-MII/OEE), with which the production line can be monitored
- a PCo, with which the connection to the physical devices is established
- a Kepware server that can be used to simulate the function of the physical devices

11.2.2 Essential Objects in SAP®-ME/MII

As particularly relevant for the core tasks of an MES, the production orders, SFCs as well as the routings of the ME system are to be explained here.

Production orders are typically created in the ERP system and transferred from there to the ME system. There, they represent a specific work to be performed, which is represented in the ERP and ME systems in parallel, but at different levels of detail. Theoretically, it is also possible to create the production order directly in the ME system, although in this case the process between the two systems is no longer integrated. When a production order is released within the ME system, the production order is divided into individual "Shop Floor Control IDs" (SFCc), which are assigned to the production order and can be broken down to a piece size = 1. This corresponds to a unique identification of the piece/a 1-piece production according to the ideas of Industry 4.0. Thus, a production order of a certain lot size n can be broken down in detail to n SFCs in production, which are all produced slightly differently in detail – this different production would then also be updated within the product genealogy with SFC accuracy in the ME (see also Table 11.1 – Product genealogy in c-MES).

A detailed, flexible routing represents an essential master data record in production control (see also Table 11.1 – "Process Management" in c-MES). In SAP®-ME, the bill of materials and the routing are transferred from the ERP system, but can be subsequently maintained there. The basis is the PP-POI interface – similar to what is required in Sect. 11.2. The routing in particular offers a range of options for flexibly mapping the structures of production – this is done with the help of constructs such as:

- **Dynamic work plans:** a work plan can be (re)defined dynamically per SFC – for example, if a short-term change is to be implemented for a specific lot or SFC. This work plan is then saved individually for the SFC.
- **Use of branches, simultaneous groups and arbitrarily arranged processes:** This is used to represent such things as operation alternatives, optional steps, loops, or rework, parallel structures (simultaneous group), and flexible structures (arbitrarily arranged sequences) that allow operations in the routing to be processed arbitrarily as long as they are only processed.
- **Sub-routings:** It is possible to insert sub-routings in routings (e.g. for rework) or to call up a separate routing in case of deviations ("nonconformity").
- **Scripts:** Furthermore, decisions in the flow of the work plan can be executed in an automated way based on scripts to support automation – similar to what business rules are proposed in the "Process Management" item from Table 11.1. Essentially, a JavaScript description is interpreted here – see [15] as well as [13, p. 149ff.], whereby EJB and SQL calls and predefined variables can be integrated.

Figure 11.5 shows an example of a simultaneous group that has been embedded in a dynamic routing, in this case for a specific SFC. Operation 20 is parallel to operation sequence 30–40; operation 10 is always to be performed, and operation 50 is to be performed as soon as 40 and 20 have both been performed – this corresponds to the logic stored in the simultaneous group. If this is done, the operations of this SFC must be in the operation queue – an example of this can be found later in Sect. 11.3.2 (Fig. 11.14). There the sketch of the operation structure and its implementation in a dynamic routing of the ME using a simultaneous group for a SFC can be seen. In a non-SFC specific routing the implementation would be the same – only the routing would be specified without reference to a SFC.

An example of a rule at the end of an operation using JavaScript to automate branching logic can be seen in Fig. 11.6. The "Exit" command is used to communicate to the next execution step. This is a slightly modified version of the "pass" script predefined in ME: if certain operations, arranged in a loop, have not been executed more than twice, the subsequent operation associated with that edge can be executed. For an application of this script see Sect. 11.3.2.

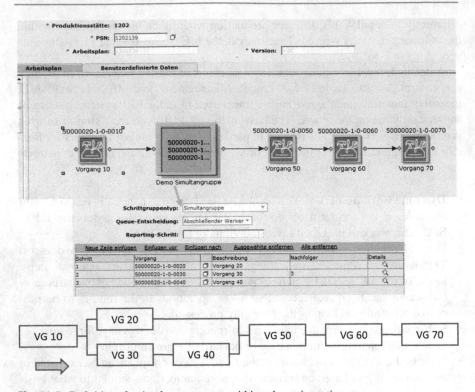

Fig. 11.5 Definition of a simultaneous group within a dynamic routing

```
// Path for SFCs that do not fail
if(LOOP_COUNT <= 2) {
  exit (true);
} else {
  exit(false);
}
```

Fig. 11.6 Simple example of a flexible business rule for outbound linking

11.3   Sample Processes in the SAP University Alliance Industry 4.0 Landscape

A case study exists for the landscape in which a production order is essentially transferred from the ERP system to the ME system [16], broken down into SFCs there, released and reported back and visualized ([17], "Part 1"). A case of "rework" is also considered, as well as a number of reporting options ([17], "Part 2"). Additionally, own processes can be mapped in the system to investigate own questions.

11.3.1 Standard Processes of the University Alliance Case Study

Figure 11.7 shows the standard process of the current case study of the University Alliance as a BPMN diagram:

- In the ERP system, production orders are created and released (steps 1–4) – of course, other activities would be conceivable here; such as detailed planning in the graphical planning board or even real sequence optimization on several production lines.[5]

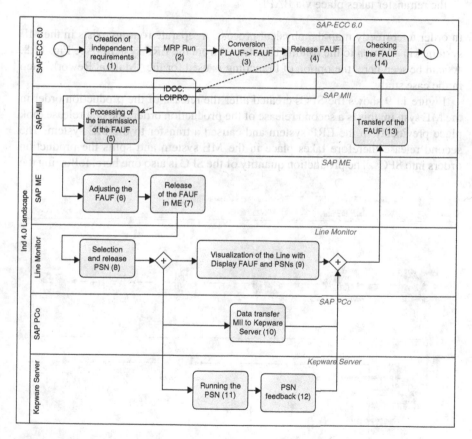

Fig. 11.7 Standard process of the landscape in case study according to [16] as BPMN diagram

---

[5] An SCM APO with the known optimization capabilities in PP/DS is not part of the landscape, but in principle it could be added – ERP only supports a single-line optimization.

- After release, the production order is passed on to the MII system as an IDOC and imported from there into the ME system (step 5).
- The production order is processed in SAP®-ME and the individual SFCs assigned to this order are generated by the release (steps 6 and 7).
- In the Line Monitor, an execution of the SFC on the production line can now be triggered and monitored – there are scenarios with and without rework (steps 8 and 9).
- The PCo synchronizes the data between the MII Line Monitor and the Kepware server (step 10)
- The Kepware server now starts the operations of the SFCs one by one (step 11) and reports them back via the PCo (step 12) (could also be done manually via POD – Sect. 11.3.2).
- At some point the order is completed and the production order should then also be correctly confirmed in the ERP system and can be checked there (step 14) – the retransfer takes place via BAPI.

In order to correctly map the physical process, a separate routing exists in the ME system – in addition to the routing transferred from the ERP system – see Fig. 11.8. As can be seen here, the option of branching is used for the "Manual Rework" step in the case study.

Figure 11.9 shows the SFCs created after the release of the production order in the ME system: this is a second release of the production order; the first release took place previously in the ERP system and caused a transfer to the ME system. The second release therefore takes place in the ME system and splits the production orders into SFCs. The production quantity of the SFC is also one here, following the

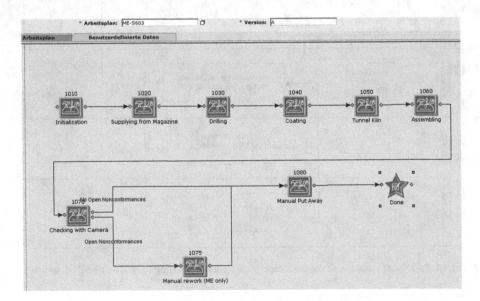

Fig. 11.8 Routing of the given standard case study of the University Alliance

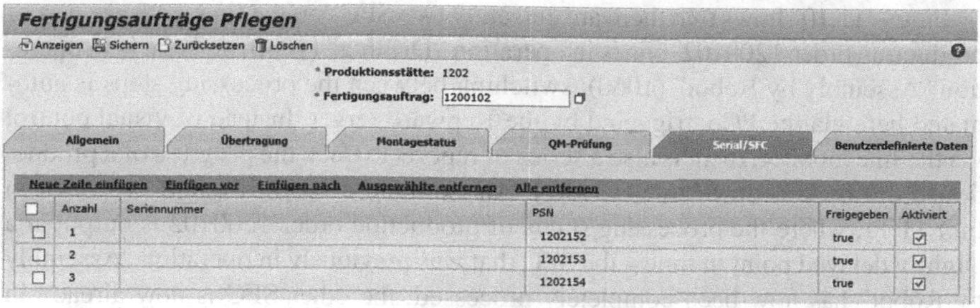

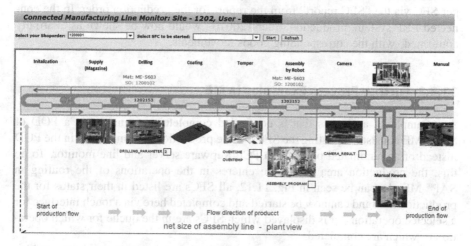

Fig. 11.9 SFCs of a production order after its release

Fig. 11.10 Line monitor with SFCs of a production order in processing status

idea of "1-piece production" in the context of Industry 4.0. However, this is not restricted to quantity 1, because the ME system splits the production orders at the event of release according to a parameter in the material master; for this purpose, the ME system has its own lot size parameter that regulates this splitting, which is located directly in the general data of the material master.

The individual SFCs can now be started, the case study mainly uses the Line Monitor for this (Fig. 11.10); in this, the SFCs can be selected for a production order and started individually. The Line Monitor is regularly refreshed by the system and thus the individual SFCs can be directly visually tracked in their processing status. It should be noted that the Line Monitor is not directly part of the ME system, but was added via the MII (and in this case as part of the "OEE" component) as part of the case study by the University Alliance. However, this also leads to a certain **inflexibility of** the case study, since a certain line structure and thus also routing structure is predefined. Own structures can then not be started and monitored via the Line Monitor, the use of PODs and reports is necessary.

Figure 11.10 shows that there are currently two SFCs on the line: both are part of production order 1200102, one is in operation "Drilling" (1030) and one is in operation "Assembly by Robot" (1060); switching between the processing steps is automated here via the PCo, triggered by the Kepware server. Instead of visual control via the line monitor, there is also a series of reports to track the progress of a production order broken down to SFC level. An example of such a report is shown in Fig. 11.11, where the processing status of production order 1200102 is output at a slightly delayed point in time – the SFC that was previously in operation "Assembly by Robot" has now been completely processed, the other SFC is now already in operation 1070 ("Checking by Camera"), and another SFC has not yet been started. For the last two SFCs, it would also be possible to drill down to the operation list per SFC via the "SFC report" from the report for the production order. In the connected ERP system, production order 1200102 would now be shown as "Partially confirmed" with the corresponding goods movements.

11.3.2 Further Process Examples in ME

An example of a process that is controlled completely manually via a POD of SAP®-ME consists of posting the SFCs of the production area manually in the POD instead of an automated posting via PCo/Kepware server and line monitor. To do this, the production area should be enteres in the operations of the routing in SAP®-ME. As can be seen in Fig. 11.12, all SFCs are listed in their status for the production area and can now be started and completed here via a touch interface for a selected operation – it is displayed which SFCs are in the queue for which operation or which are completed.

Using the "Assemble" function (Fig. 11.13), the components can be assembled into the assembly-part – the result would be evaluable in an "As-Built" report within the product genealogy, for example; however an inventory change in the connected ERP system would already take place directly based on the confirmation of the operation. It should be noted that a non-touch version of the interface also exists, as well as PODs (Production Operator Dashboards) with other delineation criteria, such as directly by SFC or by operation.

An example of processing a concurrent group, as defined in Fig. 11.5, using an area-specific POD is shown in Fig. 11.14. It is easy to see which operations of the

| | | BERICHT FÜR FERTIGUNGSAUFTRAG NACH SCHRITT | | | | |
| Produktionsstätte: 1202 | | Fertigungsauftrag: 1200102 | | | | |
SCHRITT-ID	VORGANG	ARBEITSPLAN	MENGE IN QUEUE	MENGE IN ARBEIT	MENGE ABGESCHLOSSEN	WEITERE INFORMATIONEN
010	1010	ME-S603	1	0	2	PSN-Bericht
060	1020	ME-S603	0	0	2	
070	1030	ME-S603	0	0	2	
080	1040	ME-S603	0	0	2	
090	1050	ME-S603	0	0	2	
020	1060	ME-S603	0	0	2	
030	1070	ME-S603	0	1	1	PSN-Bericht
040	1075	ME-S603	0	0	0	
050	1080	ME-S603	0	0	1	
		Ende der Daten				

Fig. 11.11 Processing status via "Shop Order by Step" report

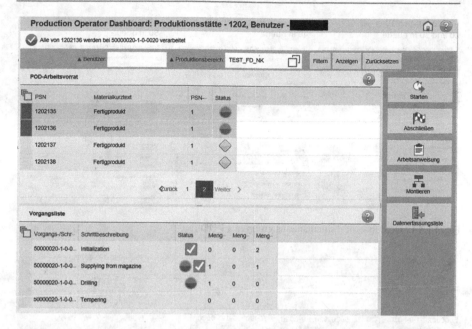

Fig. 11.12 Production operator dashboard worklist with SFC and operation list

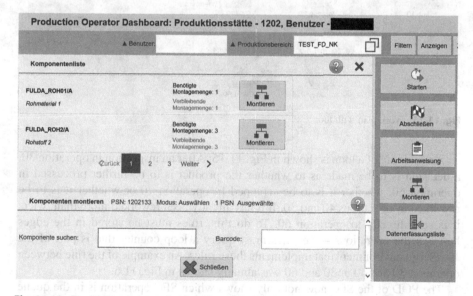

Fig. 11.13 Production operator dashboard worklist for assembly

SFC are in the queue (indicated by the circle symbol) – namely, operation 20 and 30 first, since both are part of the concurrent group, then only operation 40, since 30 has been processed. Operation 50 requires operation 20 and 40 to be processed before the SFC can be executed for this operation.

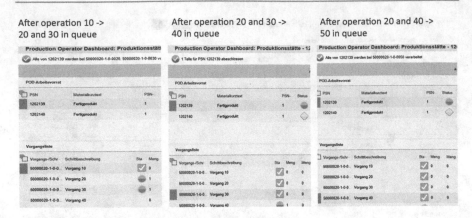

Fig. 11.14 Execution of a simultaneous group in a POD

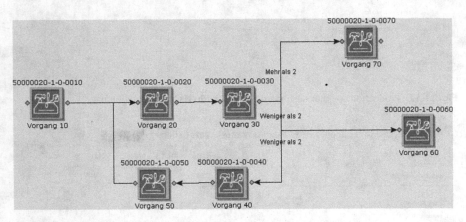

Fig. 11.15 Work plan with loop

An example of a loop is shown in Fig. 11.15: After an inspection in operation 30, a decision is to be made as to whether the product is to be further processed in operation 60, whether it is to be scrapped in operation 70 or whether it is to be reworked in operations 40 and 50. If it has already been reworked more than twice, it is sent directly to operation 60. To do this, rules must be stored in the edges between the operations – the rules must query a loop counter that is part of the JavaScript environment that implements these rules. An example of the rule between operation 30 and 40 or 30 and 60 was already shown in Fig. 11.6.

The POD of the SFC now not only shows which SFC operation is in the queue for processing and which is being processed or has already been processed; it also shows whether this is "rework". An example of this is shown in Fig. 11.16: The loop is run until the upper limit has been reached, after which the SFC is placed directly in the queue of operation 70.

Reporting of the operations is possible via predefined reports, but custom dashboards can also be defined. For this purpose, a number of so-called "portlets" exist,

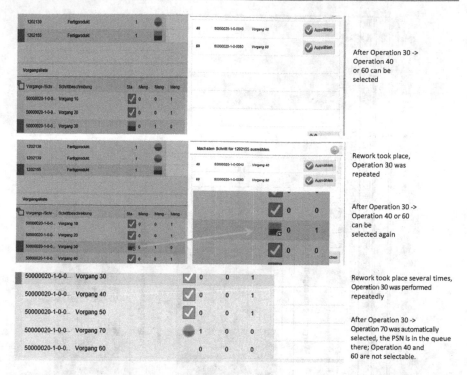

Fig. 11.16 Processing the SFC – shown in the POD

which represent a certain range of data – defined by the report to be created and the input parameters. The portlets can then be combined to create dashboards – an example of a dashboard is shown in Fig. 11.17 – it consists of two portlets ("WIP by Operation Tabular Report"/"Operation Yield by Material").

Both the VDI guideline and c-MESA speak of information management. An example of this in SAP®-ME/MII is the representation of work instructions in PODs, which can be called up for a SFC. This work instruction can be stored on different levels, such as material, routing, operation, production order or even SFC and can thus be defined very generally or also very specifically, down to a 1-piece production (see Fig. 11.18).

11.4   Outlook

ME systems and their relation to Industry 4.0 were presented and especially related to the c-MES standard. SAP®-ME/MII served as an example system, which represents the essential component of the "Industry 4.0 landscape" provided by the "SAP University Alliance". For this landscape, the core process propagated there was outlined; further processes can be mapped in it through their own configuration.

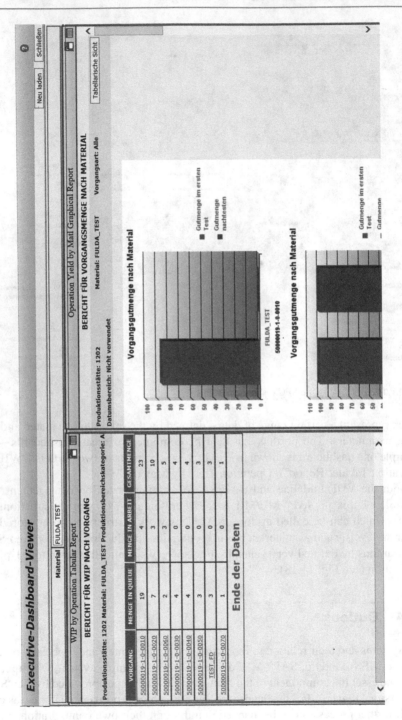

Fig. 11.17 Example of a self-defined executive dashboard

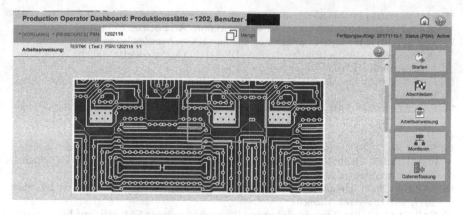

Fig. 11.18 Example of installation instructions in a POD

The number and complexity of the processes mapped there can still be increased significantly, for example if the MII system is included even more in the process definitions. One example would be a stronger interaction with surrounding systems and improved monitoring/dashboarding.

References

1. Kletti (2007) Konzeption und Einführung von MES-Systemen: zielorientierte Einführungsstrategie mit Wirtschaftlichkeitsbetrachtungen, Fallbeispielen und Checklisten. Springer, Berlin/Heidelberg
2. Kletti J (2015) MES – Manufacturing Execution System (Moderne Informationstechnologie unterstützt die Wertschöpfung), 2. Aufl. Springer, Berlin/Heidelberg
3. Louis P (2009) Manufacturing Execution Systems – Grundlagen und Auswahl, Gabler Edition Wissenschaft. Gabler, Wiesbaden
4. Müller S (2015) Manufacturing Execution Systeme – Status Quo, zukünftige Relevanz und Ausblick in Richtung Industrie 4.0. Books on Demand, Norderstedt
5. MESA (2004) Next generation collaborative Mes model, MESA white paper 8, 5.2004. MESA, Chandler
6. Brandl (2008) What is ISA-95? Industrial best practices of manufacturing information technologies with ISA-95 models präsentation. http://industrialautomation.wikia.com/wiki/ISA-95/
7. Vogel-Heuser B (2014) Herausforderungen und Anforderungen aus Sicht der IT und der Automatisierungstechnik. In: Bauernhansl T, ten Hompel M, Vogel-Heuser B (Hrsg) Industrie 4.0 in Produktion, Automatisierung und Logistik. Springer, Wiesbaden, S 36–48
8. Bauernhansl (2014) Die Vierte Industrielle Revolution – Der Weg in ein wertschaffendes Produktionsparadigma. In: Bauernhansl T, ten Hompel M, Vogel-Heuser B (Hrsg) Industrie 4.0 in Produktion, Automatisierung und Logistik. Springer, Wiesbaden, S 5–35
9. RAMI (2016) Referenzarchitekturmodell Industrie 4.0 (RAMI 4.0) – Eine Einführung. http://www.plattform-i40.de/I40/Redaktion/DE/Downloads/Publikation/rami40-eine-einfuehrung.pdf/. Accessed on 05.12.2017
10. Schell O, Schmidt-Lutz V et al (2017) Industrie 4.0 mit SAP. SAP Press Rheinwerk Publishing, Bonn

11. SAP SE (2013) PP – PDC-Schnittstelle. https://help.sap.com/saphelp_erp60_sp/helpdata/de/ad/17b753128eb44ce10000000a174cb4/frameset.htm/. Accessed on 16.11.2017
12. SAP SE (2017) Production optimization interface (POI). https://help.sap.com/viewer/fc2dff-c8238e4ce681c3496d5c1e0810/6.04.19/de-DE/811ebf53d25ab64ce10000000a174cb4.html/. Accessed on 16.11.2017
13. Jash S (2016) Implementing SAP manufacturing execution. Rheinwerk Publishing, Bonn/Boston
14. SAP SE (2017) SAP plant connectivity. https://help.sap.com/viewer/c90214be0d934eb-db6f3bce29c63c0ff/15.1.4/en-US/46a00344d44852b7e10000000a155369.html/. Accessed on 21.11.2017
15. SAP SE (2017) Setting up routing scripts. https://help.sap.com/doc/saphelp_me151/15.1.3VERSIONFORSAPME/en-US/7d/a880ae4c8e4dcc951366917f500a7f/frame-set.htm/. Accessed on 23.11.2017
16. SAP UA (2017) Introduction to industrie 4.0 – preparing orders in ERP, version 1.4, May 2017, SAP University Alliance
17. SAP UA (2017) Introduction to industrie 4.0 – production using SAP-ME (part 1 und 2), version 1.4, May 2017, SAP University Alliance

Part VI

Analysis and Optimisation of Customer Interaction

Analysis of Travel Blogs Or: What Can We Learn About Traveller Behaviour From Travelogues?

12

Marco Graf and Thomas Barton

Abstract

This paper deals with the analysis of unstructured data. It shows how travel blogs of an online platform can be analyzed. The travel blogs are stored in the document-based NoSQL database MongoDB. In order to be able to draw conclusions about regional and supra-regional issues on the basis of user-generated content, a geo-based analysis is carried out. The basis for this analysis is an aggregation framework. This paper exemplifies how a geo-based analysis of travel blogs can be performed. Typical questions are: How many travel blogs are available in a given holiday region? Which conclusions can be drawn from travel blogs for a certain holiday region?

12.1 Introduction

When traveling, people relax, experience adventures, get to know new countries and customs, acquire new knowledge and expand their own horizons. Modern technologies from the IT sector have led to travellers not only preparing and following up their trips via various websites, but also documenting their holiday experiences while travelling and sharing them with others. This is now easily possible from anywhere. In this way, travelers today are very much actively participating themselves in generating new content rather than just consuming information. This behavior leads to a huge amount of so-called user-generated content (UGC) on the

M. Graf · T. Barton (✉)
University of Applied Sciences Worms, Worms, Germany
e-mail: barton@hs-worms.de

T. Barton et al. (eds.), *Digitalization in companies*,
https://doi.org/10.1007/978-3-658-39094-5_12

web. Vacationers record their experiences on site with the help of various apps, often in the form of a travel blog or travel diary, and often share this information with other vacationers. These private travelogues contain a large amount of interesting information and facts, especially location-related information such as specific attractions (e.g. Golden Gate Bridge), styles (e.g. beach, history) and activities (e.g. diving, surfing) [1]. As a result, a large amount of information is available about different destinations, attractions, or even travel behavior, mostly in an unstructured way [2, 3]. With the rise of tourism and Web 2.0 technologies, more and more people are willing to record and share their travel experiences in weblogs, forums or travel communities in the form of textual travelogues, photos and videos taken during their trips. In order to use this information for planning a trip, the data from many different users must be aggregated and analyzed in a suitable form. Here, the information from location-based data should also be used for analysis purposes. Thus, questions such as "Which excursion is interesting locally" (e.g. national park XY near city XY) can be answered. The combination of both, the large unstructured data sets in combination with location-based information, allows to provide valuable information to travelers. Location-based information in travel reports can greatly help other travelers plan their trip if this information is extracted in an appropriate form and presented in a summarized manner. Since travel-related content not only underlies communities and social networks among travelers, but also provides rich travel-related information to other users, the use of user-generated content holds great potential. Since most travel stories are in unstructured form, and also contain a lot of information that is unnecessary for the actual research question, and important information is often spread across multiple stories, it is difficult for ordinary users to use this knowledge effectively. On the one hand, an aggregated view of information from many different contents must be possible, and on the other hand, it should focus on relevant contents of the research question in order to extract location-based knowledge from a large collection of travel reports [1, 4].

12.2 Travel Blogs

A popular and frequently used tool for recording and sharing travel information and experiences are so-called travel blogs. Via private travel blogs, users can create content in text, video or image form free of any specifications and share it with other users, similar to a digitalized diary. In contrast to services such as rating or information platforms, the information from travel blogs is not available in a structured way. Information that can be helpful for travel planning is often spread across different travel blogs and posts. Not every post to a blog contains useful information or facts that are actually helpful for travel planning. It is difficult and time-consuming for users to collect and structure all this information from different blogs and posts. This raises the question whether private travel blogs can have an impact on the choice of travel destinations and travel planning.

Does aggregated information from travel blogs really add value to travel planning and can it influence travelers' decisions? What information on travel destinations and holidaymakers' behaviour can be derived from travel blogs? This raises the question of how information from travel blogs has to be processed in a suitable form in order to derive conclusions about behaviour or even predictions about certain travel destinations. In order to use travel blogs meaningfully and efficiently for travel planning and to obtain information for certain regions or travel destinations, the content must be prepared and analyzed in an appropriate manner.

12.3   Modern Technologies for Data Storage and Analysis

In the world of database technologies, there are two main types of databases, SQL and NoSQL, also known as relational databases and databases, which are not only relational. These databases differ, among other things, in their structure, the type of information they store and how this information is held and retrieved in the database. Relational databases represent and store data in a strictly structured manner in tables, columns, and rows of a database. Thus, the database stores its relations as tables on a row-by-row basis. Each column has a fixed data type. Fields of a table can be defined to keys and indexes for quick access. There are different types of NoSQL databases such as key-value databases, column-store or wide-column store, document databases and graph databases. Generally speaking, the goal of all NoSQL databases is to map the huge amounts of rapidly growing unstructured data in the web environment into an appropriate database and also make it easily scalable. NoSQL database systems therefore offer flexible or even schema-free storage of data without the kind of "referential integrity" that is present in relational databases. The data within a NoSQL structure is highly denormalized and, in its original form, does not allow SQL operations such as JOIN or GROUP-BY statements [5]. For example, the NoSQL database MongoDB provides partially schema-less document-based management. When using a MongoDB, the database itself, collections as well as the documents of a collection have to be considered. Thus, a MongoDB process can manage multiple databases, which in turn are considered individually and can be configured accordingly. Each database consists of a set of collections, which is comparable to the table of a relational database. A collection consists of a number of documents. A document is comparable to the row of an SQL structure. It contains an arbitrary number of key-value pairs in JSON format. However, the structure of a JSON document does not have to follow a uniform schema. That is, values of the same key can have different data types [6]. Using MongoDB's built-in aggregation framework, arbitrary data sets can be processed and the computed results are returned. Aggregation operations combine values from multiple documents and can perform a variety of operations on this grouped data to produce a single result. MongoDB provides three different ways of aggregation, the aggregation pipeline, the map reduction function, and single purpose aggregation methods. The aggregation operations are therefore well suited for analysis purposes where the data needs to be summarized or grouped. The following Fig. 12.1 shows the JSON document used for a trip report.

```
// Posts
{
  "_id": ObjectId("12011"),
  "post_meta": {
    "country": "US",
    "city": "Miami",
    "latlng": [ -73.856077, 40.848447 ],
    "likes": 11,
    "type": "travel report",
    "lang": "de"
  },
  "post_status": "publish",
  "post_content": "Lorem ipsum dolor sit amet, consetetur sadipscing elitr, sed diam nonum
  "post_title": "Lorem Ipsum",
  "post_user": { "$ref": "user", "$id" : ObjectId("11007"), "$db" : "bicore"},
  "post_blog": { "$ref": "blogs", "$id" : ObjectId("12034"), "$db" : "bicore"},
  "post_date": { "$date": 1393804800000 },
  "post_modified": { "$date": 1393804800000 },
  "post_comments": [
    { "date": { "$date": 1393804800000 }, "content": "Lorem ipsum dolor sit amet, consetet
    { "date": { "$date": 1393804800000 }, "content": "Lorem ipsum dolor sit amet, consetet
    { "date": { "$date": 1393804800000 }, "content": "Lorem ipsum dolor sit amet, consetet
  ],
  "post_url": "https://traveloca.com/somepost.html"
}
```

Fig. 12.1 Example of a document for a travel report

The visualization of the data and information is done using a self-developed tool. The tool allows queries to be sent to MongoDB in text form and the returned data to be visualized as bar charts, graphs or pie charts as well as on maps.

12.4 Analysis of Travel Blogs

In the following, the blogging service Traveloca.com [7], a provider for private travel blogs, is used as an example for the analysis of travel blogs. At Traveloca, users can write their own travelogues online as well as via app for iOS and Android and share them on their travel blog. A travelogue consists of a title as well as text, photos or videos and can be tagged with a location. Users then receive a clear map of the world on which their travel reports are displayed. Other users of the platform can use the search function to look for travel reports on keywords or from specific regions and thus obtain information from many individual contributions. However, it is hardly possible for the user to display information from many posts in an aggregated form. Therefore, the goal of this paper is to filter out information of interest to tourists from the mass of articles and present it accordingly. For this purpose a NoSQL database is used, in which all data about the travel reports are contained in documents of the database. In this article only a part of the data available at Traveloca is evaluated. Geographical information, as it often occurs in the travel sector, is usually displayed on maps. The visualization on maps has the advantage that it is quite easy to draw conclusions about questions concerning certain regions and areas. In order to visualize a multitude of data on one map, so-called thematic maps are used. In contrast to reference maps, which reference exactly "where something is", thematic maps show "how something is". This means that reference maps can refer-ence, for example, every single travelogue on a blog on a map. Thematic maps, on the other hand, don't show the individual travelogue. They pull in attributes or sta-tistics about a site and present that data in an abstracted way in the form of a map. This type of representation allows for a better understanding of the relationships between location and spatial patterns in the data. There are a number of visualiza-tion techniques and thematic map types. Each of these types differs according to the type of data and type of spatial analysis. For example, the type of information rep-resentation used to study travel routes and movement profiles in a particular area require a different representation than the analysis of popular travel destinations [8].

• Choropleth maps are one of the most commonly used map types. The most impor-tant aspect of these maps is their coloring. A color scale is assigned to the numerical data which is to be visualized on the map (e.g., light green for few records and dark green for many records). The color equivalent for each region is used to colorize that region.

- Choropleth maps usually use political boundaries as regions. However, it is also possible to define your own boundaries. This type of map is quite easy to under-stand, but often leads to some perception problems.
- Heat maps represent the intensity of occurrence of an event within a data set. A heat map uses color to represent intensity. Unlike a choropleth map, a heat map does not use geographic or geopolitical boundaries to group data.
- Proportional symbol maps typically use circles or other simple shapes centered on each region. The map type can represent data tied to a specific geographic point or data aggregated to a point from a larger area.
- Dot density maps use a dot to represent a feature or attribute in your data. Dot density maps can describe "one-to-one" relationships, where each dot represents a single occurrence or data point, or they can represent "one-to-many" relation-ships, where each dot represents a set of aggregated data.

In order to initially limit the analyses to one country, it is useful to create a query about the most popular travel destinations on Traveloca. An aggregation query makes it possible to identify those countries that contain the most travel reviews. In this case, the number of travel reviews serves as an indicator of which destinations are popular with travelers. For this purpose, first all posts are scanned and their country identifier is read. In a second step, the country identifier assigned to the post is set as the ID for a new document structure and a value "count" is added for each identifier. The aggregation query then returns a JSON string containing the country identifier as ID and the number of posts as value "count".

Structure = {_id: „DE": „count": 10000, _id: „US": „count": 11000, _id: „AU": „count": 12000}

The JSON string can then be easily visualized in the form of a choropleth map.

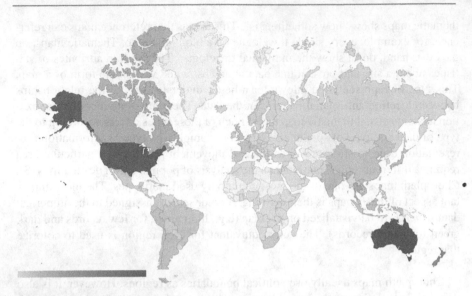

Fig. 12.2 Worldwide distribution of contributions

Figure 12.2 shows that especially New Zealand, Australia and the USA seem to be popular destinations. This analysis can still be filtered by the travellers' country of origin or the time of travel. However, the query is well suited to obtain a general overview of the popular travel destinations.

12.5   New Zealand As a Destination

A survey conducted by the "INITIATIVE Auslandszeit" from May to July 2017 concludes that especially New Zealand and Australia are popular destinations for young backpackers and "work and travel" stays [9]. Therefore, we choose New Zealand for the research conducted in the following. New Zealand as a destination offers many interesting sights that can be well analyzed geographically. The landscape of New Zealand is characterized by coasts, lakes and fjords, high mountains and glaciers, volcanoes and hot springs as well as their national parks on North and South Island. In addition, analyses can be carried out on the travel season and popular destinations such as Rotorua, the Waitomo Caves, the Coromandel Peninsula or the Fjordland with the Milford Sound.

12.5.1 Example Travel Blog

An example of a travel blog from New Zealand is the blog according to Fig. 12.3. This travel blog contained 26 travel reports from New Zealand and a detailed map of the travel route. Users can view travelogues using the reference map or the so-called blog feed.

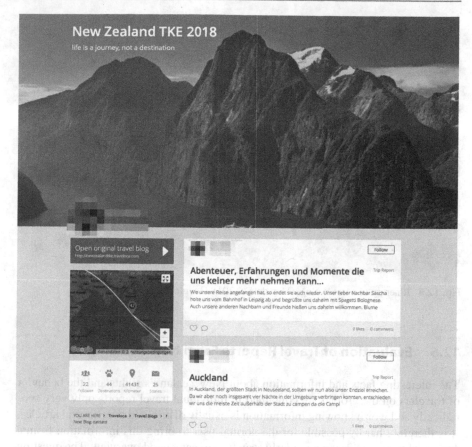

Fig. 12.3 Example of a travel blog

12.5.2 Destinations, Travel Distance, Map

Some information can already be gathered very easily from the posts and metadata of the travel blog. For example, the travel destinations can be read from the map or the blog feed. The travel route can also be clearly displayed on a map, as shown in Fig. 12.4. The route covers the North Island and the South Island of New Zealand. In the process, 44 destinations were visited and a total distance of 41,431 km was covered. The distance is determined by the destinations. Each destination is stored with a date and latitude and longitude information. The information is stored in a MyISAM table of geometry data type and a SPATIAL index is created to these points. Then the distance between two points can be determined using the MBRContains() function.

However, these are only excerpts from a travel blog with a comparatively small number of travel reports. However, in order to obtain general and touristically valuable information for the travel destination New Zealand, analyses are needed that are based on the data of many different blogs and travel reports.

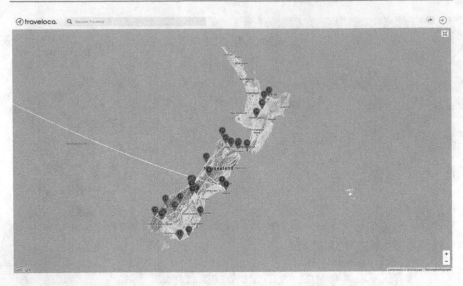

Fig. 12.4 Itinerary of a travel blog. (Map data © 2018 Google)

12.6   Evaluation of Travel Reports From New Zealand

The interesting facts and information about New Zealand's sights and the behavior of travelers on the ground are contained in individual travel reports only very sporadically and worth knowing information is usually distributed over several articles. It is therefore hardly possible for the normal user to bring this information from a variety of travel reports in an orderly structure to get a good overview. The question of the most popular travel time or the tourist hotspots, for example, can hardly be determined from the information of a few individual blogs. However, a large number of travelogues can serve as a promising resource for travel-related information, which is additionally complemented by user-generated photos and videos. Travelogues cover various travel-related aspects that can be informative for other tourists. Besides descriptive information, which can also be reflected by photos, additional contextual information such as the story behind a place, cultural info or tips are provided. With this plenty of information, travelogues could support a more comprehensive location description and location comparisons. Despite the large amount of structured travel information offered by various travel websites and online travel agencies, many travelers prefer to get experiences and advice from other travelers. Travel blogs and reviews complement the structured travel information provided by many companies with unstructured and personal descriptions, places and sights. In this section, we analyze some interesting facts about New Zealand as a travel destination using travelogues on a travel blog platform. Here, the data from MongoDB are used as a basis to extract information about New Zealand using various aggregation queries. The information obtained will show how it is possible to use many travelogues to create various analyses that contain valuable information for the user. Where possible, this data can be visualised using thematic maps.

12.6.1 Results

First, we will look at travel reviews in general. On a travel blog platform, each active user writes on average a certain number of travel reviews per week. Taking this average number of posts as a basis, the number of travel reviews in relation to certain criteria such as year or month can be an indication of the popularity of the destination at certain time periods.

12.6.1.1 Year, Development Over Time

Using the aggregation framework (see Fig. 12.5), the travel reports can be grouped by year. The query is narrowed down to posts from New Zealand (NZ) starting in 2012 ($gte: 2012) using the "$match" operator. The number of posts is grouped based on the year of publication and returned as a JSON string. Using the MongoDB operators "$year" and "$month", dates stored in the Date() format can be easily evaluated by year or month.

The returned JSON string can be visualized well with the help of a graph. The graph shows that the number of travel reports in New Zealand fluctuates per year, but always increases on average (see Fig. 12.6). On the one hand, this increase confirms the New Zealand Government's "International arrivals and departures" statistics, which show a significant increase from year to year [10]. On the other hand, this state of affairs may also be partly due to the growth of the traveloca community, as a larger number of bloggers also make more contributions.

12.6.1.2 Season

Also of interest is the time of the year when more users visit New Zealand. Unlike common travel destinations such as Italy, Spain or France, where the summer months are usually considered the main travel season, such statements cannot be made across the board for New Zealand. However, the most popular travel time for a rather abstract destination such as New Zealand can also be narrowed down using

```
db.posts.aggregate([
    { $project: { "post_meta.country": 1, "year": { $year: '$post_date' } } },
    { $match: {
            "post_meta.country": "NZ",
            "year" : { $gte : 2012 }
    } },
    { $group: { _id: "$year", total_posts: { $sum: 1 } } },
    { $sort: { _id: -1} }
])
```

Fig. 12.5 Example of an aggregation framework query

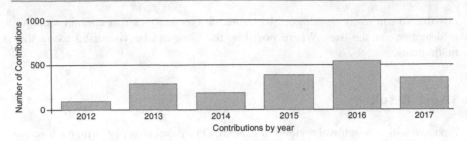

Fig. 12.6 Travel reports by year of publication

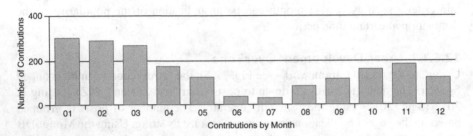

Fig. 12.7 Travel reports by month of publication

travel blog data. As before, a query is performed using the aggregation framework. In doing so, the operator "$year" is replaced with "$month". The travel reports are returned cumulatively per month (1–12) since 2012.

The analysis from Fig. 12.7 shows a clearly wave-like structure. It is precisely in the winter and spring months that most travel reports can be found. Only a few travel reports can be seen over the summer months. This analysis suggests that the beginning of the year is when most travelers visit New Zealand. During the months of April to around August, New Zealand as a travel destination seems to be less popular. Then towards the end of the year the number of travellers increases again. Comparing this graph with a climate table of New Zealand (Auckland), it can be seen that this trend is related to the climate there.

As can be seen in Fig. 12.8, temperatures are on average higher and rainy days much lower in the winter and spring months. Sunshine hours also vary between 8 h in the spring months and 4 h in the middle of the year, which corresponds quite closely to the travel months analysed.

12.6.1.3 Posts by Blogger Language

Another important aspect is the language of the travelogues. On the one hand, they give a first rough indication of where the travellers come from, on the other hand, this is also valuable information for the usefulness of the reports. If, for example, there are only a few travel reports in German, it is very likely that no informative analyses will be possible in this language. The language information is contained in the database in the metadata of the travel reports as language code. These can be also read out via an aggregation query.

	Jan	Feb	Marc	Apr	May	Jun	Jul	Aug	Sep	Oct	Nov	Dec
Maximum-Temperature	23°	22°	22°	20°	17°	16°	15°	15°	16°	18°	19°	21°
Minimum-Temperature	16°	15°	15°	14°	11°	9°	8°	7°	9°	11°	13°	14°
Sun-Hours	8h	7h	6h	5h	4h	4h	4h	5h	6h	6h	7h	7h
Water-Temperature	19°	20°	20°	19°	18°	17°	16°	15°	15°	16°	16°	17°
Reg entage	9	10	10	12	13	15	13	13	13	11	10	9

Fig. 12.8 Climate table New Zealand

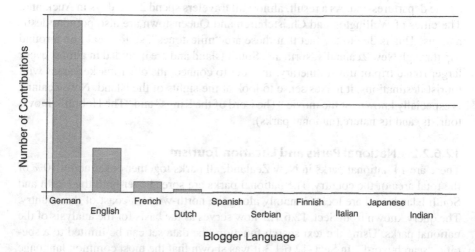

Fig. 12.9 Contributions by language

In Fig. 12.9 it can be seen that there are mainly contributions from travellers from German and English-speaking countries. French and Dutch are also represented to a lesser extent. Above all, it can be seen that, overall, a large proportion of travellers come from the European region. This is quite easily explained by the increasingly popular "Work & Travel" and backpacker tourists, who often spend a longer time abroad in the European region directly after graduating from high school or school. Popular destinations for this are, as mentioned above, especially Australia and New Zealand.

12.6.2 Distribution of Bloggers

Now the destinations and itineraries of New Zealand are considered. For this purpose, all travel reports from New Zealand are read with their latitude (lat) and longitude (lng) information using the aggregation framework. The lat and lng information gives the exact location of the post, in the form of GPS coordinates. This information can be visualized in the form of a heat map. The individual data points or contributions do not play a role here, but only the overall distribution of the contributions.

The heat map (see Fig. 12.10) shows green, yellow and red areas. It shows all coordinates of the contributions on the map and the amount of records in a certain geographical area, from red very many to green few records.

12.6.2.1 Explanations on the Distribution of Bloggers on the Island

At first glance, this distribution of travel reports is difficult to explain. However, one thing is immediately noticeable, in Auckland very many travel reports were published, because by the Auckland Airport in this area many trips begin and likewise by the departures end. As a result, almost all travelers spend 2 to 3 days in Auckland. The cities of Wellington and Christchurch and Queenstown are also popular destinations. This is due to the fact that these are "milestones", so to speak, on a round trip through New Zealand's North and South Island and are included in almost every larger round trip or travel itinerary. In order to connect the other marked areas with tourist destinations, it makes sense to look at the sights of the island. New Zealand is especially known for the movie "The Lord of the Rings" and "The Hobbit" (movie tourists) and its nature (national parks).

12.6.2.2 National Parks and Location Tourism

There are 14 national parks in New Zealand, all parks together cover about 10% of the total area of the country. The national parks are spread over both the North and South Islands and are located mainly along the north-western coast of the country. The query known from Sect. 12.6.1.2. now serves as the basis for the analysis of the national parks. Using the text search function, the data set can be limited to a specific "search word". In Sect. 12.6.1.3 it was shown that the most common language is German. It is therefore appropriate to use the keyword "Nationalpark" (german

Fig. 12.10 Heatmap depicting travelogues in New Zealand. (Map data © 2018 Google)

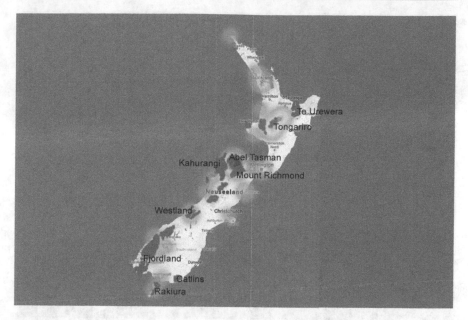

Fig. 12.11 Trip reports with the keyword "Nationalpark". (Map data © 2018 Google)

translation for national park) for this analysis. All posts containing this word are visualized again using a heat map.

To simplify the visualization, the national parks in Fig. 12.11 have been highlighted in blue on the map. The geographical data for the individual national parks was taken from the New Zealand Government [11] and placed on a new layer of the map. This layer overlays the actual map and enriches it with information about the national parks, which can then be displayed in colour. It can be seen that especially the national parks "Tongariro", "Abel Tasman" are very popular among travelers in the region. The national parks "Te Urewera" and "Catlins", on the other hand, enjoy little or hardly any popularity among tourists, as very few or no travel reports have been published here. The yellow areas in Wellington and Auckland can be explained by the fact that travellers first reported about national parks when they were back in the cities.

The film locations of the movies "Der Herr der Ringe" (german translation for "The Lord of the Rings") and "Der Hobbit" (german translation for "The Hobbit") can also be analyzed. For this purpose, further search words such can be selected for the text search analysis. For a better representation, the film locations in Fig. 12.12 have been marked in blue again.

12.7 Summary

The analysis of unstructured data is demonstrated using travel blogs about New Zealand. The travel blogs originate from one online platform. In order to be able to draw conclusions about travel behavior on the basis of this data, a geo-based

Fig. 12.12 Travelogues with the keyword "Der Herr der Ringe". (Map data © 2018 Google)

analysis and visualization has been carried out. NoSQL technologies are used for this purpose. The described approach allows general analyses of travel blogs and travel reports and shows how it is possible to obtain informative and location-based information based on a larger number of travel blogs. Travelers can use this information for their own travel planning and actively contribute to generating new data by creating UGC themselves. The analysis and visualization of travel blogs can be used to make travelers' experiences visible. Initial results confirm that the destination of New Zealand travellers is often national parks, with filming locations of the movies "Lord of the Rings" or "The Hobbit" also being visited.

12.8 Update and Outlook

Travel reports about other countries have been analyzed and visualized using different approaches. The findings for Thailand are described in [12]. The results for travel reports about the United States of America are published in [13]. In order to identify destinations, which are visited subsequently, Bayesian statistics has been used in a later study [14]. Travel destinations and both their predecessors and their successors are analyzed there, where an evaluation starts on the level of a country and ends on the level of a region. Experiences show, that Artificial Intelligence methods have become a matter of special importance.

In order to be able to use information optimally both for the planning of destinations and for that of travellers, the textual information in particular must be analysed more extensively. If aggregates of tourist information are combined with location-related information, the use of contextual content in relation to the geographical information can improve travelling enormously.

References

1. Hao Q, Cai R, Wang C, Xiao R, Yang J-M, Pang Y, Zhang L (2010) Equip tourists with knowledge mined from travelogues. Tianjin University/Microsoft Research Asia, Tianjin/Beijing
2. Barton T, Graf M (2016) Architektur, Funktionen und User Interface einer Cloud-basierten Anwendung für Reiseblogging. HMD Praxis der Wirtschaftsinformatik 53(5):712–720
3. Bundesministerium für Wirtschaft und Klimaschutz (n.d.) Dossier Digitalisierung. https://www.bmwi.de/Redaktion/DE/Dossier/digitalisierung.html. Accessed 6 March 2024
4. Yuan H, Xu H, Qian Y, Li Y (2016) Make your travel smarter: summarizing urban tourism information from massive blog data. Int J Inf Manag 36(6):1306–1319. China
5. Meier A, Kaufmann M (2016) SQL- & NoSQL-Datenbanken. Springer, Heidelberg
6. Graf M, Barton, T (2017) Einsatz einer NoSQL-Datenbank zur Analyse von Reiseblogs: Konzept und Integration. In: Barton T, Herrmann F, Meister VG, Müller C, Seel C (Eds.) Prozesse, Technologie, Anwendungen, Systeme und Management 2017: Angewandte Forschung in der Wirtschaftsinformatik, 1. Aufl. Mana-Buch, Heide, 104–112
7. Traveloca was a travel blog platform, which had been closed in 2020. https://Traveloca.com/. Accessed 6 March 2024
8. Peterson GN (2014) GIS cartography: a guide to effective map design. Apple Academic Press Inc, Ontario. (2 new edition)
9. Statista (2019) Welches Land favorisierst du für deinen work and travel Aufenthalt? https://de.statista.com/statistik/daten/studie/748079/umfrage/beliebteste-laender-fuer-einen-work-and-travel-aufenthalt-der-deutschen/. Accessed 6 March 2024
10. New Zealand Government (2013) International travel and migration: December 2013. http://archive.stats.govt.nz/browse_for_stats/population/Migration/IntTravelAndMigration_HOTPDec13/Commentary.aspx. Accessed 25 Jan 2018. The website archive.stats.govt.nz has been closed in the meantime
11. New Zealand Government: New Zealand's national parks contain some of our most treasured wilderness areas. https://www.doc.govt.nz/parks-and-recreation/places-to-go/national-parks/. Accessed 6 March 2024
12. Barton T, Graf M, Özünlü F (2020) Analysis and visualization of travel blogs by means of NoSQL techniques: set up and results. In: Böhm S, Suntrayuth S (eds) Proceedings of the IWEMB 2019: third international workshop on entrepreneurship in electronic and mobile business. PubliQation, Norderstedt, pp 9–18
13. Özünlü F, Barton T (2019) Geobasierte Analyse von Reiseberichten aus den USA. In: Wof MR, Barton T, Herrmann F, Meister VG, Müller C (eds) Angewandte Forschung in der Wirtschaftsinformatik 2019. mana-Buch, Heide, pp 95–105
14. Barton T, Peuker A (2024) Analysis of travel blogs by means of bayesian statistics: first insights for destinations in Australia and New Zealand. In: Böhm S, Suntrayuth S (Eds) Proceedings of the IWEMB 2020 and 2021: fourth international workshop on entrepreneurship in electronic and mobile business, to be published

Optimization of Customer Interaction in Online Wine Trade Using the Example of the VICAMPO iOS App

13

Karsten Würth and Thomas Barton

Abstract

This chapter describes how the use of an online shop can not only be simplified by a mobile app, but how customer interaction can be significantly increased at the same time. The simplification from a customer's point of view is illustrated by different functions like recommendations, offers, rating of wines, reordering of wines as well as the check-out. An increase in the frequency of interaction is achieved through the use of so-called push notifications. The importance of a modern interaction design in a mobile environment is exemplified in the article as well as the use of a modern software architecture using a RESTful API. The implementation of the developed VICAMPO iOS app is done as a Minimum Viable Product (MVP), which convinces the customer by simplicity and clarity and at the same time offers clear advantages for developers, because the complexity of the application is kept as low as possible.

13.1 The VICAMPO App

The Vicampo.de GmbH, an online wine retailer from Mainz, has developed an app for existing customers. For this purpose, a "Minimum Viable Product" (MVP) was created. An MVP is a product that fulfills the minimum requirements of the market. It is therefore competitive, but only offers a very limited range of features. However,

K. Würth (✉)
VICAMPO.de GmbH, Mainz, Deutschland
e-mail: karsten@karstenwuerth.com

T. Barton
Worms University of Applied Sciences, Worms, Germany
e-mail: barton@hs-worms.de

© The Author(s), under exclusive license to Springer Fachmedien Wiesbaden GmbH, part of Springer Nature 2024
T. Barton et al. (eds.), *Digitalization in companies*,
https://doi.org/10.1007/978-3-658-39094-5_13

this should be sufficient for the launch and enables a quick release with as little development effort as possible. The VICAMPO app offers three main functions:

1. Recommendations

Wine recommendations, matching the purchases of the customer

2. Current offers

Offers, matching the purchases of the customer

3. My wines

A list of wines already purchased by the customer

As shown in Fig. 13.1, all main features can be accessed with the TabBar located at the bottom of the screen. In this way, the user can quickly switch between the areas while having the most important functions always in view. Additionally badges (visible in the tab bar on the far left) can be used to draw the user's attention to a specific area. Some of these main areas combine several pages of the homepage. In the Offers view, for example, the user can find all offers from different landing pages (white wine, red wine, mixed) at a glance. This provides a significantely larger amount of products, which can be refined with filters individually so the customer keeps a clear overview. In the personal wine shelf "My Wines", numerous customer-specific functions have been merged. The user finds his purchased wines there and

Fig. 13.1 The main functions of the VICAMPO app

thus a kind of order history. Mixed packages are already divided into their individual wines, so that the user directly receives his individual post-purchase offer for each product and with only one more click, he directly gets to the evaluation of it. In addition to a much better overview, the general use of the rating feature can be increased, which ultimately gives other customers more meaningful opinions on the wines and generates more content for the shop. This means that four functions, which are divided into several pages on the homepage, could be united in one screen. Besides the main areas, the app includes further indispensable components of an e-commerce app, like a shopping cart or the check-out, where the user finally completes the purchase by specifying address and payment method. All in all, the MVP initially provides access to features that are particularly useful on the move. These are implemented on around 35 screens, which access 22 API endpoints. More functions will subsequently be delivered with updates.

13.2   RESTful API in the Mobile Environment

Nowadays, apps exist for the most diverse purposes, in countless designs and very diverse target groups. But what (almost) all of them have in common is the communication with a server. Whether synchronizing contacts, loading the latest recipes, or saving a game score, the data of all these interactions are rarely stored locally on the executing device, but are synchronized with a server. On the one hand, this saves storage space on the device, and on the other hand, the data is stored securely and can be made available to other services (e.g. a homepage). In this way, the user can use his applications on a wide variety of devices and no longer has to worry about porting the data. For this communication between server and client, the RESTful API is one of the most popular methods. It uses the standard HTTP methods GET, POST, OPTIONS, HEAD, DELETE, TRACE and CONNECT for data exchange. For using such a RESTful API in the mobile environment, developers should pay attention to some specifics [1]. An introduction to RESTful services in the context of applied business informatics can be found in [2].

13.2.1 JSON Instead of XML

Today JSON has largely replaced XML in the area of data transmission. The data format offers various advantages, where one of the most important is undoubtedly the saving in data volume. Due to its simple syntax, savings of up to 60% [3] are possible using JSON, depending on the XML notation. In the mobile sector, this topic may have lost importance due to advances such as the LTE and 5G, but due to still very low volume tariffs, this point is not negligible, at least in Germany. But not only the data volume decreases, also the processing time on devices is significantly lower. In a test by Infragistics, a 1.3 MB file in JSON format was processed about 1 s faster than its XML counterpart of the same size [4].

13.2.2 HTTPS Instead of HTTP

Mobile apps are often used in unsecure mobile networks, hotspots or similar. The user usually does not know the operator of the access point and its users, nor whether they are trustworthy. It is therefore very important in the mobile environment that all endpoints use an encrypted HTTPS connection in order to protect the data of the user, but also of the operator of the API. The WPA2 security vulnerability KRACK [5] illustrates the importance of this point.

13.2.3 Servers Do Most of the Work

Data volume and battery life are probably the least favorite topics of smartphone users. In the development of mobile apps it is therefore all the more important that as little work as possible is done on the device. On the one hand, only data that is needed in the app should be transmitted from the server: This means that the API user should be able to limit the output by a filter. On the other hand, the transmitted data should be ready for use. Complicated filtering and sorting options, calculations, data aggregations, or a search, for instance, should be implemented on the server side. With the help of pagination, data output can be further limited so that the user has full control over which and how many records he wants to receive. Moving the work from the device to the server also benefits developers. For example, these operations no longer have to be implemented for different platforms such as iOS or Android, but both systems can access the finished data of the API and only have to output it.

13.2.4 Versioning Is Clearly More Important

Since app users update their apps at very different frequencies (or not), API versioning plays a much more important role in the mobile app context than in other, more controllable use cases. So it's not uncommon for users to have installed an outdated version of the app instead of the latest one, even after several months. These cases need to be considered and taken care off. It is therefore imperative that the API can respond to requests of the latest version as well as for requests of deprecated versions. However, at a certain point, support can be more of a hassle than a benefit. The app should be prepared for this situation and able to show an inevitable update screen for example.

13.3 User Interface and Design

When users interact with an application, visual feedback is very helpful. Especially if the target group of the application does not belong to the digital natives. The ripple effect is one of these supporting elements. It is part of the Material Design motion

Fig. 13.2 Ripple effect

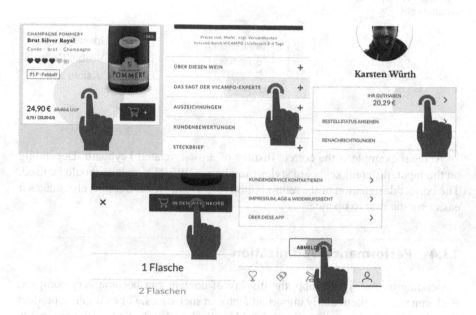

Fig. 13.3 Examples of the use of the ripple effect in the VICAMPO app

concept [6], which was first introduced at Google's developer conference I/O in 2014 and has received a lot of attention since then. The Ripple effect in particular is modeled after a wave and represents a circular animation that is executed as soon as the user interacts with an element. A simple example can be seen in Fig. 13.2.

In this way, it can be made clear to the user which elements are interactive and whether an interaction was successful. A selection of areas in which the ripple effect was used in the VICAMPO app can be seen in Fig. 13.3.

Furthermore, there are numerous details that simplify the usage of apps. For example, it should always be visible what is to be entered in text fields. A placeholder should not disappear completely after the first letter has been typed in. Figure 13.4 shows a text field from the VICAMPO app. Initially, only the placeholder is visible. It disappears as soon as the user starts writing. The placeholder then shows up as a label above the text field so the context is clear to the user at all times. Furthermore, it can be displayed whether the field is optional or whether an error occurred during validation.

Fig. 13.4 Text field before
and after entering text

E-Mail

E-MAIL

kars|

Fig. 13.5 Principle of
reusable cells

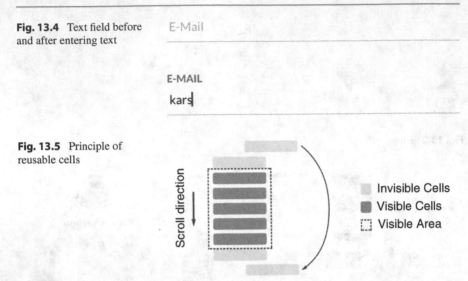

Another example is the correct display of a topic-related keyboard. Depending on the input, different keyboard styles (numbers, QWERTY, email) should be used. The correct designation of the return button (e.g. Next, Done, Submit) also makes it easier for the user to operate.

13.4 Performance Optimization

Depending on the type of app, the display of content can become very complex. Performance is a particularly important factor in such cases. For example, a product list with a lot of information, which should be displayed at the first level, can already lead to performance drops if implemented suboptimally. In native apps, the use of reusable cells is therefore indispensable (Fig. 13.5). With the help of these cells, only the elements located in the viewport as well as one cell above and one below are created. Depending on the scroll direction, the cell at the end – outside of the visual area – is then removed and placed at the beginning. With this approach, only a limited number of cells need to be instanciated, which then can be reused and filled with new content.

In addition to this technique, it is also important to ensure that all information is present when the cell is to be displayed. This means that all calculations, formatting or loading processes have been completed and the content only needs to be inserted.

13.5 Development Under iOS

The proprietary operating system iOS is used to develop the VICAMPO app. Apple makes it easy for developers to get started. There are only a handful of devices and fragmentation is usually limited to two or three of the latest versions. However, both a curse and a blessing is the rapid distribution of new iOS versions. As of September 2017, after about 1 year iOS 10 was clearly the leading iOS version with 89% [7] market share. Developers could therefore easily start developing for apps from version 10 and rarely had to worry about users of earlier versions. However, this behavior can also become a disadvantage. For a significant number of users it can quickly lead to crashes, layout issues or the like if developers do not tak into account when the release of an app is around the publication of a new iOS version. For example, iOS 11 was released in September 2017 and after just 1 day, over 16% of all users had installed the new version [8]. About a month later, the distribution was already around 56%, ahead of iOS 10 [7]. It is therefore essential to pay attention to future iOS versions during development and to consider pre-release versions for the implementation. If bugs are fixed in these early versions, a release during the period of an iOS update is usually not a problem. Another advantage of iOS development is the fact that there are no initial costs to get started. Programming takes place in the free development environment Xcode, where simulators for all common iOS devices are integrated. Only for the publication in Apples App Store or testing via Testflight an annual fee of 99 USD [9] must pe paid. The first version of the development environment came up in 2003 – at that time primarily for software that runs on OS X. It was Xcode 3 which integrated the support for iOS for the first time in 2007 in favor of the first iPhone. From this point on, developers could also make use of an integrated iPhone simulator. The programming language at that time was Objective-C. Numerous years and updates later, in 2014, Xcode is now available in version 9 and Apple introduced its own programming language called Swift. It was meant to replace Objective-C for iOS programming. Swift relies on a variety of ideas from other programming languages. Among them ideas of the predecessor Objective-C, but also concepts from Rust, Haskell, Ruby, Python, C#, CLU and many more [10]. Swift has also been open-source since 2015 [11] and releases a new version every year. Since September 2017, version 4 is available, which, for

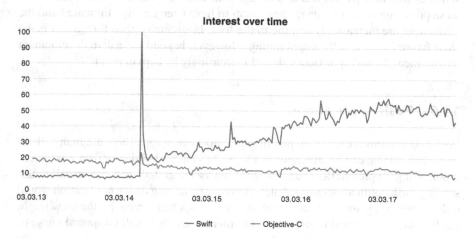

Fig. 13.6 Since release, Swift is significantly more in demand than Objective-C [15]

example, significantly improves the handling of strings and collections as well as working with the package manager [12].

The release of the first Swift version in 2014 can be clearly seen in Fig. 13.6. Since then, interest in both languages has visibly diverged. However, it is striking that interest in Swift has increased significantly more than it has decreased in the case of Objective-C. This fact can be attributed to the circumstance that many apps, but also third-party code, are written in Objective-C and the conversion is sometimes time-consuming. Many frameworks, libraries and code samples are therefore still available in this "old" language, which may also be a reason why Objective-C is still only one place behind Swift in the TIOBE index for October 2017. Also on GitHub, there is a request in Objective-C for about every second Swift pull request [13]. Swift's predecessor can therefore by no means be written off, and Swift developers must be prepared for the fact that third-party code may still be written in Objective-C. In every project, it is therefore important to carefully check which frameworks are used and in which language they are written. The integration of Objective-C frameworks into Swift projects is possible, but may require effort, which must be taken into account. In addition to interest drifting apart, Fig. 13.6 also shows that interest in Swift has stagnated in 2017. In the meanwhile it has overtaken Objective-C in the TIOBE index, but both languages have fallen four respectively seven places compared to the previous year. According to the publishers of the index, this development is due to the increasingly strong hybrid apps:

> Until recently it was quite common to program Android apps in Java and iOS apps in Swift/Objective-C. This is quite cumbersome because you have to maintain two code bases that are doing almost the same. So frameworks for mobile hybrid apps were developed and now that they have grown mature these are becoming very popular. Market leaders in this area are Microsoft's Xamarin (C#), Apache's Cordova (JavaScript) and Ionic (JavaScript). The consequences of all of this are that languages such as C# and JavaScript are gaining popularity at the cost of languages such as Java and Swift. [14]

Whereas hybrid apps still had to struggle with teething problems a few years ago, these problematic disadvantages now seem to have been largely eliminated and the advantages are increasingly coming to the fore. In summary, therefore, Swift is the clear future in native iOS programming. However, beyond the native development environment, hybrid approaches should increasingly be kept in mind.

13.6   Push Notifications

Push notifications are common practice in almost every app. There are many all-in-one solutions that can be integrated via SDK, or you can build your own implementation using Apples SDK. Once the solution is integrated, you can usually start sending push notifications immediately. However, clicking on the notification would only open the app and the user would see the last opened screen. So the view might not be related to the notification at all. In order to be able to call up special views or

Table 13.1 Open-direct URLs of the VICAMPO app

URL prefix	Function
recommendations	Calls the recommendation screen. If a product_id (with campaign_id, if applicable) is passed, a product is called within the recommendations
recommendations? **product_id=12**	
recommendations?product_id=12& **campaign_id=81**	
Offers	Calls the offers screen. If a product_id (possibly with campaign_id) is passed, a product is called within the offers
offers? **product_id=34**	
offers?product_id=34& **campaign_id=8**	
Mywines	Calls the My Wine screen. If a product_id (with campaign_id, if applicable) is passed, a product is called within the My-Wine screen
mywines? **product_id=23**	
mywines?product_id=23& **campaign_id=1**	
Profile	Calls the profile

even products, a mechanism must be implemented where a URL can be attached to the push message, which is then registered by the app and responded to appropriately. VICAMPO uses ExactTarget from SalesForce for its existing customer marketing. In addition to pure email marketing, the service also allows sending of push notifications including links. SalesForce calls it OpenDirect URLs. By working out a schema, prior defined actions can afterwards be executed in the app. In the VICAMPO iOS app, these links are introduced by the suffix "vicampoApp://". The exact action is defined with the help of the various prefixes from Table 13.1.

The corresponding behavior must be implemented in the app, after which messages can be created and automated via the user interface from Fig. 13.7.

Via the field "OpenDirect" in Fig. 13.8, the URL can be entered, which is transferred to the app. In this way, the user can be made aware, for example, that one of his wines is on sale. When opening the notification, the user is then taken directly to the product within the "My Wines" screen.

13.7 Status and Further Steps

From concept development to release, the functions and design of the VICAMPO app have always been validated through tests in collaboration with customers. This is to ensure that the functions of the app meet the expectations of the customers. Even after implementation, the app is therefore subjected to alpha and beta testing. In the alpha tests, user interactions, layouts and other functionalities are tested that

Fig. 13.7 Creating a push notification in ExactTarget

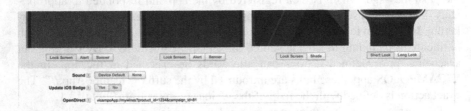

Fig. 13.8 Adding an OpenDirect URL to ExactTarget

could not be simulated by prototyping during the conceptional phase. This includes, for example, real customer-specific content, animations or transitions. So with the help of alpha testing, minor concept errors can be uncovered, which then can be corrected in the remaining time until release. With the completion of the alpha tests and the determination of the resulting changes, the feature set for version 1.0 is final. From this point on, only existing features will be tested for functionality and stability in the subsequent beta phase. After the app has reached an appropriate level of quality through extensive testing, it is published in Apples App Store and available for download since October 2017. Since the first version is an MVP, numerous future features are already fixed at this point – for example, support for additional languages. But despite the constantly growing range of functions and in order to guarantee a high level of quality as easy and efficient as possible, the app is first subjected to an extensive refactoring, which includes the integration of unit and UI tests. Through this maintenance of the code, the existing functions can then be tested automatically to the greatest possible extent, whereby release cycles are significantly shorter.

References

1. Tea M (2017) A massive guide to building a RESTful API for your mobile App. Savvy Apps. https://savvyapps.com/blog/how-to-build-restful-api-mobile-app/. Accessed 19 Nov 2017
2. Barton T (2014) Grundlagen für E-Business. In: E-Business mit Cloud Computing. IT-Professional. Springer, Wiesbaden
3. Wikimedia Foundation Inc (2021) JavaScript object notation. Wikimedia Foundation Inc. https://de.wikipedia.org/wiki/JavaScript_Object_Notation. Accessed 30 Nov 2021
4. Betts T (2016) Mobile performance testing – JSON vs XML. infragistics. https://www.infragistics.com/community/blogs/b/torrey-betts/posts/mobile-performance-testing-json-vs-xml. Accessed 30 Nov 2021
5. Geiger J (2017) Sicherheitslücke in WPA2. CHIP Digital GmbH. http://www.chip.de/news/Sicherheitsluecke-in-WPA2-Wie-Sie-Ihr-WLAN-jetzt-trotzdem-verwenden-koennen_125521601.html/. Accessed 30 Nov 2021
6. Google LLC (2021) Material motion. https://material.io/design/motion. Accessed 30 Nov 2021
7. Mixpanel (2021) Mixpanel trends. https://mixpanel.com/trends/-report/ios_11. Accessed 30 Nov 2021
8. Floemer A (2017) iOS 11 nur zwei Tage nach Release weiter verbreitet als Android 7 und 8 zusammen. yeebase media GmbH. http://t3n.de/news/ios-11-update-verbreitung-859691//. Accessed 18 Nov 2017
9. Apple Inc (2021) Choosing a membership. https://developer.apple.com/support/compare-memberships//. Accessed 30 Nov 2021
10. Lattner C (2021) Chris Lattner's Homepage. http://nondot.org/sabre//. Accessed 30 Nov 2021
11. Apple Inc (2016) Swift 2.0. https://developer.apple.com/swift/blog/?id=29/. Accessed 30 Nov 2021
12. Grüner S (2017) Swift 4 erleichtert Umgang mit Strings und Collections. Golem Media GmbH https://www.golem.de/news/apple-swift-4-erleichtert-umgang-mit-strings-und-collections-1709-130158.html/. Accessed 30 Nov 2021
13. GitHub Inc (2017) GitHub Octoverse 2017. https://octoverse.github.com//. Accessed 18 Nov 2017
14. TIOBE software BV (2017) TIOBE index. https://tiobe.com/tiobe-index//. Accessed 15 Oct 2017
15. Google LLC (2021) Google trends. https://trends.google.de/trends/explore?date=2013-03-03 2017-11-30&q=%2Fm%2F010sd4y3,%2Fm%2F05q31. Accessed 30 Nov 2021

Part VII

Opportunities and Risks in Implementation

Implementing the Digital Transformation: Digital Leadership Principles and Tools

Claudia Lemke, Kathrin Kirchner, and Walter Brenner

Abstract

Digitalisation is changing our everyday life.Digital and networked technologies are determining the current transformation in society and economy and are bringing the world into the digital age. The opportunities and risks of these technologies must be recognised, understood and used to successfully shape this change. Based on the characteristics, development stages and challenges of the so-called digital transformation, this article shows the necessary management tools for a successful business change. The focus is on the changing principles of digital leadership and associated effects on the management of organisations. The establishment of digital governance steers this cultural change and is complemented by the presentation of essential recommendations for management action. Following this, an overview of some of the central instruments for the implementation of a digital transformation is presented.

C. Lemke (✉)
Berlin School of Economics and Law, Berlin, Germany
e-mail: claudia.lemke@hwr-berlin.de

K. Kirchner
Technical University of Denmark, Kgs. Lyngby, Denmark
e-mail: kakir@dtu.dk

W. Brenner
University St. Gallen, St. Gallen, Switzerland
e-mail: walter.brenner@unisg.ch

T. Barton et al. (eds.), *Digitalization in companies*,
https://doi.org/10.1007/978-3-658-39094-5_14

14.1   Introduction

In 2017, a comparative study by the digital consultancy firm etventure [1] on the state of digitisation of companies in Germany and the USA came to the conclusion that Germany is still lagging far behind when it comes to its opportunities for digitisation. The large companies surveyed showed a need to catch up in all areas, from the importance and challenges of digitisation to the methods for implementation and creation of an adequate corporate culture. Although 50% of the German companies surveyed stated that digitisation is one of their top three topics and also a senior executive responsibility for 35% of the companies, implementation has been failing because of a number of factors. The obstacles cited include general uncertainty among employees, too few specific organisational units to assume responsibility and a lack of experience and qualifications among the workforce. A comparative look at the USA shows that only 3% of board members are responsible for digital issues, and 81% of the companies surveyed use their internal IT departments for this purpose. The advanced digital skills of 90% of employees lead to visible success in the USA, meaning that half of all US companies can already come up with concrete results in the short term.

The results of this study make it clear that once again, specific organisational questions about structures, management principles and tools are decisive for the sustainable success of digitisation in companies. Data-driven algorithms and further emerging technologies like artificial intelligence (AI) applications, blockchain technologies or cloud-based services are undoubtedly the enablers for the further digitisation of companies. However, only the organisational alignment of the entire company with the different technologically opportunities will ensure success and a sustainable impact on the business model, including its processes, products and services.

Starting from a definition, classification and systematisation of the term 'digital transformation', this book chapter outlines a set of management principles and tools that can be used to methodically realise the challenges of digital transformation.

14.2   Essence of the Digital Transformation

14.2.1 Concept and Development

The fact that we are in times of fundamental, technology-driven change is demonstrated when looking at the changed individual behaviour towards social communication and interaction through digital and networked technologies. It is this fundamental paradigm shift that has led to no longer viewing information and communication technology as a tool but as an inherent part of everyday life. These digital and networked technologies "become environmental, anthropological, social, and interpretative forces. They are creating and shaping our intellectual and physical realities, changing our self-understanding, modifying how we relate to each other and ourselves, and upgrading how we interpret the world, and all this pervasively, profoundly, and relentlessly" [2]. The changed individual behaviour in values and norms is impacting companies in an increasingly powerful way. The management has to find new ways for defining and executing the business strategy aligned with the digital and networked technologies. Additionally, companies must recreate their leadership principles, the forms of employee management as well as all management tools to ensure a sustainable and successful digital transformation. Thus, it is essential for the successful digitisation of companies to rethink and implement their cultural values and norms. Only this changed 'mindset' towards digitisation makes it possible to successfully realise actual technological challenges.

In this context, **digital transformation** can be understood as 'emblematic of all the social, political, economic and environmental profound upheavals resulting from the predominance of digitalisation and networking' [3]. The essence of digital transformation is based on the ability of hyperconnectivity through digital and networked technologies. **Hyperconnectivity** means the complete interconnection of people, organisations, and the smart objects of the Internet of Things with all imaginable combinations. That creates entirely new forms of digital or digitally interwoven products and services, forms new corporate structures and processes and redefines business models. This capability of digital and networked technologies line up various organisational and technological drivers, such as security and privacy issues, cloud computing, Internet of Things, Industry 4.0 or 'Smarter World' issues [4], as well as robotics, AI and Big Data. As a result, digital transformation is changing the entire value creation structures and networks, thus determining business models.

A closer look at the term digital transformation encompasses various dimensions and perspectives [5–8]. Fundamentally common to the various definitions is the perspective as a process of change combined [3]. Digital transformation consists of different phases that allow companies a stepwise digitalisation in terms of hyperconnectivity. Furthermore, these phases also show the different evolution stages with which the digital technologies have enterprise-wide effects.as shown in Fig. 14.1.

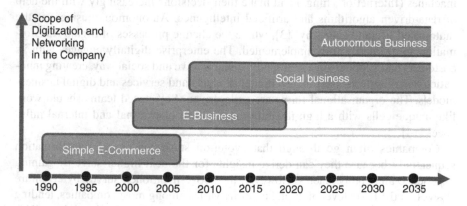

Fig. 14.1 The evolution stages of digital transformation. (Based on Lemke et al. [3])

The first stage of digital transformation evolution began with simple website creation, mostly for business reasons having a basic internet presence. For example, in 1993, there were about 130 websites, while by 1996, there were over 100,000 [9]. Companies such as Yahoo and Alta Vista started their first digital business models with the idea of searching the increasing amount of web pages. This was followed by the start-up Amazonin 1994 with the vision of online bookselling. Even at that time, there was already a discourse about the disruptive effects of such business models [10, 11], but the incumbents (still) believed in a one-hit wonder. The term e-commerce was coined during this first stage, which is generally understood as trade or the processing of transactions via the internet.

The concept of e-business (second stage in Fig. 14.1.) expanded the view of e-commerce by a technology-driven integration intothe core business processes [12]. Some leading companies established new forms of interaction and transaction with their business partners using digital marketplaces, for example, to foster the purchasing processes or to increase their sales activities, achiving competitive advantages.

Since the third stage Web 2.0 [13] has allowed companies to directly involve customers in their digitisation efforts. Customers can influence the company's business processes by participating in various social networks, via crowd sourcing or recommendation platforms. Co-creation and co-consumption are becoming the drivers of customer-centric digital business models [3]. This is what the term 'social business' stands for. Companies are increasingly recognising the necessity to consistently identify the real needs and interests of their customers. The knowledge about customer buying behaviour allows the development of customer journeys [3] for tailoring digital products and services. This knowledge can be combined with customer feedback and validated learning loops within the company to develop personalised customer experiences [7]. They guarantee that companies will successfully master this stage of digital transformation.

Autonomous business represents the pursuit of a complete fusion of the real and digital worlds of business. Companies are highly automated, produce almost completely autonomously with the help of robotics, us the capabilities for networking machines (Internet of Things) and make their decisions increasingly with the help of data-driven algorithms and artificial intelligence. Autonomous business is the 'automated life and economy' [3], where the change processes of digital transformation are primarily fully implemented. The enterprise digitally engages with its customers and suppliers in a profoundly collaborative and social way, creating innovation that manifests itself in new digital products and services and digital business models. The organisational forms are agile-driven. Self-paced teams should work like unique cells with a high flexibility in the face of external and internal influences [14].

Companies often go through that evolution stages of digital transformation sequentially because they can derive insights for the next higher stage by gaining experience and competencies. However, the above-mentioned survey by etventure shows that the basic level of digital maturity varies among most companies, tending to range between the second and third stages, as other studies also have shown [15,

16]. As before, the need to renew existing business models through digitalisation is seen only to a limited extent in established companies [17].

14.2.2 Effects of the Digital Transformation

The opportunities and risks of digital transformation act on different levels [18]. The effects are of an individual, corporate and societal nature and address the various potentials and challenges we face in the digital age. Figure 14.2 shows some examples of significant individual effects within the three levels.

14.3 Leadership Principles for Enterprise-Wide Digitalisation

14.3.1 Digital Leadership

The fundamental changes in the global economy, accompanied by the high dynamics of technological developments and the changed social behaviour of individuals and groups, present today's managers with a whole new set of challenges. In the context of digital transformation, managers need a digital-drivenskill set and new leadership qualities to successfully shape higher levels of digitalisation in the

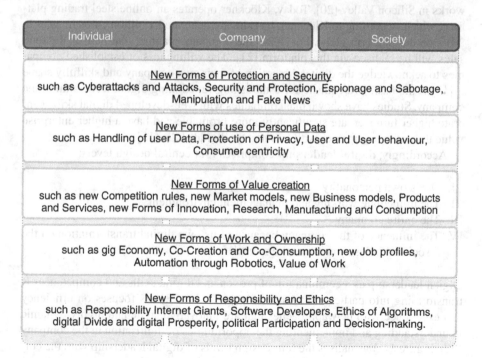

Fig. 14.2 Positive and negative effects of digital transformation

company. At its core is the ability to recognise the disruptive power of technologies and harness them for the company [14]. This disruption – or positive destruction of existing market and business structures – causes companies to fail or be reshaped precisely by technological possibilities [19]. A modern leader must apply this capability on multiple levels. The core level focuses on the profound usage of various digital tools to enhance the manager's working environment and foster the manager as a role model for a successful digital cultural change. A second level contains the leadership and management opportunities through social media insights, among other data gathering for need-finding and creating new customer-centric digital solutions. On a third level, managers consciously use advanced digital data analysis insights to support their decision-making processes better [8].

Managers must become 'engaged leaders' [6] with strong digital skills for building relationships with the different groups of people inside and outside the company. They can use these skills strategically to enforce the defined business goals and lead the company accordingly [6]. Only with this empowerment can a leader work at eye level with their employees, motivate heterogeneous and distributed teams, align them flexibly in the face of change [14] and lead them whileimplementing the strategic dimensions of a digital transformation for the company's value creation. The CEO of the steel trader Klöckner, Gisbert Rühl, well demonstrated the mode of action of an engaged leader with his changed mindset for leading the company. Starting from the latent threat of digitalisation, he embarked on the journey of understanding and learning such digital skills by learning the basics of digital innovation and how it works in Silicon Valley [20]. Today, Klöckner operates an online steel trading platform which, according to Klöckner, has already generated 1 billion euros in sales in 2017 on the platform alone. For 2020, the company planned that half of the total sales will be realised via this platform [21]. The willingness of established companies to acknowledge the digital disruption of their own company and skilfully shape it [17] is the basic prerequisite for establishing functioning digital leadership in the company. Studies have shown that companies with well-developed digital skills generate higher turnover, are significantly more profitable and have a higher enterprise value than other companies with less mature digital skills [15].

Accordingly, **digital leadership** comprises four central design levels:

I. One's own personality
II. The immediate working and management environment
III. The entire company
IV. The influence of the company because of its own digital transformation on the associated industry or the entire market

Digital leadership as a combination of proven and digital skills and competences is transforming into participative leadership [6, 7, 22, 23]. Its focuses on efficiency and excellence with new approaches that are innovative, agile and highly dynamic in understanding and implementing the opportunities of digitisation in the company [22]. Figure 14.3 visualises the four design levels of digital leadership with the corresponding necessary methods and competencies.

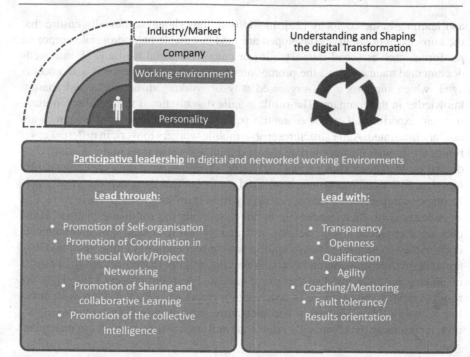

Fig. 14.3 Participative leadership principles. (Based on Lemke et al. [3] and Raskino and Waller [8])

In the digital age, individuals' professional and private spheres are increasingly shifting into a public role, caused by people's digital omnipresence [18]. As a result, individual attitudes and behaviour towards work are also changing [3]. Employees, especially digital natives [24], identify more strongly through networks and communities, share and generate knowledge and skills together and consciously resort to the data-driven exploration of information and its interpretation for solving problems. They accept the parallelism of creative and automated activities in what they see as a unified real and digital networked world.

Above all, today's managers must promote the self-organisation of their employees. Employees want to complete the tasks assigned to them in a self-determined and autonomous manner and tend to see their superiors as coaches, sparring partners or experts in specific problem solutions. The promotion of network-like cooperation, here also beyond departmental and company boundaries, which offers an exchange in communities and with expert groups, is a necessary realisation of this self-organisation. The manager only must coordinate the work in the networks to conformity with the corporate objective. Platforms such as GitHub (www.github.com) or real places such as coworking spaces illustrate the benefits of network-organised collaboration. Encouraging sharing information and knowledge and a willingness to learn together also characterise digital leadership. The leader should create the conditions and set incentives that strengthen the sharing of knowledge and learning in the company [25]. In addition, they should technically ensure that the knowledge or solutions developed are made available on appropriate corporate platforms, such as social intranets [26] or enterprise social media [27], in a well-documented manner. Thus, the promotion of collective intelligence is also encouraged, which supports a self-organised way of working in networks and sharing knowledge in the company. The result is agile organisational forms in which iterative and experimental customer-centric solutions are developed and resources are flexibly integrated. Agile structuresenable mobile workers to work in different environments through the appropriate use of digital and networked tools. A study conducted by McKinsey showed that such agile structures were only implemented by less than 25% of all performance-oriented teams but that these achieve greater performance compared with classic, relatively rigid team structures [28].

A leader with these leadership methods exhibits the following competencies: they are transparent in their actions, instructions and feedback; they communicate openly; they consciously create conditions to further empower employees; and they are agile in their thinking and decision-making. Digital leaders accept the benefits of making mistakes and use them in a validated learning process [29]. They are results-oriented and act more as coaches or mentors and less as leaders with directive authority. Thus, leadership becomes more indirect, primarily providing direction, representing the company's value code and empowering to meet organisational goals [3].

14.3.2 Digital Governance

The company's sustainable and effective digitisation can only succeed through an accompanying cultural change, just as many new organisations and reorganisations have only worked successfully through an organisational change. At the same time, digital technologies also support and force the necessary corporate cultural change of a company's values and norms. This feedback results from changes in employee attitudes and the positive effects of increasing automation and a more data-driven decision-making space.

On the one hand, this cultural change draws on the fundamental findings in organisational development. For example, Lewin's three-stage model shows how organisations should first prepare for change (unfreezing), then implement the actual change (moving) and before finally stabilising this new state through appropriate measures and incentive systems (refreezing) [30]. Transferred to the challenges of digital transformation, this approach applies in this realm as well. The organisation should also be prepared for the change and then actively pursue the change before finally securing the new state. Several models exist in the literature for this purpose, for example, the approach of 'The Digital Transformation Compass' according to Westerman et al. [7] or 'Digital to the Core' by Raskino and Waller [8].

Digital governance provides a regulatory framework for effective digital transformation. It forms the cornerstone of digital transformation and is based on the results of a digital corporate strategy [31], with which new business models can become feasible. Digital governance creates the conditions for empowering all employees to work successfully with the changed structures and processes through digital transformation. These new structures include the further dissolution of hierarchies favouring internal and external company networks in the direction of agile organisations in which knowledge sharing and collective learning are promoted. Communication and interaction increasingly take place via digital platforms, various digital tools, and corporate social networks. These structures accelerate the further increasing digitalisation of all work processes, regardless of their basic level of automation [32].

The establishment of digital governance in a company can be guided by digital mastery [7, 15]. Digital masters possess a uniform digital vision with different strategic goals, generate measurable success in digitisation through established specific structural units, and have a distinct digital corporate culture [15]. These involve a combination of digital leadership skills and the basic entrepreneurial skills to digitise the enterprise [7]. This digital mastery enables digital leadership and governance of the overall enterprise to enforce all strategic goals and operational tasks. Thus, the path to digital mastery can also serve as a yardstick for the level of digital transformation achieved and enable the company to become the 'game changer' [33] in its industry.

The functioning of digital governance includes some organisational design aspects [3]. For example, specific governance units should be defined, with which the various digital activities, initiatives and plans can be bundled and a uniform view of the innovation impact can be taken for the entire company. The focus is on coordination, where a prioritised assessment of resources is made, and uniform rules and standards are introduced. Thus, an optimised and coordinated approach to implementing the various digitisation efforts can be achieved. However, this already requires relatively established digital governance structures. Furthermore, digital governance is often enforced through the explicit introduction of a new leadership position. The so-called chief digital officers (CDO) create a unified digital vision and can assume the coordination function between the different enterprise-wide digital projects. In addition, this leader can act as a driver of cultural change, creating a balance of interests between the established and new digital corporate world. These two structural units should be supplemented by decentralised, distributed digital units with which digitisation can be implemented operationally in individual departments. Digital governance enables the identification and use of synergies for shared infrastructures, competencies, and other resources within the different digital projects and initiatives.

Digital governance contains the guidelines according to which digitisation should be advanced in the company, which should have the following [3]:

- Presentation of the digital business scenario for the company's value creation, its products and services, and its overall business model
- Presentation of the potential of customer centricity for the company and the possibilities for innovative implementation

- Demonstration of the potential for disruption for the entire business model or parts of the model and for the products and services
- Presentation of the criteria for centralised and/or decentralised decisions on digital projects
- Presentation of the criteria for a digital investment portfolio, also in relation to the company's traditional IT portfolio
- Presentation of the structures and processes for coordination, decision making and coordination of all digital plans and projects
- Presentation of the positions, responsibilities, tasks and competences within the framework of digital governance and their cooperation
- Outline basic IT security and risk criteria and the processes and roles for enforcement

14.3.3 Recommendations for Action for Enterprise-Wide Digitisation

Successful digitisation of the enterprise requires the synchronous and simultaneous management of traditional IT. This address the core systems or systems of record and the agile and innovative systems of engagement [3, 18]. The core systems are the robust, durable and secure transactional systems of the enterprise, such as the Enterprise Resource Planning (ERP) systems, and they form the backbone of the enterprise and the technological prerequisite par excellence for successful digitisation. The systems of engagement – or systems of innovation – reflect the social and mobile communication and interaction systems empower for a strong customer centricity. Those systems are externally focused and allow the execution of a defined digital strategy. Digitisation gradually becomes feasible through that systems. Such systems include digital platforms, apps, social network components or digitally interwoven products, for example, through the capabilities of the Internet of Things. The different dynamics in the management of traditional IT and innovative IT are also referred to as bimodal IT [34]. Figure 14.4 shows the different modes used in the management of these systems.

That two worlds, the continuous management of classic IT solutions and the agile management of the innovative, user-centered digital solutions involve the definition of rules and standards for unified management so that a enterprise-wide digitisation can be operated permanently. That implementation requires the extension of the field-proven perceptions of the classic IT management life cycle with plan, build and run. Such a broader life cycle allows a holistic perspective of all essential management tasks for asuccessful implementation of an enterprise-wide digitisation [3].

This extended IT management lifecycle could onsist of four central building blocks ('innovation', 'planning', 'development' and 'operation') that are supplemented by another cross-sectional building block – 'organisation'. The first building block, 'innovation', within this IT process life cycle focuses on management for recognising and implementing the innovative and disruptive forces of digital technologies. At its core, this is about identifying, here based on a customer-centric

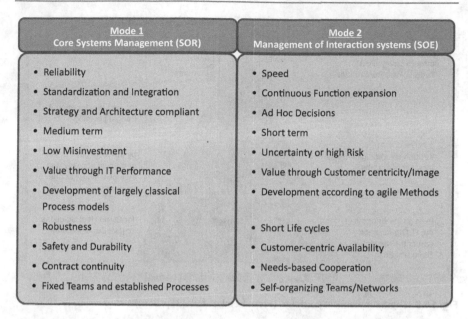

Mode 1 Core Systems Management (SOR)	Mode 2 Management of Interaction systems (SOE)
• Reliability	• Speed
• Standardization and Integration	• Continuous Function expansion
• Strategy and Architecture compliant	• Ad Hoc Decisions
• Medium term	• Short term
• Low Misinvestment	• Uncertainty or high Risk
• Value through IT Performance	• Value through Customer centricity/Image
• Development of largely classical Process models	• Development according to agile Methods
• Robustness	• Short Life cycles
• Safety and Durability	• Customer-centric Availability
• Contract continuity	• Needs-based Cooperation
• Fixed Teams and established Processes	• Self-organizing Teams/Networks

Fig. 14.4 Simultaneous and synchronous design of a bimodal IT system. (Based on Gartner [34])

mindset, which digital solution ideas the company can develop to innovate its business model, products, and services. The search for such digital ideas should always be done from the customer's perspective. This perspective not only provides the guarantee of actually developing valuable solutions for the customer, but it also enables internal realignment to the customer's needs. According to the capabilities of agile organisations [28], these ideas should be tested and evaluated as experiments via prototypes. In the 'planning' building block, the focus is on the definition and adoption of all digital ideas and plans and their strategic synchronisation. A digital investment can be guided by the nature of the digital endeavour, its effectiveness in enforcing that endeavour for the entire organisation and the strategic and competitive dimensions of such initiatives [7]. Figure 14.5 shows a possible portfolio for investment decisions in digital projects.

The 'development' building block deals with the concrete implementation of digital initiatives in the company and produces executable digital solutions that are subsequently handed over to the 'operation' building block for the permanent maintenance of these solutions. The cross-cutting building block 'organisation' comprises the management tasks for implementing the digital transformation, such as creating the conditions for a cultural change, building digital leadership competencies, and establishing digital governance. Clear approval and identification of the management for these changes, and a communicated vision and strategy about the path of digitalisation in the company, are essential for this [15].

The most essential management tasks in their assignment to the building blocks of the IT management life cycle are summarised in Fig. 14.6 and can serve as minimum recommendations for action for effective enterprise-wide digitisation.

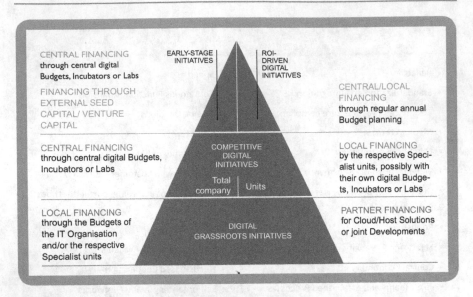

Fig. 14.5 Digital investment portfolio. (From Lemke et al. [3, p. 256])

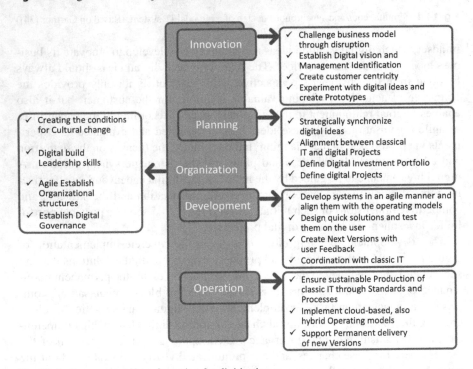

Fig. 14.6 Recommendations for action for digitisation

14.4   Instruments for Enterprise-Wide Digitalisation

14.4.1 Overview of Instruments

Each effective and efficient management requires a set of appropriate tools for execution. These include essential management tools like instruments or methods for strategic planning or the design of business models [35, 36]. A digital-driven reorganisation also needs the usage of various IT-specific management tools such as requirements management [37], architecture management [38], or data and process modelling as well as security and risk management [39]. Additionally, an successful execution of digitisation transformation contains new management instruments, for example, methods like lean start-up management for a digital entre- and intrapreneurship [29], crowdsourcing for collective and open idea search and evaluation [40], exploration and visualisation of data [41] or the design of modular digital platforms or ecosystems [42]. These tools can be used for one specific management task at a time; they are also partly suitable for several task areas and can be used more universally. The following paragraphs present some selected new instruments – one for each defined building block of recommendations of action. These include the following:

- Design thinking for the building block 'innovation'
- Tech screening for the building 'planning'
- Agile software development for the building block 'development'
- DevOps for building block 'operations'

For the cross-cutting building block 'organisation', the three-stage model of organisational change has already been referred to in the context of digital governance. Therefore, there is no explicit presentation of a further instrument.

14.4.2 Presentation of Selected Instruments for Enterprise-Wide Digitalisation

Design thinking is currently regarded as the innovation method with which iterative user-centred results can be developed leading to the solution of even complex problems [43]. This encompassesthe three principles of customer centricity, iteration and prototyping, and the openness to solutions, that make design thinking one of the most effective tools for designing digital innovations. The combination of empathy towards the customer or user and their problems with a creative search for suitable solutions using rational reasoning in the analysis, evaluation and selection of possible alternatives [44] offers innovation, even in areas with complex, multilayered and diffuse problems. Thus, design thinking is a mindset, process model and method kit [45] in equal measure. The following principles demonstrate this mindset:

- Innovations are made by people for people.
- It is a cycle of divergent thinking in the sense of searching for unconventional solutions to problems through creative ideas and convergent thinking that produces feasible solutions.
- Continuous learning from mistakes provides positive learning effects.
- Prototypes and test scenarios test and experience diverse ideas from divergent thinking and provide valuable feedback for further design.

The process model for design thinkingdifferentiates between a superordinate macro-process, which takes up the divergent and convergent way of thinking, and a micro-process, which should be run through in each phase of the macro-process [43]. This micro-process demonstrates the iterative approach towards design thinking. Each cycle begins with a problem definition or redefinition. The need finding and synthesis phase is used to identify user needs and to deliver valuable insights. The evaluation of these insights allows to define a pool of ideas, which are then produced as prototypes, before being tested in the last stage of the cycle. That kind of micro-process is valid for each macro-process step and defines the journey through a concrete design thinking project. That also is the path, which steadily concretises possible problem solutions. The two processes arevisualised in Fig. 14.7 [43].

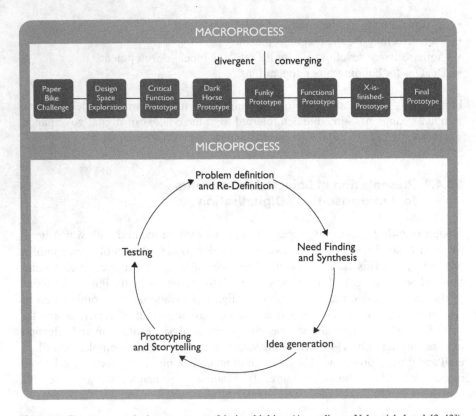

Fig. 14.7 The macro- and micro-processes of design thinking. (According to Uebernickel et al. [3, 43])

A toolbox of methods is available for the variety of tasks in design thinking, which allows interdisciplinary teams to work systematically and in a structured way [43]. Such as toolbox is a combination of behaviour-oriented tools, project management techniques and methods for creating and testing prototypes. The *Design Thinking Handbook* by Uebernickel et al. contains an extensive collection of design thinking methods [43].

Today's innovation management, even more so in the context of digital transformation, draws on the benefits of design thinking. Software manufacturers such as SAP or IBM also use design thinking to manage their projects in a new manner and to develop customer-centric products and services. However, design thinking is the most viable because of its extreme focus on the user, actually identifying customer needs to quickly develop digital solutions based on them. This is why design thinking is now firmly interwoven with the potential of digital transformation.

The rapid advancement of the landscape of digital and networked technologies indicates an observing, evaluating, and forecasting of technological solutions toward the potentials, chances and risks, and impact for the business. The instrument of **tech screening** should have a permanent place in planning processes. Tech screening involves searching for, detecting and filtering out technologies with specific characteristics that currently have the potential for digitalisation and networking in general [3]. This involves the systematic early detection of trends and tendencies, and their observation for the assessment of the maturity levels of the technologies and the estimation of possible business use.. The technology radar technique is well suited to support the management in fulfilling such tasks, because it systematises technologies via a four-stage process, evaluates them and develops a portfolio of suitable technologies on this basis (see Fig. 14.8).

In the identification, initial selection and evaluation phase, the most diverse technologies are recorded without precise knowledge of whether and to what extent they will actually be used later. Thus, this phase corresponds to a fundamental environment scanning and preoccupation with technological trends and new technologies.

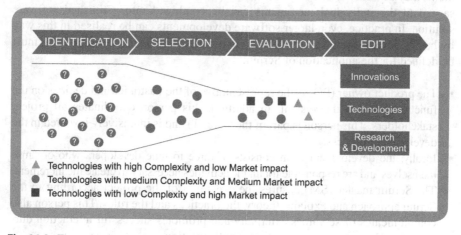

Fig. 14.8 The technology radar technique. (According to Rohrbeck et al. [3, 46])

A time horizon is also not immediately considered in a limiting manner. The next phases examine the technologies, which are covered in more detail, and select based on fixed criteria. The maturity level is a typical decision factor and can divide technologies into those with high innovation potential, with high media perception, or with a first successful or unsuccessful practical application [3]. Mature, productive technologies can also be considered in this context, but these are usually not captured by the first stages because they are generally already on the 'radar screen'. The criteria for further evaluation can be seen in the Fig. 14.8 and can lead to the utilisation of the technologies in the company in the fourth phase.

Even though tech screening is a tool associated with planning, it can also be used for innovation tasks because a systematic preoccupation with trends can also reveal innovation potential at an early stage. That helps companies better react to the high dynamics of technology development and the shortened life cycles of technologies [3]. At the same time, it may be possible to discover the fundamental trends that cannot yet be translated into concrete technologies but that already show how certain topics may develop.

Agile software development [47] is a new, alternative approach to the rapid development of software but without using classic process models, such as the waterfall or spiral model. It is an incremental form of software development based on the close cooperation and communication among all participants and project stakeholders Individual software products – the so-called increments – are developed in small steps that are tested directly by a later user; this allows for finished software solutions to be delivered quickly. Scrum (www.scrum.org) is one of the best-known representative of agile software development and is currently the most widely used in practice for the development of digital solutions.

Scrum is an iterative procedure that consists of several 'sprint' units, in each of which a usable software increment is created. Each sprint lasts 4–6 weeks and consists of typical development tasks such as requirements gathering, implementation and quality assurance, as well as code reviews or systematic tests. No new requirements may be added within a sprint. These sprints are run through as often as necessary until the individual increments can be combined into a finished software solution. In practice, even larger software developments can be realised in this way by having several Scrum teams develop in parallel [48]. Three essential roles must be defined for the application of Scrum:

- The product owner (PO) is the representative of the customer and decides on the functionalities of the system. In addition, this person coordinates all project stakeholders. This person is part of the team (T) and is intensively involved in the development process.
- Ideally, the development team consists of three to nine developers who organise themselves and are responsible for all the activities necessary to create the increment.
- The Scrum master (SM) ensures the execution of the project according to the Scrum approach and explains theory, the practices and the rules. This person also communicates these values externally and promotes successful interaction during the project, thus helping optimise collaboration.

Two essential documents support the entire development process:

- The product backlog contains all prioritised requirements for the system and contains an effort estimate. It forms the basis for processing in the respective sprints. After each sprint, this document can be adapted if customer requirements change.
- The sprint backlog contains all the requirements to be implemented in a sprint as the so-called items.

Four different meeting structures exist for the communication and realisation of the necessary cooperation of all roles:

- The sprint planning meeting opens each sprint session and decides on the tasks and content of the current sprint.
- The sprint review serves to give the PO feedback on the sprint result. The developed increment is demonstrated and serves as the basis for feedback.
- The sprint retroperspective meeting is an internal team meeting that contributes to the reflection of the collaboration within the team.
- The daily Scrum meeting is conducted on a daily basis using fixed communication rules, records the sprint progress of each team member and synchronises all necessary tasks of the day.

Figure 14.9 shows the Scrum approach. The upstream and downstream phases of pre- and postgaming help prepare and postprocess the software development

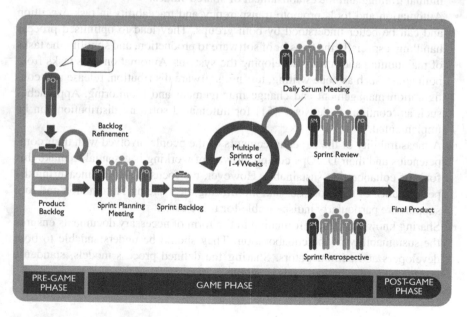

Fig. 14.9 The Scrum approach. (According to Lemke et al. [3, p. 309])

process. The gaming phase is the actual development phase in which meetings and sprints take place iteratively.

As a dynamic approach, this tool supports diverse development tasks in the context of implementing the digital projects of a digital transformation. At the same time, the idea of an iterative approach also serves for all other tasks within the digital transformation framework. An agile approach involving the consumer promotes the success of digital innovations and thus customer-centric solutions. Nevertheless, the implementation of an autonomous, self-organised way of working is also strengthened by the ideas of agile methods.

The **DevOps** tool is considered an approach for promoting cooperation between the previously organizationally separate task areas of software development and the operation of these systems. It stands for a common set of cultural values, processes and instruments for the realisation of an operationally compliant development of software, thus also promoting the self-image of all employees involved [3]. It supports agile thinking of development with the stability of operations management. These two areas are classically characterised by different communication and task areas. Coordination in the sense of DevOps with an integration of the involved parties, defined processes and explicit tool support ensures the challenges of a continuous delivery of systems to the users [49]. DevOps is characterised by the following principles [50]:

- A culture of collaboration that enables open communication and where alignment works through respect and responsibility bridges the traditional barriers between development and operations. Examples of this are attentive listening, mutual training and the establishment of shared values.
- Automation and tools promote transparency and traceability in task execution and can be better understood by both groups. They lead to optimised process handling, especially the transfer of software to production, and simplify the tasks of maintaining and further developing the systems. Automation adds tasks from both areas, such as code writing, testing, software distribution, release and configuration management and change management and monitoring. Approaches such as 'continuous delivery' [51] for automated software distribution can be implemented.
- A measurability of the target agreements of the people involved with their competencies and their DevOps-compliant way of working is essential to make this form of collaboration sustainable. However, the focus is also on measuring the performance of the processes and monitoring the systems. Automation and tool support are particularly indispensable for these tasks.
- Sharing knowledge and information in the form of necessary documents ensures the sustainability of the collaboration. They should be understandable to both developers and administrators. Sharing the defined process models, standards and methods also includes this principle.

- Software quality assurance is an integral part of DevOps. Thus, the data from automation and tool support should also be used to draw insights into how systems can be developed with a high quality.
- Structures and standards promote continuous and goal-oriented collaboration. They provide a framework for a reliable usage of DevOps. These standards often represent common market reference models like CMMI as reference model for software development or ITIL® as best practice for IT Service Management. DevOps also aims to implement a service-oriented approach in IT and foster the idea of customer-centered solutions in IT departments where the defined IT service will meet users' requirements.

DevOps is now widely used, even by established companies and not just those with complete digital business models, such as Zalando [3], to take advantage of seamless software development and operations management. Combined with agile development methods, it is the perfect way to establish customer-centric solutions. These can be rolled out quickly and continuously while guaranteeing stable operation. In this way, the company ensures the overall sustainability of its digital business models.

14.5 Summary and Outlook

Most established companies today face the challenge of the greater digitisation and networking of their businesses. In the meantime, it is clear to most company leaders that this change is irreversible and, therefore, not a strategic option but a necessity for securing the future of the company. This article provides approaches to how a digital transformation can be realistically implemented with sustainable success. First and foremost, this includes changing one's own leadership principles and structures. Digital leaders have internalised the effects of digitisation and networking [3] and apply them to their tasks on a daily basis. They have charisma, can motivate, inspire and intellectually stimulate their work environment while being able to lead in an individualised way. Thus, they create network-like organisational structures in which employees can work digitally in a self-organised manner. As a framework for this new form of leadership, every company needs established digital governance that provides the guidelines and rules for managing digitally shaped structures and processes and ensures that the necessary cultural change can also succeed. To effectively implement digitalisation, managers must draw on a toolbox of tried-and-tested instruments and expand them with new, modern ones. In the current article, four selected techniques were presented to design, implement and operate customer-centric digital solutions in an agile and aligned manner. At the end of the day, digitalisation is IT management, which is becoming more complex and must reconcile the new and old worlds of information systems.

References

1. Etventure (2017) Studie 2017: Digitale Transformation und Zusammenarbeit mit Startups in Großunternehmen in Deutschland und den USA. https://www.etventure.de/innovationsstudien/ Accessed on 10 Dec 2021
2. Floridi L (2016) The fourth revolution. How the Infosphere is reshaping human reality. Oxford University Press, Oxford
3. Lemke C, Brenner W, Kirchner K (2017) Einführung in die Wirtschaftsinformatik. Band 2: Gestalten des digitalen Zeitalters. Springer Gabler, Berlin
4. Oswald G, Kleinmeier M (2017) Shaping the digital enterprise, trends and use cases in digital innovation and transformation. Springer, Cham
5. Bounfour A (2016) Digital futures, digital transformation, from lean production to acceluction. Springer, Cham
6. Li C (2015) The engaged leader, a strategy for your digital transformation. Wharton Digital Press, Philadelphia
7. Westerman G, Bonnet D, McAfee A (2014) Leading digital: turning technology into business transformation. Harvard Business Review Press, Boston
8. Raskino M, Waller G (2015) Digital to the core, remastering leadership for your industry, your enterprise and yourself. Bibliomotion, New York
9. Gunelius S (2013) The history and evolution of the internet, media, and news in 5 infographics. ASCI. http://aci.info/2013/10/24/the-history-and-evolution-of-the-internet-media-and-news-in-5-infographics/ Accessed on 10 Dec 2021
10. Kelly K (2016) The inevitable: understanding the 12 technological forces that will shape our future. Viking
11. Shapiro C, Varian HR (1999) Information rules, a strategic guide to the network economy. Harvard Business School Press, Boston
12. Kalakota R, Robinson M (2000) E-business 2.0: roadmap for success, 2nd edn. Addison Wesley
13. O'Reilly T (2005) What is web 2.0, design patterns and business models for the next generation of software. O'Reilly. http://www.oreilly.com/pub/a/web2/archive/what-is-web-20.html Accessed on 10 Dec 2021
14. Wouter A, De Smet A, Lackey G, Lurie M, Murarka M (2018) The five trademarks of agile organizations. https://www.mckinsey.com/business-functions/organization/our-insights/the-five-trademarks-of-agile-organizations Accessed on 10 Dec 2021
15. Westerman G, Calméjane C, Bonnet D, Ferrraris P, McAfee A (2011) Digital transformation: A roadmap for billion-dollar organizations. MIT Center for Digital Business. https://www.capgemini.com/resources/digital-transformation-a-roadmap-for-billiondollar-organizations/ Accessed on 10 Dec 2021
16. Mulesoft (2018) Mulesoft connectivity benchmark report 2018. Mulesoft. https://www.mulesoft.com/de/lp/reports/connectivity-benchmark Accessed on 10 Dec 2021
17. Bradley C, O'Toole C (2016) An incumbent's guide to digital disruption. McKinsey Quarterly May 2016. https://www.mckinsey.com/business-functions/strategy-and-corporate-finance/our-insights/an-incumbents-guide-to-digital-disruption Accessed on 10 Dec 2021
18. Lemke C, Brenner W (2015) Einführung in die Wirtschaftsinformatik. Band 1: Verstehen des digitalen Zeitalters. Springer Gabler, Berlin
19. Christensen C (2016) The innovator's dilemma, when new technologies cause great firms to fail. Harvard Business Review Press, Boston
20. Keese C (2016) The silicon valley challenge. A wake-up call for Europe. Penguin Verlag, München
21. Stüber J (2017) Wie Klöckner zum 'amazon des Stahlhandels' werden will. Gründerszene.de. https://www.gruenderszene.de/allgemein/kloeckner-amazon-des-stahlhandels-transformation Accessed on 19 Feb 2018

22. Sheninger, EC (2019) Digital leadership – changing paradigms for changing times. 2nd rev edn. Sage Publications, Thousand Oaks
23. Hesselberg J (2018) Unlocking agility: an insider's guide to agile enterprise transformation. Addison-Wesley Signature Series, Boston
24. Prensky M (2001) Digital natives, digital immigrants, part 1. On Horizon 9(5):1–6
25. Razmerita L, Kirchner K, Nielsen P (2016) What factors influence knowledge sharing in organizations? A social dilemma perspective of social media communication. J Knowl Manag 20(6):1225–1246
26. Mergel I (2016) The social intranet, insights on managing and sharing knowledge internally. IBM Center of the Business of Government, Using Technology Series
27. Leonardi PM, Huysman M, Steinfield C (2013) Enterprise social media: definition, history, and prospects for the study of social technologies in organizations. J Comput-Mediat Commun 19:1–9
28. McKinsey (2017) How to create an agile organization, Survey October 2017. https://www.mckinsey.com/business-functions/organization/our-insights/how-to-create-an-agile-organization Accessed on 10 Dec 2021
29. Ries E (2011) The lean startup – how constant innovation creates radically successful businesses. Crown Business
30. Lewin K (1947) Frontiers in group dynamics, concept, method and reality in social science, social equilibria and social change. Hum Relat 1:5–40
31. Bharadwaj A, El Sawy OE, Pavlou PA, Venkatraman N (2013) Digital business strategy: towards a next generation of insights. MIS Q 37(2):473–491
32. Arntz M, Gregory T, Zierhahn U (2016) The risk of automation for jobs in OECD countries: a comparative analysis, OECD social, employment and migration working papers. No. 189. OECD Publishing, Paris
33. El Sawy OA, Pereira F (2013) Business modelling in the dynamic digital space, an ecosystem approach. Springer, Heidelberg
34. Mingay S. Mesaglio M (2016) Deliver on the promise of bimodal. Gartner. https://www.gartner.com/en/documents/3216217/deliver-on-the-promise-of-bimodal Accessed on 10 Dec 221
35. Osterwalder A, Pigneur Y (2010) Business model generation, a handbook for visionaries, game changers, and challengers. Wiley, Hoboken
36. Gassmann O, Frankenberger K, Csik M (2014) The business model navigator – 55 models that will revolutionise your business. Pearson Education Limited, Harlow
37. Heath F (2020) Managing software requirements the agile way: bridge the gap between software requirements and executable specifications to deliver successful projects. Packt Publishing, Birmingham
38. Winter R (2014) Architectural thinking. Wirtschaftsinformatik 56(6):395–398
39. Krcmar H (2015) Informationsmanagement. Springer Gabler, Berlin
40. Howe J (2006) The rise of crowdsourcing. Wired Mag 6(14):1–4
41. Keim D (2001) Visual exploration of large data sets. Commun ACM 44(8):38–44
42. Parker GG, Van Alstyne MW, Choudary SP (2016) Platform revolution: how networked markets are transforming the economy and how to make them work for you. W. W. Norton, New York/London
43. Uebernickel F, Jiang L, Brenner W, Pukall B, Naef T (2020) Design thinking: the handbook. WS Professional, Singapore
44. Kelley D, Kelley T (2013) Creative confidence, unleashing the creative potential within us all. Crown Business, London
45. Brenner W, Uebernickel F (2016) Design thinking for innovation, research and practice. Springer International, Cham
46. Rohrbeck R, Heuer J, Arnold H (2006) The technology radar – an instrument of technology intelligence and innovation strategy. In: Proceedings of the 3rd IEEE international conference on management of innovation and technology, pp 978–983

47. Cockburn A (2006) Agile software development, the cooperative game. Addison-Wesley, Upper Saddle River
48. Larman C, Vodde B (2016) Large-scale scrum: more with less. Addison Wesley Signature Series, Boston
49. Verona J (2016) Practical DevOps. Packt Publishing, Birmingham
50. Erich F, Amrit C, Daneva M (2014) Report: DevOps Literature Review. University of Twente Tech Rep, Twente51. Farley D (2021) Continuous delivery pipelines: how to build better software faster. Independently Published

Secure Digitization

15

Sachar Paulus

Abstract

Digitization cannot be implemented seriously without security – the two essential features of digitization, standardization and networking, make systems easily vulnerable to attack. In order to be able to control the increasingly rising risks, an information security management system (ISMS) is required. This is already expected by many companies from their suppliers, and represents the state of the art. Software architectures for digitization must also take into account certain design patterns and procedures. It is recommended that users of digitization operate an ISMS.

15.1 Introduction

Digitization sounds easy and fast – at least that's what we're promised: Digitization makes everything easier and faster. And indeed, digitalization enables many new usage scenarios, savings and faster processes [1]. But this is not without risks: the networking of systems and the standardization of protocols make attacks increasingly easy, and without appropriate measures, digitalization exposes you to considerable risks [2].

This article therefore asks the question: How can one dare to digitize while taking as few unacceptable risks as possible? To this end, various aspects of IT and information security in the concept of digitization are considered, requirements are discussed and recommendations for implementation are given.

This paper first gives an overview of the dangers of digitization, then discusses what exactly could be meant by security in digitization, and introduces information

S. Paulus (✉)
Hochschule Mannheim, Mannheim, Germany
e-mail: paulus@hs-mannheim.de

253

security management systems. Subsequently, the currently valid legal requirements are considered and finally requirements for software architectures of digitalization are derived. In the conclusion, recommendations for dealing with security in digitization are given.

15.2 Overview of the Dangers of Digitisation

15.2.1 Examples

Digitization is approached very cautiously by many people – and "security problems" are cited as the reason for this. But which security problems are specifically meant by this? There are many kinds of digital risks – from very technical risks such as dependence on the Internet when using cloud solutions, to application risks such as fear of "hacking" bank accounts, to more personal risks such as "cyber dependency"; all these aspects are commonly subsumed under "security problems of digitalization".

15.2.2 Delimitation

There are, of course, other risks associated with digitalization. For one thing, those that occur as a result of changes to business models – new players have the potential to succeed quickly in the market, often at the expense of existing players. If they are not able to adapt quickly enough, they fall by the wayside – which is why such companies perceive digitization as a threat, especially since they often do not understand what opportunities digitization can bring for them. Or, on the other hand, those that involve changes for staff. These types of risks are not covered in this chapter; the reader is invited to consult the relevant chapters in this book.

This chapter focuses on the risks of digitalisation that arise directly and immediately as a result of technical innovation. These are also referred to in the literature as "cyber risks" or "cybersecurity risks". As a rule, they emanate from external, active attackers. Security risks that can arise without attackers (such as the fact that access to critical company data in the cloud is no longer possible due to a loss of the Internet connection) are normally also to be considered, but do not represent a fundamental threat and can be compensated for by better service qualities from providers. These risks are therefore also not considered further.

15.2.3 Types of Attack

The attacks can be classified as follows: espionage is an attempt to extract interesting information from companies – such as production secrets, customer data or new developments. Sabotage aims to maliciously change information or production in order to damage the company. Information is encrypted for the purpose of blackmail. To achieve these goals, attackers use various attack methods, including attack via the web (e.g. by attempting to penetrate the company via a web application), by using malware (viruses, Trojans) which is leaked to the target company and, last but not least, by enticing employees to disclose information (e.g. via phishing) or to visit websites (via so-called drive-by exploits) which then install malware in the company. Finally, the theft of computing power for cracking passwords, or the sending of SPAM e-mails and the theft of identities (login data, or even credit cards) are part of these criminal activities.

Digitization allows attacks to be carried out remotely – networking and the use of standardized protocols make access via the Internet easy.

15.2.4 Attack Groups

Who are the attackers? Essentially, one can distinguish three different groups of attackers today. On the one hand, there is a still growing group of state actors, usually intelligence services, whose aim is to gain advantages for states (both strategically and tactically, e.g. through economic espionage) or to stabilise the existing regime (usually by monitoring their own citizens). On the other hand, the criminal scene is now highly organized, and primarily mafia-like structures can be found. These offer corresponding interested parties to take on hacking services on behalf of them. Finally, there is also a scene of petty criminals who take advantage of opportunities when they arise, such as encryption Trojans or identity theft.

15.2.5 Carelessness/Awareness

As technology has become more secure in recent years, the focus of attacks to get inside companies has shifted to people. This is because in most cases, an attack on a company's IT systems is only successful if there is an "internal" person who opens the door, so to speak. Accordingly, persuasion techniques to exploit employees are becoming more sophisticated. We explain this with the example of phishing: Phishing is a made-up word and is composed of "password" and "fishing", i.e. fishing for passwords – the first phishing emails asked the victim to log on to a website under a flimsy reason in order to get their login data. Nowadays, logging in is usually no longer necessary, as websites infected with malicious code are often enough to take over computers.

The attention and sensitivity of employees is therefore all the more important – because security software is usually powerless against the type of attacks described. Only if the IT system used has the latest updates installed can the damage perhaps still be limited, but the attack itself can only be avoided if people think along with it. Whereby this can be quite difficult, since the deceptive manoeuvres can appear very real and credible. Therefore, a constant occupation with the latest techniques is mandatory to keep the attention and decision-making ability high.

In general, when considering the security of an IT system, it is important to take the people involved into account – because it is only possible to draw an overall picture of the security situation if the people and their decisions and actions are also taken into account. Researchers use the term "socio-technical system" [3] for the overall view, which can be used to examine – and also promote – the trustworthy behavior of a system.

It is of great value to consider the different archetypes. An interesting classification comes from Deutschland sicher im Netz e.V. [4]: there, users are classified along two dimensions, namely motivation to behave correctly and competence to make the right decisions. Thus, this model results in four archetypes of users (the names stand for themselves): naive, uninvolved, carefree and competent.

15.2.6 Digitisation as a Divide in Society

Digitalisation offers a whole host of opportunities – but it can also widen the gap between rich and poor. In any case, it is already creating a rift in our society – namely between those who are able to use their devices in a responsible manner and those who are not. The latter will fall victim to attackers much more easily – which makes it all the more important to advance digitization as securely as possible and thus ensure a balance in society.

15.3   What Is Security?

There is no unique definition for security, or alternatively there are too many. Furthermore, security is subjective, or it is very difficult to agree on an "equal", objective security in an organisation. It therefore makes sense to use a definition that takes this subjectivity into account, and yet can be used uniformly. We use the following definition: "Security is freedom from unacceptable risks" (according to IEC 61508). The risks can be objectified and evaluated with classical methods – but it is still up to the individual (or in the business context, the decision-maker or the person responsible for the risk) to decide where his or her limit of acceptability lies.

In this context, a risk is an expected loss, and is calculated by the product of the probability of occurrence/frequency of occurrence in a given period (usually 3 years) and the amount of loss. A risk is usually valued in a financial currency – after all, from a business point of view, provisions are required for risks in the order of magnitude of the risks (the expected values for the possible losses). For simple applications, however, it is also sufficient to define levels for probability of occurrence and amount of damage (for example: 3×3).

15.3.1 Perfect Security Does Not Exist

With this definition, it is clear that there can be no one hundred percent security: in practice, there are always risks that are acceptable, and therefore one will not protect oneself against precisely these risks (for economical reasons or the associated restrictions) (e.g. that the computer is stolen at home). It is also possible that one does not have certain risks "in mind" and does not protect oneself against them (e.g. the already mentioned drive-by exploits when clicking on foreign/subverted websites). It should therefore be noted that security is a relative state, depending on the risk situation and the (individual) need for protection.

Security is, more precisely, even a very volatile state, i.e. it is subject to frequent changes, and it takes a lot of effort to keep the level of security approximately the same. The following essential variables influence the current state of security:

- Motivation and competence of the attackers – a sudden interest in a company or a technology (e.g. by the attackers' clients) can drastically influence the security situation – just as vice versa: a decrease in interest can suddenly lead to a strong increase in security.
- Effectiveness of the measures already taken – the most essential factor for the existing security is that the measures planned for the reduction of risks actually work as expected – and do not add further risks. For example, a password policy that requires a minimum level of complexity works well against hacking and password guessing, but it encourages passwords to be written down – digitally or in paper form – and so a good measure actually creates a higher risk.
- Flawlessness of the systems used – most technical attacks (when the firewall has been overcome by social engineering) exploit technical flaws in software, so-called vulnerabilities. These are caused by carelessness and unprofessionalism on the part of software developers and are inherent in software; however, as soon as they are discovered, so-called exploits are built (these are programs that exploit the vulnerability for a hacker's purposes) and released into the world. Monitoring announcements about vulnerabilities in software and information about when and how the software producer intends to fix the bugs is therefore also very important for an up-to-date assessment of the security situation.

15.3.2 Security Is a Process

Due to the volatility of security and especially the extremely fast possible change of the security state, it is said in IT and information security that "security is a process" [5]. This means that only well-functioning, sustainable processes can maintain an acceptable (albeit fluctuating) security state. These processes include activities such as Risk analysis, identification of measures, effectiveness control of measures, or vulnerability management.

15.3.3 Security Objectives and Protection Needs

How can we describe the target concept of "security"? Of course, all risks can be considered simultaneously – and this is exactly what management systems do, as we will see – but this very individual and fine-grained approach is not helpful, for example, in identifying suitable basic protection measures, i.e. measures that address a large number of risks, or, conversely, in minimizing a large part of the risks "in one fell swoop". To achieve this, one uses a simplification: one maps the risks to security properties of information or processes. Typical information security objectives are availability, confidentiality and integrity; typical process security objectives are traceability, non-repudiation and integrity. These are then referred to as security objectives (or protection goals). Depending on the author/security model, there are also other security goals – but theoretically all security goals can be traced back to the three goals of availability – confidentiality – integrity of information [6].

Therefore, security measures are usually classified according to their security goal to be achieved: Anti-virus, for example, to ensure the integrity of a system; encryption, for example, to ensure confidentiality; and load-balancing or back-up, for example, to ensure availability. Conversely, it is also possible to identify minimum measures for an item of information, a system or a process that reduce the risks affecting it to an acceptable level. This is referred to as the need to protect information, systems or processes.

15.3.4 IT Security vs. Information Security vs. Data Protection

The exemplary assignment of security measures to the security objectives already shows a certain preference for one or the other measure – depending on which security perspective one prefers. This takes on even clearer forms when one considers the strongly overlapping but not identical subject areas of "IT security", "information security" and "data protection".

- IT security aims to protect the IT infrastructure, IT systems and IT applications. The most important stakeholder of IT security is the IT manager: his interest is that the services he provides run as trouble-free (and cost-effectively) as possible. Protecting the actual information being processed is not the primary concern. Technical measures are predominantly used for IT security.
- The aim of information security is to protect the processed information and the processes in accordance with their protection requirements. This involves ensuring the security objectives for the information or processes – the systems performing the processing are not in focus. On the contrary: the information owner may not even care which systems are used for the processing (if necessary with pencil and paper) as long as the security objectives are ensured. Therefore, non-technical measures are often used to guarantee the security objectives.
- Data protection aims to protect personal rights, namely when processing personal or personal-related data. The risks must be considered from the perspective

of the data subjects and suitable risk-reducing measures must be identified (in data protection these are called "TOMs" = technical and organisational measures).

The objectives are very different and may even be contradictory in some cases; however, the measures are very often (almost) congruent.

15.3.5 Assessment of Risks

In addition to the processes for determining the effectiveness of measures and assessing the impact of vulnerabilities, the key parameters for assessing the security situation are statements about risks (probability of occurrence, extent of damage, risk-reducing effect of a measure, and possibly even risk propagation and aggregation in the case of advanced models). The determination of the associated parameters is therefore of particular importance with regard to the informative value of a risk analysis and assessment.

The amount of damage of a risk, i.e. an expected loss, can be calculated by two approaches: in the first approach, the direct and indirect costs of a loss are added up (for example, in the case of successful espionage: loss of competitiveness due to a decline in sales figures). In the second approach, the costs are estimated to restore the original state before the damage (this is well suited in the case of image risks).

The probability of occurrence, unlike systemic risks (where occurrence can be spread across all aspects of a system, such as severe weather, vehicle accidents or accidental fire), cannot be determined by statistics. Here, therefore, it is more helpful to look at characteristics about attack routes (= the vulnerabilities) and about the attackers. For example, knowledge and exploitability of a vulnerability, and motivation and competence of attackers can be used as criteria to determine the probability (OWASP Risk Rating). Of course, this means that a "scalar" probability is no longer possible, or the result must be artificially mapped onto a scale.

When working in detail with risk management, the devil is in the detail; ultimately, the same "margin of error" should be applied to all risks to get comparability of results – after all, the goal of risk management is to accept certain risks in order to reduce the effort required to take action.

15.3.6 Resilience

Currently very much in vogue are systems with artificial intelligence, or at least with the ability to perform machine learning. From a security point of view, the long-term objective is that the systems should be able to heal themselves to a certain extent and thus provide the services defined and expected by the users with little or no disruption. This is referred to as resilience, i.e. the ability to continue to provide the expected services even under disruptions – similar to the ability of the human organism to continue to function under virus and bacteria attack, but also to be able to initiate healing processes in order to return to full functionality.

15.4   Security Management

In order to keep the constantly changing security status at an acceptable level, a management system is used – quite analogous to quality management – which defines a target level and uses a wide variety of measures to pursue the achievement of or compliance with this target. Such a management system is called security management – or, depending on the focus, also information security management system (ISMS) or IT security management. Everyone is currently talking about the ISO/IEC 27001 standard, according to which you can have your ISMS certified.

Important for an ISMS are the so-called scope, as well as the defined protection goals. The scope states in which part of an organization (a site, a department, a process) the information is kept secure, and the protection goals which security properties are ensured. IT service providers often advertise that they have ISO 27001 certification – but since they don't know the customer data, it's not clear what protection goals they are adhering to. Customers of IT service providers are much better served if the latter has an ITIL® or ISO 20000 certification, because then they can prove that they provide their services sustainably in the same quality (incl. security!). ISO 27001 is rather intended for the organizations that are responsible for information to be able to prove that they can handle it in a sustainable and uniformly secure manner.

The main difference to quality management is the speed with which reactions must be able to take place in order to maintain the level of security. Furthermore, most of the elements, especially those concerning the control of the management system, are essentially identical. So there are some synergies between information security management and quality management, even if there are specificities. The situation is similar with data protection: the data protection management system required by the new EU General Data Protection Regulation (see also later) is essentially identical to an information security management system – with one major difference: the perspective from which risks are recorded and assessed. Common to all is the requirement to continuously strive for improvement and to document thoroughly.

The essential components of an information security management system are described below.

15.4.1 Mission Statement and Objectives

The first step is to determine the security objectives. For this purpose, the information processed in the organization must be recorded and assessed for its importance for the company. Security objectives and protection requirements are derived and recorded in a central document (mission statement or guideline). This definition is important because it subsequently determines the activities that are to be used to maintain the security of the information, and as already mentioned it is simply not possible to keep all information 100% secure. The mission statement should be reviewed on a more regular basis to see if it is still relevant (or if, for example, the business activities have changed and the security objectives need to be adjusted).

15.4.2 Managing Risks

At the heart of an ISMS is the most up-to-date knowledge possible about the risks that affect the security objectives. For this, some processes have to be set up in the organization: risks have to be regularly recorded and evaluated in each area, the risks have to be combined and compared, the effectiveness of the measures has to be known, and of course changes in the security situation (attackers, attacks in the "neighborhood", vulnerabilities, etc.) and their evaluation on the risks have to be recorded.

This information must be presented to the management responsible in each case, and a decision must be made there as to whether the risks are acceptable or whether further risk-reducing measures (up to and including the discontinuation of the potentially critical business activity) must be taken. Due to the fundamentally very volatile security situation, management should deal with the security and risk situation on a regular basis – and, depending on the importance of information security for the business activity, also very frequently. While a monthly cycle may be appropriate for manufacturing companies, a daily update may be advisable for banks or similar. As a general rule, the following rule of thumb can be applied: the interval between two management meetings on information security should not be longer than the time in which the company can be significantly affected by hacker attacks [7].

15.4.3 Prevention

Preventive measures are used to avoid the occurrence of risks from the outset. These include standard IT security measures (firewalls, network segmentation, anti-malware solutions, etc.) but also additional measures that specifically address individual risks, such as encryption of certain information, or use of dedicated IT systems for certain applications. There are various collections of best practices for such preventive measures; the following are recommended:

- the measures in Annex A of ISO/IEC 27001: 135 measures are listed there, which are basically required for certification (basically means that they can also be deselected with appropriate justification). These measures essentially form a generally accepted catalog and cover all important areas.
- the measures in the BSI (Bundesamt für Sicherheit in der Informationstechnik)'s basic protection catalogues: this collection is very exhaustive and includes concrete recommendations for action to close vulnerabilities and reduce risks for many systems.

- the measures of the VdS standard 3473: the association of damage insurers has further slimmed down the catalogue of measures of ISO/IEC 27001 and developed it into a good recommendation.

The measures must be regularly checked for their effectiveness – because only if the measures work do they protect against attacks and damage. This is usually done by (random) audits, e.g. all measures are audited regularly in 3 years; if two audits are carried out per year, approximately. one sixth of the measures are audited in each audit. If it is found that the measures do not work or do not work completely, the risks that are reduced to an acceptable level by these measures must be reassessed – and additional measures may have to be taken to remedy the (hopefully temporary) gap.

15.4.4 Reaction

As emphasized several times, a security state is very volatile. Therefore, the response processes of an information security management system are of great importance. The response processes include the following processes:

- Vulnerability management: as part of this process, new vulnerabilities in IT systems that have become known are examined to determine whether they are relevant to the company and, if so, what measures are to be taken. In many cases, patches are available, in which case their implementation in the systems must be planned. But even if there are no patches, appropriate measures must be taken to minimize the attack surface that has been briefly increased by the vulnerability. In any case, the impact of vulnerabilities on risks must be evaluated and communicated to the responsible person. The prerequisite for a functioning vulnerability management is the knowledge of all systems and applications used in the organization – often this is already a major challenge.
- Incident management: while vulnerabilities only represent potential new attacks and "only" increase the risk, incidents are actual attacks (or signs of them). Thus, all employees should be able to report anomalies to an incident handling team, which evaluates them and initiates further escalation steps if necessary. In the case of information security incidents, the damage can be very great in a very short time (e.g. internal information can often be sent quickly and unnoticed), so it is important to be able to react very quickly. Accordingly, affected persons as well as experts must be available quickly and be able to come together at short notice (if necessary also virtually) – they then form a so-called Computer Emergency Response Team (CERT). If the incident cannot be contained at the working level, the next escalation step may be to declare a crisis within the framework of crisis management processes.
- Crisis management: if incidents take on developments that can significantly affect the entire company (and in the case of information security incidents, this can happen very quickly for reputational reasons), then a crisis team consisting

of second-level management personnel trained in this should completely take over the handling of the crisis. To this end, training, alerting and exercise processes should be set up in preparation.

15.4.5 Responsibilities

In principle, management is always responsible for the appropriate handling of risks (see also the section on commercial due diligence). In this context, management can decide on the appropriateness itself – as long as the decisions are not negligent.

An information security officer is usually appointed to implement the activities of the information security management system described. He is not responsible for security, but for the proper and timely implementation of the processes and activities. As a rule, it should be an expert who also recommends measures and assists in the evaluation.

If the organization is too large to be fully covered by one officer, an information security organization is required, consisting of – in addition to the officer – additional local contacts per division or site.

Basically, it is not a good idea to place the responsibility for information security within the IT department for the following reason: IT provides the applications and services with which the business departments process the information relevant to them. A realistic assessment of the risks from the company's point of view is therefore only possible in the respective specialist department; the IT department would always view the risks through "their" glasses and thus come to completely different assessments. Therefore, the ideal staffing for the information security officer is a staff position.

15.4.6 Security Awareness

The biggest gateway for attackers today is the human being. The IT systems are already quite secure if they are well managed. Only when an employee helps – usually unknowingly – will an attacker be successful. In order to reduce this risk, it is necessary to educate employees (as well as external parties) about the risks and to encourage them to behave in a security-compliant manner. This is best done with awareness measures adapted to the culture of the organization. A distinction should be made between the two important learning objectives: increasing the competence of employees, e.g. in assessing the harmlessness of their own actions, and increasing the motivation to behave securely, for example when confidential files are not sent to a partner via a messenger application. Competence-enhancing measures should tend to be topic-oriented (e.g. espionage risks on trips abroad), while motivation-enhancing measures should tend to be target group-oriented (e.g. for engineers separately from sales people), as the target groups generally have different motivations.

15.5 Legal Requirements and the State of the Art

Which of these activities are legally binding? At first glance, IT and information security activities, especially for digitalization, appear to be voluntary. But this is by no means the case!

15.5.1 IT-Sicherheitsgesetz

The European Cybersecurity Regulation mandates local specific laws to address the challens of Cybersecurity. The IT Security Act (IT-Sicherheitsgesetz, ITSG, [8]) aims to ensure adequate IT security in critical areas in Germany. This therefore concerns critical infrastructures on the one hand and IT services via the Internet on the other. Critical infrastructures are companies and organizations from the sectors of energy, information technology and telecommunications, transport and traffic, health, water, food, finance and insurance, state and administration, and media and culture, which serve more than 500,000 citizens. Critical infrastructure operators must implement an information security management system (the details are regulated by ordinances and downstream authorities, such as the Federal Network Agency (BNetzA) and the Federal Office for Information Security (BSI)), and have it certified, i.e. have its effectiveness confirmed by external independent experts. IT service providers must also operate an ISMS, but do not have a certification obligation.

As part of their responsibility, operators of critical infrastructures can also impose requirements on their suppliers in order to reduce the risk along the supply chain. Here, IT security requirements can cascade "downwards". There are already industry-specific requirements for secure collaboration in the context of Industrie 4.0, e.g. in the automotive industry (TISAX model).

15.5.2 Basic Data Protection Regulation

The EU General Data Protection Regulation (GDPR, [9]) replaces the Federal Data Protection Act as of May 2018 and regulates a uniform data protection standard in Europe. The regulation is directly applicable law; however, there are still federal and state data protection laws that specify further details – but they cannot override the contents of the regulation. New aspects of the GDPR include the following:

- the penalties are very sensitive (up to 4% of the parent company's annual turnover) and the supervisory authorities can impose penalties without cause on the basis of the documents,
- the rights of data subjects with regard to the "right to be forgotten" or the "right to take data with them" have been significantly strengthened, and
- a data protection management system is required, which differs from an information security management system in exactly one respect: it requires that the risk

assessment be carried out from the perspective of those affected. The core operational processes of a DSMS are completely identical to those of an ISMS, only the assessment and the content considered are "different" (at least from a different perspective).

Thus, the GDPR requires the same competences, processes and transparency as the IT Security Act (plus further activities to fulfill; data subject rights).

15.5.3 Commercial Due Diligence

It is part of the commercial duty of care to deal appropriately with unreasonable risks. For this purpose, the state of the art is to be used (in the legal sense, not in the sense of patents and inventions). By anchoring an ISMS in the two laws mentioned above, an ISMS (or at least a management system, one could also treat information security risks with a quality management system) is thus quasi mandatory to use – even if not to certify.

In summary: Every company must now operate an information security management system in order to adequately deal with the risks of digitalization – at least in basic terms.

15.6 Necessary Security Concepts

Digitization has two essential features that are of particular importance for security: Standardization and networking. While networking makes it possible for attackers to prepare and carry out their attacks remotely and at their leisure, standardization ensures that attackers do not first have to familiarize themselves with the technology of their target organization, but are ready for action, so to speak. As a consequence, this means that all protection mechanisms should assume that the attacker has access to all interfaces on the one hand and has mastered the protocols on the other – a sort of analogue to Kerckhoff's principle from cryptography, which states that the security of an encryption method must not depend on the secrecy of the method.

This assumption excludes some software architecture patterns that are common today. Unfortunately, such elements are still too often found in today's implementations for digitized solutions, for the most part the changing requirements are considered in the reference architecture to Industry 4.0 [10]. In the following, some concepts are discussed.

15.6.1 Separation of Application Logic and User Administration

A secure and well usable user administration is very complex to implement. User administrations allow attackers to penetrate at many points if the security aspects are not taken into account appropriately. Stumbling blocks exist, for example, in session management, in password storage, or in role management.

Ideally, modern applications no longer have a user administration themselves, but use the possibilities offered by external user administrations. Here, federation and entitlement processes can be used, which enable dedicated controlled access to resources, implementing roles and authorization structures (groups, etc.) without having to keep user information in the application. The protocols for integrating external user management are standardized (such as SAML, OAuth 2.0) and libraries are available for easy use.

15.6.2 Message-Based Protection Concepts Instead of Network-Based Approaches

There is still a persistent belief that by appropriately separating applications and systems at the network level one can ensure the security of systems. This worked in a time when protocols were not yet standardized and not all devices were networked – now this protective measure no longer works. Firewalls, for example, are now there to intercept mass attacks over Internet protocols, and to enforce rules on outbound communications. However, since a large part of the communication takes place via http, moreover on a few, always the same ports, and moreover even secured via https, this task is also increasingly difficult.

The right approach in times of digitalization is for the individual pieces of information exchanged between systems to protect themselves – so that they ultimately do not care where the information is flowing and what the protection at the transmission level looks like. The standards and protocols for this are available, and are also used by modern Industrie 4.0 approaches: digital signature and policy-based encryption of individual messages (XML, JSON) [10].

15.6.3 Security and Privacy by Design Instead of Functionalisation of Security

Many solutions for digitalization are developed according to the principle: "someone else will take care of security later on". The basic assumption behind this idea is that the required security properties can be functionalized. This means that security properties of an overall solution can be achieved by implementing certain security-related features (and selling them as a separate product). For example, to prevent malware in e-mail programs, an antivirus solution is developed and sold.

The functionalization approach has its limitations in complexity – simple features are fine with it; however, if the security property is increasingly complex and heavily interwoven into the application, then functionalization fails. Instead, applications must be secure "by themselves." This is realized by the concepts of "security by design" or "privacy by design" (for privacy properties) [11–13].

Security & Privacy by Design require that systems and applications do not rely on external, specialized security products and instead provide for the often non-functional security and privacy properties themselves. This requires additional investments on the part of system and application manufacturers, but makes it significantly easier to achieve the overall security goals of an integrated system [2, 14].

15.7 Conclusion

Digitization without security is like flying without a parachute: you will either take unreasonable risks or only maneuver in harmless situations. In other words: only information security enables a serious use of digitalization.

New innovations and interesting prototypes are often developed very quickly; productive and professional use, on the other hand, only becomes possible when the necessary security is also available. Since security follows significantly slower innovation cycles than "normal" innovation due to its high complexity, security delays digitization, so to speak.

An information security management system makes it possible to take risks in a controlled manner – accordingly, it is perfectly possible to start digitisation projects if you have the risks "under control", use alternative, time-limited preventive measures if necessary and are well prepared for incidents.

In the author's opinion, the legal situation will become even more acute – the more networked the world becomes, the more need there will be to regulate security in order to be able to protect critical aspects.

The author's central recommendation is therefore: Implement an information security management system. This offers you the opportunity to dare digitalization with security!

References

1. Baums A, Schössler M, Scott B (2015) Industrie 4.0: Wie digitale Plattformen unsere Wirtschaft verändern – und wie die Politik gestalten kann. Kompendium Digitale Standortpolitik, Bd 2
2. Paulus S, Mohammadi NG, Weyer T (2013) Trustworthy software development. In: IFIP international conference on communications and multimedia security. Springer, Berlin/Heidelberg, S 233–247
3. Baxter G, Sommerville I (2011) Socio-technical systems: from design methods to systems engineering. Interact Comput 23(1):4–17
4. Deutschland sicher im Netz e.V. https://www.sicher-im-netz.de//. Accessed on 05.03.2018
5. Sowa A (2017) Wichtige Begriffe rund um Informationssicherheit. In: Management der Informationssicherheit. Springer Vieweg, Wiesbaden, S 5–15
6. Eckert C (2013) IT-Sicherheit: Konzepte-Verfahren-Protokolle. de Gruyter, München
7. Paulus S (2005) Informationssicherheit. In: Müller KR (Hrsg) Handbuch Unternehmenssicherheit. Umfassendes Sicherheits-, Kontinuitäts- und Risikomanagement mit System. Vieweg, Wiesbaden
8. Deutscher Bundestag (2015) Gesetz zur Erhöhung der Sicherheit informationstechnischer Systeme (IT-Sicherheitsgesetz). Bundesgesetzblatt I(31):1324–1331

9. Europäische Union (2016) Verordnung (EU) 2016/679 des Europäischen Parlaments und des Rates vom 27. April 2016 zum Schutz natürlicher Personen bei der Verarbeitung personenbezogener Daten, zum freien Datenverkehr und zur Aufhebung der Richtlinie 95/46/ EG (Datenschutz-Grundverordnung). EG (Datenschutz-Grundverordnung) Amtsblatt der Europäischen Union
10. Adolphs P, Bedenbender H, Dirzus D, Ehlich M, Epple U, Hankel M, Koziolek H et al (2015) Reference architecture model industrie 4.0 (rami4. 0). ZVEI and VDI, Status report
11. Danezis G, Domingo-Ferrer J, Hansen M, Hoepman JH, Metayer DL, Tirtea R, Schiffner S (2015) Privacy and data protection by design-from policy to engineering. arXiv preprint arXiv:1501.03726
12. Mohammadi NG, Bandyszak T Paulus S, Meland PH, Weyer T, Pohl K (2014) Extending development methodologies with trustworthiness-by-design for socio-technical systems. Trust, S 206–207
13. Mohammadi NG, Paulus S, Bishr M, Metzger A, Könnecke H, Hartenstein S, Pohl K et al (2013) Trustworthiness attributes and metrics for engineering trusted internet-based software systems. In: International conference on cloud computing and services science. Springer, Cham, S 19–35
14. Paulus S (2012) Basiswissen Sichere Software: Aus-und Weiterbildung zum ISSECO Certified Professionell for Secure Software Engineering. dpunkt, Heidelberg

Printed in the United States
by Baker & Taylor Publisher Services

Printed in the United States
by Baker & Taylor Publisher Services